3000 800068 12681
St. Louis Community College

Florissant Valley Library
St. Louis Community College
3400 Pershall Road
Ferguson, MO 63135-1408
314-513-4514

WITHDRAWN

D1295803

# THE ELIXIR OF THE GNOSTICS

Islamic Translation Series
Al-Ḥikma

**EDITOR IN CHIEF**
Parviz Morewedge
*Rutgers, The State University of New Jersey*

**EXECUTIVE EDITOR**
Daniel C. Peterson
*Brigham Young University*

**ASSISTANT EXECUTIVE EDITOR**
D. Morgan Davis

**ASSOCIATE EDITOR**
Muhammad Eissa

**ADVISORY BOARD**
Jalal Badakhchani
Charles E. Butterworth
William C. Chittick
Farhad Daftary
Majid F. Fakhry
Hermann Landolt
Muhsin S. Mahdi
Michael E. Marmura
Seyyed Hossein Nasr
Ismail K. Poonawala
Nasrollah Pourjavady
Anthony Preus
John Walbridge
Hossein Ziai

**COSPONSORS**
The Foundation for Interreligious Diplomacy

Institute for the Study and Preservation of Ancient Religious Texts
Brigham Young University

*Mullā Ṣadrā*

# The Elixir of the Gnostics

# اكسير العارفين

*A parallel English-Arabic text*
*translated, introduced, and annotated by*
William C. Chittick

*Brigham Young University Press • Provo, Utah • 2003*

©2003 by Brigham Young University Press. All rights reserved.

LIBRARY OF CONGRESS CATALOGING-IN-PUBLICATION DATA

Sadr al-Dīn Shīrāzī, Muḥammad ibn Ibrāhīm, d. 1641.
[Iksīr al-ᶜarifīn. English & Arabic]
Mulla Sadra, the elixir of the gnostics : a parallel English-Arabic text / translated, introduced, and annotated by William C. Chittick.
p. cm.—(Islamic translation series)
Includes bibliographical references and index.
ISBN 978–0–934893–70–5 (alk. paper)
1. Philosophy, Islamic. I. Title: Elixir of the gnostics. II. Chittick, William C. III. Title. IV. Series.
B753.M82 E54 2002
181′.5—dc21 2002013549

PRINTED IN THE UNITED STATES OF AMERICA

03 04 05 06 07 08 09 9 8 7 6 5 4 3 2 1

*First Edition*

# Contents

## Part Two

*On the Knowledge of the Soul, which is a Receptacle for the Sciences*



## Part Three

*On the States of the Beginnings*

# Foreword to the Series

The Islamic Translation Series: Philosophy, Theology, and Mysticism (hereafter ITS) is designed not only to further scholarship in Islamic studies but, by encouraging the translation of Islamic texts into the technical language of contemporary Western scholarship, to assist in the integration of Islamic studies into Western academia and to promote global perspectives in the disciplines to which it is devoted. If this goal is achieved, it will not be for the first time: Historians well know that, during the so-called Middle Ages, a portion of the philosophical, scientific, and mathematical wealth of the Islamic tradition entered into and greatly enriched the West. Even Christian theology was affected, as is brilliantly evidenced in the works of St. Thomas Aquinas and other scholastics.

Manuscripts submitted to ITS for consideration are, of course, evaluated without regard to the religious, methodological, or political preferences of the translators or to their gender or national origins. The translator of each text, not the editors of the series nor the members of the advisory board, is solely responsible for the volume in question.

On behalf of Daniel C. Peterson, the executive editor, and members of the advisory board, I wish to express deep appreciation to the cosponsoring institutions—the Institute for the Study and Preservation of Ancient Religious Texts at Brigham Young University and the Foundation for Interreligious Diplomacy (and its director, Charles Randall Paul)—for their gracious support of this project.

—Parviz Morewedge
*Editor in Chief*
*Rutgers, The State University of New Jersey*

◆ ◆ ◆

Brigham Young University and its Institute for the Study and Preservation of Ancient Religious Texts are pleased to sponsor and publish the Islamic Translation Series: Philosophy, Theology, and Mysticism (ITS). We wish to express our appreciation to the editor in chief of ITS, Parviz Morewedge, for joining us in this important project. We are especially grateful to James L. and Beverley Sorenson of Salt Lake City for their generous support, which made ITS possible, and to the Ashton Family Foundation of Orem, Utah, which kindly provided additional funding so that we might continue.

Islamic civilization represents nearly fourteen centuries of intense intellectual activity, and believers in Islam number in the hundreds of millions. The texts that will appear in ITS are among the treasures of this great culture. But they are more than that. They are properly the inheritance of all the peoples of the world. As an institution of The Church of Jesus Christ of Latter-day Saints, Brigham Young University is honored to assist in making these texts available to many for the first time. In doing so, we hope to serve our fellow human beings, of all creeds and cultures. We also follow the admonition of our own tradition, to "seek . . . out of the best books words of wisdom," believing, indeed, that "the glory of God is intelligence."

—Daniel C. Peterson
*Executive Editor*
*Brigham Young University*

## *Notes on References and Spelling*

References internal to this edition of *The Elixir of the Gnostics* specify either part and paragraph number or part and endnote number. For example, 3.21 means part 3, paragraph 21; while 4 n. 56 means note 56 of part 4, in the endnotes. References to *Jāwidān-nāma* specify book and chapter numbers separated by a period. Most dates are given according to both the Muslim (Hijra) and Common Era calendars, in that order, separated by a slash.

Also, in this work, terms of Arabic derivation found in *Webster's Third New International Dictionary* generally follow the first spelling given therein and are treated as regular English words. Otherwise, Arabic or Persian words and proper names have been transliterated following, with few exceptions, the standard recommended by the *International Journal of Middle East Studies*.

# Preface

Ṣadr al-Dīn Muḥammad Shīrāzī, more commonly called Mullā Ṣadrā (d. 1050/1640), has lately become one of the best-known Muslim philosophers. For many years he was almost completely ignored by Western scholarship, even though Max Horten had published two books about him in German in the early twentieth century. Gradually, however, the studies of Henry Corbin, Seyyed Hossein Nasr, and Fazlur Rahman helped break down the resistance of Western scholarship to later Islamic philosophy in general and Mullā Ṣadrā in particular, and recently increasing numbers of scholars have been looking carefully at his works.[1]

In Iran, Ṣadrā became the focus of philosophical attention after the revolution, and this has much more significance than it would have had in other countries, given the role that the ulama—within whose circles philosophy has traditionally been cultivated—are now playing in politics and the media. In May 1999, the "World Congress on Mullā Ṣadrā" was held in Tehran. The president of the republic, Mr. Khatami, who has written thoughtful books about contemporary philosophical issues, opened the Congress and spoke on the importance of the philosophical tradition. Over 150 foreign scholars attended together with several hundred Iranians. Although relatively few of the papers dealt specifically with Mullā Ṣadrā, a significant number did, including half a dozen by young non-Iranians who had chosen Mullā Ṣadrā as the topic of their Ph.D. dissertations. Twenty years ago, it would have been difficult to find more than a handful of scholars outside of Iran who had read any of Mullā Ṣadrā's works.

The Congress was organized by the "Ṣadrā Islamic Philosophy Research Institute," which has also undertaken to publish Ṣadrā's works in new, critical editions and has encouraged scholars to translate his books into foreign languages. It was the Institute's request that led me to translate the present treatise.

Among the first publications of the Institute is *Bibliography of Mullā Ṣadrā,* a five-hundred page book detailing manuscripts, editions, and studies in all languages.[2] The Persian title declares that the work is "comprehensive," but already treatises of Mullā Ṣadrā have been published that are not included. Specifically I have in mind *Majmūʿah-i rasāʾil-i falsafī-i Ṣadr al-Mutaʾallihīn,*[3] a six-hundred-page book edited by Ḥāmid Nājī Iṣfahānī, who was not working under the auspices of the Ṣadrā Institute. It includes eighteen "unknown and unpublished" treatises, four of which are not mentioned in the *Bibliography,* though Iṣfahānī declares that they are certainly genuine.

Mullā Ṣadrā deserves the attention he is getting. He is one of the grand scholars of the later period, and the fervor and energy with which he tackles all the issues discussed over the history of Islamic philosophy are difficult to match. He wrote at least fifty major books and substantive treatises, not to mention a good number of minor works. His knowledge of the history of the Islamic intellectual tradition was extraordinary. In his magnum opus, *Al-asfār al-arbaʿa* (The four journeys)—whose full and proper name is *Al-ḥikma al-mutaʿāliya fī al-asfār al-ʿaqliyya* (The transcendent wisdom: On the intellective journeys)[4]—he cites all the great authorities in order to bring them under the scope of his project.

The modern scholarship on Ṣadrā has discussed the vast range of his undertaking and the manner in which he combines and synthesizes the various currents of Islamic thought, especially philosophy, theoretical Sufism, and Kalam (dogmatic theology). It has also been pointed out that he constantly cites the Qurʾān and the hadiths of both the Prophet and the Shiʿite Imams to support his positions, and that he wrote voluminous philosophical commentaries on parts of the Qurʾān and works of Hadith, so he is able to integrate the traditional religious rhetoric into his perspective in a manner that has no real parallels among the earlier philosophers. Nonetheless, despite his constant attention to the Qurʾān and the transmitted sciences, he is primarily a philosopher, by which I mean to say that he wants to engage the great ideas that were first given systematic form by the Greek philosophers.

There is much to be learned about how Ṣadrā developed these ideas if we study his sources and compare his arguments with those of his predecessors. However, if we were to limit ourselves to this, we should have failed to engage him on his own level. He often tells us where the issues he discusses were originally posited in the form in which he knows them, but this is not of any great importance for him. Rather, he thinks that these issues deserve to be thought about by any rational person. If we refuse to think about them and concern ourselves only with historical questions, we treat him and the Islamic philosophical tradition with disdain. Parviz Morewedge, among others, has argued forcefully that the Muslim philosophers deserve to be dealt with as important thinkers in their own right, just as Greek and European philosophers are still treated as figures with something significant to say, not simply as products of peculiar historical circumstances.[5]

The secondary literature on Ṣadrā has made a good deal of progress in laying down the philosophical background and historical context of his works, but such studies can never take the place of translations, and, up until now, to my knowledge only two of his works have been published in English translation, a small fraction of his total output.[6] We cannot engage his philosophical ideas on the basis of the secondary literature, which invariably fits his thinking into preconceived frameworks and fails to allow him to argue out his positions by himself. Of course, translations also have their drawbacks, but they take us a few steps closer to the original texts. For those still in the process of learning the requisite skills, nothing can be more useful than text and translation together.

Finally, I wish to express my gratitude to Professor Michael Fishbein, to whom the Islamic Translation Series editors sent my manuscript for evaluation. He went far beyond the call of duty by drawing up a detailed list of suggested corrections and revisions. In my long career as a translator, I have never before had the benefit of a careful reading by an accomplished scholar. I have put all his suggestions to good use, either by adopting them, or by opting for a third alternative that avoids the problem. His comments have also led me to add quite a number of footnotes to clarify the meaning of technical terms and explain the rationale for my choice of English equivalents. Naturally, I remain totally responsible for the final form of the text.

—William C. Chittick
*25 February 2001*
*Mt. Sinai, New York*

# Translator's Introduction

*Iksīr al-ᶜārifīn* seems to be unique among Ṣadrā's works in that it is, in a certain sense, a translation of an earlier work in Persian. This is *Jāwidān-nāma* (The Book of the Everlasting) by Afḍal al-Dīn Kāshānī (d. ca. 610/ 1213–14), commonly known as Bābā Afḍal.[7] Although Kāshānī was a sophisticated and original philosophical thinker, he was largely ignored by the later tradition, at least partly because he wrote his works mainly in Persian. Ṣadrā's *Iksīr al-ᶜārifīn* is one of the few instances in which Bābā Afḍal's direct influence can be traced, though he does not mention him by name in the text (nor does he mention him in the *Asfār*).

In the introduction to *Iksīr*, Ṣadrā states that he has taken its pearls of wisdom from the books of "the folk of God" *(ahl Allāh)*. In the *Asfār* he uses this expression only seventeen times, invariably to refer to the masters of theoretical Sufism *(ᶜirfān)*—that is, to Ibn al-ᶜArabī and his followers. He often tells us that he has been able to combine the "tasting" *(dhawq)* and "finding" *(wijdān)* of "the folk of God"—that is, their intuitive and mystical perception—with the "investigation" *(baḥth)* and "demonstration" *(burhān)* of the philosophers.[8]

The fact that Ṣadrā includes Bābā Afḍal among the folk of God in the introduction to *Iksīr* may at first sight seem curious. Ostensibly, Bābā Afḍal's treatises are purely philosophical. They make little reference to theological issues and have practically no similarity with the writings of Ibn al-ᶜArabī's school of thought. However, closer study shows that they focus on achieving self-knowledge and human perfection in a style that could only have been dear to Mullā Ṣadrā's heart, and the simplicity, clarity, and even luminosity of Bābā Afḍal's works have few parallels among other philosophical writings. It may have been these qualities that made Ṣadrā place him in the same category as Ibn al-ᶜArabī.

Only three passages in *Iksīr* can be traced directly to anyone else whom Ṣadrā may have considered one of the folk of God. One is a rather long section drawn from Ibn al-ʿArabī's *al-Futūḥāt al-makkiyya,* the second derives from the *Rasāʾil* of the Ikhwān al-Ṣafāʾ, and the third is borrowed from al-Ghazālī's *Iḥyāʾ ʿulūm al-dīn.* There is also a short passage apparently taken from Fakhr al-Dīn Rāzī's commentary on the Qurʾān. Several other passages have no exact parallels in *Jāwidān-nāma* or any other source that I was able to find, but their similarities with Ṣadrā's other writings make me fairly certain that they are his own compositions.

Relatively little of *Iksīr* can be called a "translation" in the modern sense of the word. What Ṣadrā has done is to write a new treatise, using *Jāwidān-nāma* as his model, but revising the contents to fit his own teachings and adding ample clarification to the sections actually taken from Bābā Afḍal. The two books are structured exactly the same. Each has four parts for a total of thirty-five chapters, and the Arabic chapter titles are often translations from the Persian. However, the contents of the chapters can be quite different. *Iksīr* is fifty percent longer than *Jāwidān-nāma,* which already suggests that Ṣadrā added a good deal to it. But he also dropped about forty percent of the text. Hence, in reality, only about one-third of the passages in *Iksīr* can be judged to be actual translations of passages from *Jāwidān-nāma,* and even these are loose translations with commentary.

Ṣadrā does not tell us why he rewrote *Jāwidān-nāma* in Arabic, so I can only offer tentative suggestions:

First, Ṣadrā wanted to make some of the contents of this Persian work available to students of philosophy and the religious sciences. All the important texts of the philosophical curriculum were in Arabic, and few scholars bothered to look at the exceptional books that had been written in Persian.

Second, the general theme of *Jāwidān-nāma* is "the Origin and the Return" *(al-mabdaʾ wa'l-maʿād),* one of Ṣadrā's constant concerns, and indeed the title of one of his earliest books.

Third, in all his writings Bābā Afḍal focuses with extraordinary clarity and simplicity on one issue, which is self-knowledge. He explains that training the intellect is the only way to achieve human completion and perfection. Perhaps his key teaching is the "unification of the intellecter, the intellect, and the intelligible" *(ittiḥād al-ʿāqil wa'l-ʿaql wa'l-maʿqūl),* one of the cornerstones of Ṣadrā's philosophy.[9] Ṣadrā often invokes Porphyry, whom he calls "the most excellent student of . . . Aristotle,"[10] as the first to formulate this issue properly, and he frequently criticizes Avicenna for denying it. He must have appreciated the fact that Bābā Afḍal was one of his predecessors who highlighted this teaching and considered it the goal of the philosophical quest.

Fourth, *Jāwidān-nāma* has a strong Qurʾānic flavor, and this would have attracted Ṣadrā because of his own concern to bring the Qurʾān into the center of the philosophical arena. In this use of the Qurʾān, *Jāwidān-nāma* differs not only from most early works on philosophy but also from Bābā Afḍal's other treatises, which rarely mention Qurʾānic verses. He says in the conclusion that he has written the book "by way of reminding, not by way of argument and demonstration," which is to say that he had his eye on the Qurʾān and Hadith rather than on philosophical reasoning. This makes the text somewhat similar to Ṣadrā's Qurʾān commentaries, which are philosophical but also written with attention to the rhetorical needs of readers without much philosophical training.

If we can only speculate on why Mullā Ṣadrā rewrote *Jāwidān-nāma,* we stand on firmer ground in guessing when he accomplished the task. Nasr and others have discussed the difficulty of dating Mullā Ṣadrā's works. Ṣadrā rarely provided dates himself, often composed works simultaneously, and added cross-references to later books in earlier books. In the introduction to his seven-volume edition of Ṣadrā's Qurʾān commentaries, Muḥammad Khwājawī claims to have made some progress in dating the works.[11] He provides a table of twenty-five books in a rough sort of chronological order, though only half a dozen actually have specific dates. According to him, Ṣadrā's first datable book is *al-Mabdaʾ wa'l-maʿād,* written in 1015/1606–7. He then wrote *Sharḥ al-hidāya,* a commentary on a philosophical work by Athīr al-Dīn Abharī (and in both of these early books, he refers to his *Asfār*). Next he began writing his Qurʾān commentaries. Khwājawī lists eight of these as Ṣadrā's next eight compositions (he mentions four others as written later). The first that Ṣadrā himself dates is the third, that on *āyat al-kursī,* written in 1020/1611–12. The next dated commentary is that on *āyat al-nūr,* written in 1030/1621. Ṣadrā also tells us that he completed the commentary on *Sūra yāsīn* in the same year.

All this allows us to be fairly certain that Ṣadrā had completed *Iksīr al-ʿārifīn* by 1030/1621. In his commentary on *Sūrat yāsīn,* he employs fourteen passages drawn from *Iksīr,* usually in the context of a much expanded discussion. Eleven of these are in turn based on the text of *Jāwidān-nāma.* It is unlikely that he wrote the commentary on *Yāsīn* before

*Iksīr,* because *Iksīr* already modifies the text of *Jāwidān-nāma* significantly, and then the *Yāsīn* commentary modifies it even further. In fact, it would often be difficult to recognize Bābā Afḍal's text in this commentary without the intermediary of *Iksīr.*[12] An exception to this is one of the few sections of the commentary to which Mullā Ṣadrā gives a title—"On how man receives inspiration and disquietening from the angel and the satan" (5:229ff.). This might be enough to call to mind *Jāwidān-nāma* 3.8 and 3.9, "That inspiration and disquietening are in several respects" and "That just as benefit arrives from the angel's inspiration, so also God's saints take benefit from the devil's disquietening." And indeed *Iksīr* 3.8 and 3.9 form the substance of the discussion.

I conclude that Ṣadrā probably wrote *Iksīr* at the same time as or shortly before he wrote his commentary on *Yāsīn*—that is, in the year 1030/1621. Another indication of its relatively early date is his denial of substantial motion in part 3, chapter 3. This doctrine was to become a centerpiece of his teachings in his later works (he also denies it in *Sharḥ al-hidāya*).

If this dating of *Iksīr* is correct, Khwājawī may have to revise his dating of Ṣadrā's commentary on *Sūrat al-jumuʿa,* which he places among his later works. Khwājawī gives it a late date because Ṣadrā does not mention it in the introduction to the commentary on *Sūrat al-sajda* along with the other commentaries that he had written by 1030/1621. However, two pages from Ṣadrā's commentary on *Sūrat al-jumuʿa,* explaining the three levels of perfection *(kamāl)* possessed by prophets, are repeated almost verbatim in *Iksīr,* part 1, chapter 5.[13] The fact that the *Iksīr* version is slightly expanded suggests that it was written later. Moreover, in his *Shawāhid al-rubūbiyya,* Ṣadrā provides a fifty-page enumeration of the teachings and proofs specific to himself, listing about 180 points. One of these teachings is stated in the same two-page passage from *Sūrat al-sajda* that is also found in *Iksīr.* He writes in *Shawāhid,*

> The substance of prophecy comprises three levels, each of which is a perfect individual of its kind. Thus the Prophet is an angel *[malak],* a celestial sphere *[falak],* and a king *[malik],* just as we have mentioned in detail and clarified in our commentary on *Sūrat al-jumuʿa.*[14]

It is significant that Ṣadrā mentions here the commentary on *Sūrat al-jumuʿa* as the book in which he set down this teaching, because he rarely mentions the names of his books in *Shawāhid.* One can reasonably conclude that he first put this teaching into writing in this commentary and later added it to *Iksīr al-ʿārifīn.*

## Ṣadrā's Perspective

Mullā Ṣadrā is famous for the formulation of a number of issues, such as the "principiality"[15] *(aṣāla)* of *wujūd* (existence or being) and its "gradation" or "systematic ambiguity" *(tashkīk)*. Neither of these expressions plays any role in *Iksīr,* even though the text might be read as an analysis of their implications in philosophico-religious terms. Nonetheless, the underlying theme of *Iksīr* is a teaching that stands at the heart of Mullā Ṣadrā's writings and those of many other Muslim thinkers, not least Bābā Afḍal and Ibn al-ᶜArabī. This is the importance of self-knowledge. Ibn al-ᶜArabī focuses on this topic by following the route of the prophetic saying, "He who knows himself [or 'his soul'] knows his Lord." For him, knowledge of self and knowledge of God are inextricably linked, and the only way to find true and certain knowledge is by means of *kashf* or "unveiling," that is, the "tasting and finding" that is given to the folk of God. For his part, Bābā Afḍal takes the route of the philosophical maxim "Know thyself," and he rarely mentions God as essential to the philosophical quest. His tools are "investigation and demonstration." Nonetheless, the ultimate state of self-knowledge for which he asks his readers to strive—in which the knower, the known, and knowledge become one—is difficult to differentiate from "tasting and finding."

More than all the specific philosophical issues for which he is famous and all the technical arguments that he brings to support them, Mullā Ṣadrā's primary concern is self-knowledge, or knowledge of one's own soul—remember here that *nafs* literally means "self," but in these sorts of contexts it has become customary to translate it as "soul." This becomes most explicit, perhaps, in his repeated discussions of the Origin and the Return. Especially important here is his emphasis on the connection between knowledge of self and the situation of the soul in the afterlife.

There is probably no issue that Ṣadrā discusses more voluminously than *maᶜād,* the Return or eschatology. He takes as one of his starting points the eschatological events described in great detail in the Qurᵓān and Hadith, and he interprets these as descriptions of the unfolding of human selves in the next world. He is especially proud of the manner in which he is able to demonstrate philosophically the literal accuracy of the Qurᵓānic accounts. He takes a great deal of help here from Ibn al-ᶜArabī, who covered much of the same ground but without the philosophical apparatus. For his part, Bābā Afḍal exhibits relatively little interest in the afterlife, and this helps explain many of the additions that Ṣadrā made to *Iksīr.*

Ṣadrā's philosophical project, then, appears as a sort of marriage between the two routes to self-knowledge exemplified by Ibn al-ᶜArabī and Bābā Afḍal. If he is constantly correcting or criticizing the experts in Kalam, or philosophers such as Avicenna, it is because they show few signs of having achieved true self-knowledge, the goal that was reached by the folk of God. True knowledge of the self, as he often tells us, is "the mother of wisdom" *(umm al-ḥikma).*[16]

The very title *Iksīr al-ᶜārifīn* suggests the importance that Mullā Ṣadrā gives to knowledge of self. His use of the term *iksīr* parallels al-Ghazālī's use of the word *kīmiyā*ᵓ in his famous Persian work, *Kīmiyā-yi saᶜādat* (The alchemy of felicity), the first section of which Bābā Afḍal epitomized in one of his works. The *ᶜārifūn* or "gnostics" are those whose knowledge or "gnosis" *(ᶜirfān, maᶜrifa)* comes by way of tasting and finding, and these are precisely the folk of God.[17] This sort of knowledge acts as an elixir to transmute their souls into mirrors reflecting God and the cosmos.

Ṣadrā uses the term *iksīr* only four times in the *Asfār* (and he does not use the term *kīmiyā*ᵓ). On three of these occasions he is making passing reference to the activities of alchemists *(ahl al-iksīr, aṣḥāb al-iksīr)* in the context of the natural sciences, and on the fourth he uses the word in a manner that clarifies the significance of the title *Iksīr al-ᶜārifīn.* Knowledge of self—which is identical with knowledge of the soul's Origin and Return—is the gnostic's elixir, allowing him to reach the ultimate goal, which is human perfection (notice that the passage uses the word *felicity,* surely an allusion to al-Ghazālī's "Alchemy").

> [Philosophical] demonstration and the Qurᵓān agree entirely that learning the divine wisdom *[al-ḥikma al-ilāhiyya]* and the knowledge *[maᶜrifa]* of the human self—I mean knowledge of the Origin and the Return—is to win endless subsistence, and rejecting it is the source of eternal loss. . . .
>
> This knowledge makes man the possessor of a great kingdom, because it is the most magnificent elixir. It necessitates universal unneedingness *[al-ghinā al-kullī],* the greatest felicity, becoming similar to the Furthest Good *[al-tashabbuh bi'l-khayr al-aqṣā],* and assuming as one's own the character traits of God *[al-takhalluq bi akhlāq Allāh].*[18]

In *Iksīr al-ᶜārifīn* itself, other than in the title, Ṣadrā mentions the word *iksīr* only once (4.11), in a context very similar to the passage quoted above. He uses it in the unusual expression "red elixir." He clearly has in mind what is commonly called "red sulfur," the rarest form of sulfur and the most efficacious in bringing about alchemical transmutation. He identifies it with knowledge of the Origin and the Return.

To sum up, Bābā Afḍal's *Jāwidān-nāma* explains the necessity for self-knowledge in the context of the Origin and the Return, and as such it coincides with Ṣadrā's major focus of interest. Ṣadrā liked the book, but he was not completely happy with it, so he dropped the parts that did not please him and added clarifications concerning those dimensions of the philosophical and religious quest that he felt it had ignored.

The centrality of self-knowledge to Mullā Ṣadrā's project means that he puts all his philosophical teachings at the service of the human quest for perfection. Human beings were created in the divine image with a purpose, i.e., to bring the image to full actualization through self-knowledge. Philosophy is the most direct means, in Ṣadrā's view, to achieve this purpose. Teachings like "the gradation of existence" illustrate how the one, simple reality of God, who is sheer *wujūd,* embraces everything. As Ṣadrā's famous dictum puts it, *basīṭ al-ḥaqīqa kull al-ashyāʾ*, "That whose reality is simple is all things." The multiplicity of created things is real enough, but it derives from the infinite gradations that issue forth from the One *Wujūd,* whose utter simplicity and transcendence is never compromised.

If budding philosophers need to know how existence has come to appear in degrees of greater and lesser intensity, or how it displays its systematic ambiguity in the infinite beings of the cosmos, this is because they need to understand how their own souls originated with God and then came into the world. Without this knowledge, it will be impossible for them to undertake the return journey. By understanding *wujūd*'s gradations, they can grasp how the soul came down on the arc of descent *(qaws al-nuzūl),* and how it has begun the process of climbing back on the arc of ascent *(qaws al-ṣuʿūd).* Once they know where they stand on the ascending trajectory, they can undertake practices that will ensure a felicitous homecoming.

In a section of the *Asfār* on evil, Ṣadrā explains that evil's presence in the cosmos is necessitated by *wujūd*'s gradation. In itself, *wujūd* is the summum bonum, the Sheer Good *(al-khayr al-maḥḍ)* that is the source of every good. Everything other than absolute *wujūd* is deficient in good. The levels of descent that stretch down to the corporeal world become differentiated to the degree in which they fall short of the perfect good of the First. Ultimately, when the lack of good reaches its fullest possible measure, we are dealing with a domain that is almost, but not quite, sheer evil. But this lack of good is itself the potential for good. Hence, good begins to appear once again, and this gives rise to the arc of ascent, which reaches its fulfillment in the Return to the One, a return that is the reestablishment of all things in Sheer Good. Most of this discussion takes place in terms of the word *naqṣ* (and its virtual synonym *nuqṣān*), i.e., deficiency, falling short, imperfection.

> The deficiencies of the *wujūd* that is beneath the level of the First *Wujūd* are disparate, for the body falls short of the Necessary more than does the soul, and the senses fall short of the degree of the First Intellect more than does imagination. Were deficiency exactly similar in all the possible things, all the species would be one species, and all the quiddities *[māhiyyāt]* would be one quiddity. And, just as the quiddities are disparate in their realities, so also the ipseities *[huwiyyāt]* of the individuals included under one species are disparate.
>
> In short, innovation *[ibdāᶜ]* necessitates that the innovated fall short of the Innovator. Otherwise, for one of them to be Innovator and the other innovated would not be more appropriate than the contrary.
>
> So, it is incontestable that no possible thing is empty of deficiency and inadequacy, and it is incontestable that deficiency is greater in the world of the souls than in the world of the intellects; that it is greater and more ample in the world of the natures than in the world of the souls; and that it is greater and more intense in the world of the elements than in the world of the celestial spheres.
>
> So it continues, until it comes to an end at a common matter in which there is no good save the potency and preparedness to receive things. You will come to know that, although this matter reaches the utmost meanness and evil in its essence, it is the means for the approach to all good things, and, because of it, *wujūd* goes back and returns to perfection after deficiency, nobility after meanness, and ascension after fall.[19]

Just as the doctrine of *wujūd*'s gradation serves to explain the ontological basis for the route that the soul follows in her Origin and Return, so also Ṣadrā's well-known concept of "substantial motion" *(al-ḥaraka al-jawhariyya)* demonstrates how the soul's *wujūd* increases in intensity and undergoes an endless unfolding of possibilities, for the human essence, made in the image of God, is unlimited and indefinable. All creation renders service to the soul's devolution from the One and her evolution back into the One, helping her break her link with the material realm and gain independence in her own substance.

> As long as the soul is in her body, she increases her substance and her actuality. Little by little she becomes something stronger in *wujūd* and more intense in actual being *[taḥaṣṣul]*—whether in the last abode

> she is to be one of the felicitous or one of the wretched. The potency of *wujūd* necessitates independence in substantiality and not needing any locus or thing to which one is attached. Finally the conjoined becomes the disjoined, and the linked the separate.[20]

In her embodiment in this world, the soul is conjoined with the body and linked to matter, and thus she dwells in the depths of deficiency and imperfection. In her ascent back to her Origin, she gradually breaks this conjunction and linkage. She returns to her own essence *(dhāt)* and finds that she has no real linkage with anything below the First Intellect, because her essence is separate *(mufāriq)* and disengaged *(mujarrad)* from matter.

> God created the human soul as an image *[mithāl]* of His Essence, His attributes, and His acts, for He is incomparable with any likeness *[mithl]*, but not with an image. So, He created the soul as His image in essence, attributes, and acts, so that knowledge of her may be a staircase to knowledge of Him. He made her essence disengaged from beings, confines, and directions, and He made her become the possessor of power, knowledge, desire, life, hearing, and eyesight. He made her the possessor of an empire similar to the empire of her Author. *He creates what He* desires *and chooses* [Qur'ān 28:68] for the sake of what He desires. However, although she derives from the root of the Sovereignty [*malakūt,* i.e., the spiritual realm], the world of power, and the mine of magnificence and ascendancy, she is weak in existence and establishment, because she has fallen into the levels of the descent, and she has intermediaries between her and her Author.[21]

Few terms are more important to the philosophers' explication of the soul's becoming and her ultimate goal than "disengagement" *(tajarrud)*. The term has a long history of use, but its significance has often been missed in the secondary literature.[22] The technical use goes back at least to the *Theology of Aristotle,* where Plotinus writes in a famous passage, "On occasion, I withdraw into my soul and discard my body off to the side. I become as if I were a disengaged substance without body."[23] Its centrality in Ṣadrā's teachings is suggested by the fact that he and his commentator use the word and its derivatives in this meaning several hundred times in the *Asfār,* while they mention the word *aṣāla* or "principiality" only forty-five times and the word *tashkīk* or "gradation" (in the context of *wujūd*) only a handful of times. Even the expression "substantial motion" can give us no more than about two hundred instances. The secondary literature keeps on coming back to these three doctrines—principiality, gradation, and substantial motion—because they appear as original contributions. The disengagement of the soul is more basic to Ṣadrā's teachings, but there is nothing unusual about it, except perhaps the degree of Ṣadrā's stress upon it, so the secondary literature tends to ignore it.

By suggesting that principiality and gradation are not quite as important to Mullā Ṣadrā's teachings as one might assume from reading the studies, I am not suggesting that existence itself is unimportant. Quite the contrary, as in much of Islamic philosophy, *wujūd* is the primary topic of discussion (in the *Asfār* and its commentary the word itself is employed 15,000 times, not to mention its verbal forms and derivatives). The question is not about the significance of *wujūd,* which is discussed at least implicitly in all issues. Rather, the question is this: Why is *wujūd* so important? And, why must we know that it is so important? It is certainly necessary to know that *wujūd* is principial and gradational, but only because the human soul is the key to everything, and its ontological status can best be explained—in Ṣadrā's view—by reference to principiality, gradation, and substantial motion.

In one passage of the *Asfār,* for example, Ṣadrā criticizes Avicenna and his followers for denying the unification of the intellecter and the intelligible. The reason they denied it, he says, is that "They did not firm up the foundation of the science of the soul, because they neglected the issue of *wujūd,* its deficiency, its origins, and its final goals."[24] In order to achieve this true and certain knowledge of the soul, one must grasp the true nature of the gradational, principial *wujūd.* But this knowledge can be actualized only by experiencing the soul's disengagement from everything other than God.

In the purest sense of the term, "disengagement" is an attribute of the Divine Essence, which has no attachment or connection to anything other than itself. It is also an attribute of the First Intellect, which is the initial point on the descending arc that yields the created world. Disengagement enters into the discussion of the human soul in questions of the soul's reality and essence, and also in questions of modalities of perception, knowledge, and understanding.

Ṣadrā and a number of other philosophers see the soul's climb to perfection as a gradual disengagement from all embodiment and materiality and a return to her transcendent essence. This does not mean that souls will no longer have any connection to the things of the world. Rather, it means that they gradually come to see things clearly. They no longer fall into the nearsightedness of seeing realities as embodied. They come to see that all realities and essences are found in the Intellect from which all things have descended, and that their embodiment in corporeal or imaginal appearance is a temporary affair.

The soul begins its sojourn in this world as a potential intellect. She must ascend on the trajectory of the Return in order to become an "actual intellect" *(ʿaql bi'l-fiʿl)*. Once she does so, she will see that all realities are found in herself. The seer, what is seen, and the seeing will all be one. This is the "unification of the intellecter, the intelligible, and the intellect." When she reaches the stage of what is usually translated as the "acquired intellect" *(ʿaql mustafād)*, she "acquires," or, more literally, "takes the profit" *(istifāda)* of intelligence directly from the Fully Active Intellect *(ʿaql faʿʿāl)*. Ṣadrā writes in the *Asfār:*

> The human soul climbs from form to form and from perfection to perfection. At the first stages of configuration, she begins from unqualified bodiment and goes to the elemental forms, then from them to the mineral and vegetal, then from them to the animal, until she achieves fully all the animal potencies. Finally she reaches the essence from which derive the first things that are ascribed to bodily matter. When she begins to climb from it, she climbs to the first level of the existents that are entirely separate *[mufāriq]* from matter. This is the "acquired intellect," and it is nearly like the Fully Active Intellect.
>
> The difference between it and the Fully Active Intellect is that the acquired intellect is a separate form that had been linked *[muqtarin]* to matter. Then it became disengaged from matter after its transformation in the stages. But the Fully Active Intellect is a form that has never been in matter, and it is impossible for it to be anything but separate.[25]

In short, all of Ṣadrā's teachings focus on the necessity of freeing the soul from ignorance and allowing her to rejoin the intelligence from which she emerged. In the process of proving that this is in fact what being human is all about, Ṣadrā looks at the great intellectual authorities to illustrate the degree to which their teachings focus on the true goal of learning. His constant attention to the afterlife is nothing but his constant attention to the reality of the soul in her full actualization. As he puts it, "The key to knowledge of the day of resurrection and the return of the creatures [to God] is the knowledge of the soul and her levels."[26] His discussions of cosmology and psychology, under the rubric of the Origin and the Return, serve to illustrate how *wujūd* unfolds through an infinity of gradational degrees until it reaches the nothingness of pure possibility; then it gathers itself once again as the soul goes home to her own essence, which is nothing but pure intelligence, the radiance of God.

If, as Ṣadrā demonstrates, every human being becomes an independent world in the afterlife, it is because the divine image is nothing but a pure ray of *wujūd,* the "simple in reality that is all things," and hence it embraces all existence and is capable of indefinite intensification and diminution. Moreover, just as souls in the afterlife undergo a never-ending variety of manifestations, so also human beings in this life are necessarily ranked in degrees according to their actualization of *wujūd* in themselves. From the womb ad infinitum, the soul experiences endless efflorescence. In Ṣadrā's famous dictum, the soul is "bodily in occurrence, spiritual in subsistence" *(jismāniyyat al-ḥudūth rūḥāniyyat al-baqāʾ).*

> At the first of its configuration, the human soul is only a material body, like other species-specific forms. Then she comes to be disengaged in essence, but not in act. Then at death she comes to be separate from sensory, dense, material bodies in both essence and act. So, she is either felicitous, or—if her attachment to those bodies remains—she is wretched. Or, she is one of those brought nigh [to God]—if she is disengaged totally from the bodies and all her attachments.[27]
>
> As long as the human soul is an embryo in the womb, her degree is the degree of vegetal souls. When the infant emerges from its mother's belly, its soul is like the souls of the other animals until the time of formal adulthood *[bulūgh ṣūrī].* Then she becomes rational *[nāṭiq]* after that. If she has the preparedness to climb to the limit of the holy soul and the Actual Intellect, then, when she reaches forty years of age, which is the time of supraformal adulthood *[bulūgh maʿnawī],* she becomes a holy soul—if she is assisted by the divine success-giving.
>
> Hence, as long as it is in the womb, the embryo is actually a plant and potentially an animal. Once it emerges from its mother's belly, before adulthood it is actually an animal and potentially man. When it reaches the limit of formal adulthood, it is actually man and potentially angel. As for the level of the holy potency, it may be that not one of thousands of human individuals reaches it.[28]

For Mullā Ṣadrā, the discussions of the different degrees of the natural world, so popular with the philosophers, are nothing but an exposition of the different powers and potencies that are latent in the human soul. As a microcosm, the human soul embraces all the degrees of the descent from the One *Wujūd,* and she has the potential to pass through all the degrees of the ascent. Thus she goes through stages of coinciding with the elements, the mineral kingdom, the vegetal kingdom, the animal kingdom, and the various degrees of humanness.[29] When she knows the world around her—the minerals, plants, and animals—in truth she knows herself. But it is necessary to know things by disengaging them from their matter and seeing them in the holistic perspective that is provided by a grand overview like the "transcendent wisdom."

> As long as the Adamic soul is an embryo in the womb, her degree is the degree of the vegetal souls in keeping with their levels, and she obtains the degrees of the mineral potencies only after having crossed over nature. So, the human embryo is actually a plant and potentially, but not actually, an animal, because it has no sensation and movement. The fact that it is potentially an animal is its specific difference *[faṣl]*, distinguishing it from the other plants and making it a species different from the vegetal species.
>
> When the infant emerges from inside its mother, it becomes a soul in the degree of the animal souls until the time of its formal adulthood. Then the individual is actually a human animal *[ḥayawān basharī]* and potentially a soulish man *[insān nafsānī]*.[30] Then he becomes a soul that perceives things through reflection and deliberation and uses the practical intellect. He continues in this way until the time of supraformal adulthood and inward maturity *[rushd bāṭinī]* through the consolidation of inward habitudes *[malakāt]* and character traits *[akhlāq]*. This is usually around the age of forty.
>
> At this level, he is actually a soulish man and potentially an angelic or a satanic man. At the resurrection, he will be mustered either with the party of the angels or the party and troops of the satans. If the [divine] success-giving assists him and he travels the pathway of the Real and the path of *tawḥīd*, if his intellect is perfected through knowledge, and if his intellect is purified through disengagement from bodies, then he becomes actually one of God's angels, those who have the attributes of the knowers brought nigh. If he goes astray from the even road and travels the pathway of misguidance and the ignorant, he will become one of the satans or be mustered among the beasts and the crawling things.[31]

In Ṣadrā's way of looking at things, everything in existence is traveling on a path that ends up at its rightful place with God. Like Ibn al-ᶜArabī, he understands divine mercy as the guiding force of creation. He sees the movement from Origin to Return and from First to Last as a great manifestation of God's wisdom and compassion, all of it leading to a final fruition in which everything in the universe will find permanent happiness.

> The root of innovation *[ibdāᶜ]* and giving existence *[ījād]* is the Author's munificence and mercy, His conveying everything to its perfection and utmost end, and His moving all things to their final goals

> and destinies—making the low reach the high, giving to every matter the form befitting it, and inducing each to become the most excellent of what can be conceived for it.
>
> Just as the natural moving thing's arrival at its confines is its stillness, and just as nature's arrival at the soulish potency is its final goal, so also the soul's arrival at the degree of intellect is its stillness. This is the utmost end of the soul, just as the Author is the utmost end of the intellect and everything below it. At this there is perpetual ease, complete serenity, and the greatest good.
>
> This is the furthest purpose in building the cosmos, moving the heavens, and setting in motion the stars, the orbs, and all the other transformations and vicissitudes; and in sending down the angels and the messengers from heaven with books, revelation, and news-giving. I mean that the whole purpose is for all the cosmos to become the good. So, evil and deficiency will disappear from it, and it will return to that from which it began. Thus its last will become joined with its first, and the utmost end of its cycle will bend back upon its origin. Wisdom will be completed and creation perfected. The world of being *[kawn]* and corruption *[fasād]* will be removed and this world *[dunyā]* will be nullified. The Greater Resurrection will stand forth, evil and its folk will be effaced, unbelief and its party will be toppled, the null will be nullified, and the Real will be realized through His words. This is the furthest goal and the most magnificent wisdom.[32]

Let me conclude this brief overview by letting Ṣadrā expand upon the purpose and goal of his "transcendent wisdom." The following passage is taken from his introduction to the *Asfār,* in which he is explaining why it is necessary for all human beings to pursue wisdom. Understanding the nature of things, he tells us, is a precondition for and a concomitant of achieving human status. What we need to know and understand is outlined by the topics that designate the articles of faith in Islamic creeds. It is not sufficient simply to accept them. There is no "imitation" or "following authority" *(taqlīd)* in matters of faith. Each person must understand the truth for himself and commit himself to it by himself.

> The human species has an unsurpassed and unprecedented perfection specific to the substance of his essence and his true reality *[ḥāqq ḥaqīqatihi],* and that is conjunction with the intelligibles, adjacency with the Author, and disengagement from material things. However, with respect to every faculty found within man, he shares with what is equal to him or near to him in that respect. With other bodies [he shares] coming to be within confinement and space; with plants nourishment

and growth; and with dumb animals the life of breaths, volitional movement, and sense-perception. The human specificity is obtained only through sciences and knowledge along with cutting off from attachment to superficialities.

The sorts of knowledge have many branches, the varieties of perception are diverse, and encompassing all of them is impossible or difficult. Hence man's aspiration has split into many branches, just as the feet of the world's folk walk diverse paths in the crafts. The ulama have divided themselves into classes, and their concerns have split them into groups between the intellective [sciences] and the transmitted, and between the branches and the roots. Some concern themselves with things like grammar and astronomy, others with things like jurisprudence, biography, and Kalam.

It is incumbent upon the intelligent person to turn his full attention to occupying himself with the most important. He must resolutely avoid pouring away his lifespan in what does not pertain specifically to the perfection of his essence—after he obtains the other knowledges and sciences to the measure of his need for them in livelihood, the final Return, and deliverance from what prevents him from reaching the station of integrity and the Day of the Rendezvous. The most important are the sciences that pertain to the perfecting of the first of his two potencies. These two are the direction of his essence, or his face *[wajh]* turned toward the Real, and the direction of his ascription *[iḍāfa]*, or his face turned toward creation.[33] That first potency is the theoretical, which accords with the true substance of his essence without sharing in the ascription to the body and its passivities.

Other than the divine wisdom and the lordly sciences,[34] every knowledge is needed only by virtue of the intervention of the body and its faculties and the pursuit of the flesh and its desires. Only the sheer intellective sciences are able to undertake the perfecting of the human substance and the elimination of its blemishes and uglinesses when it cuts itself off from this world and everything within it, returns to its true reality, and turns totally toward its Author, Configurer, Existence-Giver, and Bestower. These sciences are knowledge of God, His attributes, His angels, His books, and His messengers; the manner of the emergence of things from Him in the most perfect mode and the most excellent arrangement; the manner of His solicitude toward and knowledge of them; His governance of them without defect, incapacity, blight, and slackening; and knowledge of the soul, its path to the afterworld, its conjunction with the Higher Plenum [the angels], its separation from its shackles, and its distance from hyle.[35] For, through all this she is completed by being released from the constraints of possibility and saved from calamitous mishaps; she is plunged into the oceans of the Sovereignty and strung on the string of the inhabitants of the Jabarūt.[36] Thus she is delivered from captivity to the appetites, confusion by appearances, passivity before the effects of movements, and domination by the revolution of the heavens.[37]

## *Jāwidān-nāma* and *Iksīr al-ᶜārifīn*

Readers who want to know exactly how Mullā Ṣadrā revised *Jāwidān-nāma* in writing *Iksīr al-ᶜārifīn* can compare this translation with the translation of *Jāwidān-nāma* that I have provided elsewhere.[38] Here I offer a summary of how he dealt with the text.

### *Part One*

Ṣadrā revises Baba Afḍal's first four chapters simply by expanding his classification of knowledge. Chapter five, however, "On the science of the afterworld," contains one of Ṣadrā's major additions to the text. In *Jāwidān-nāma,* Bābā Afḍal merely points out that knowledge of afterworldly things has a benefit that transcends this life, whereas knowledge of worldly things is like a dream that ends with death. Knowledge of the afterworld is "knowing the horizons and the souls," that is, the macrocosm and the microcosm; the first profit of this knowledge is *tawḥīd,* the recognition and acknowledgment of God's unity. Its second profit is knowing the self's place of return *(maᶜād)* after this life. But this is all that he says in the chapter. For the rest, he refers the reader to the next three parts of the book. And notice that he lists two of the three principles of Islamic faith—*tawḥīd* and *maᶜād*—but he does not mention the third, prophecy *(nubuwwa),* though he speaks of its importance later on. He leaves the implications of these two principles to the later text. In contrast, Ṣadrā provides several pages of explication concerning the three principles of faith, devoting the largest amount of space to the third, that is, the Return to God. He does not mention the other two principles added by Shiᶜites: imamate and justice.

### *Part Two*

In chapter one Ṣadrā translates the first half of Baba Afḍal's chapter, which explains the four roots of disagreement among schools of thought. He drops the second half, which traces these roots to the nature of language.

Chapter two is half expanded, half dropped.

Chapter three is partly revised, mostly dropped.

Chapter four entails a total revision of the discussion. There is much more reference to Qur'ānic verses, a more systematic classification of the sorts of subjection, and several of Bābā Afḍal's points are dropped.

Chapters five and six contain translation and revision.

Chapter seven is dropped; the argument is replaced with a shorter, parallel discussion. Bābā Afḍal provides what may be an original explanation of the correspondences between seven macrocosmic signs (heaven, fire, air, water, earth, plants, animals) and seven microcosmic signs (hearing, eyesight, smell, taste, touch, rational speech, writing). Mullā Ṣadrā may have found this discussion too far from the mainstream of Islamic philosophy.

Most of chapter eight is dropped, but what is kept is elaborated upon in detail. The dropped material explains the correspondence between the four levels of numerals (units, tens, hundreds, thousands) and four levels of the microcosm (reflection, memory, rational speech, writing), and then expands on the microcosm/macrocosm correspondences begun in the previous chapter.

In chapter nine Ṣadrā expands on some of Bābā Afḍal's points, adds some material, and drops the one-third of the chapter that deals with the number correspondences discussed in chapter eight.

About half of Ṣadrā's chapter ten expands on a few of Bābā Afḍal's points, and the other half summarizes, in quite different language, a rather long discussion on understanding *tawḥīd* through macrocosm/microcosm correspondences.

*Part Three*

Chapter one adds a good deal of material and drops some.

Chapter two is retained basically the same, with the exception of the last paragraph, which makes a point that Ṣadrā mentions in *Shawāhid* as among his own contributions to philosophy.

About half of the original chapter three is dropped and replaced by a different discussion.

Chapter four is revised.

Chapter five is revised, with two short additions.

Chapter six is half revised, half dropped. The dropped section discusses the four archangels and their microcosmic correspondences (Seraphiel = reflective thought; Michael = memory; Gabriel = speech; Azrael = writing). In later chapters, however, Ṣadrā keeps the discussion of these angels.

Perhaps he dropped this section because of the odd classification of human faculties, in particular the inclusion of "writing," concerning which Bābā Afḍal has already said a good deal in passages that Ṣadrā has not translated.

In chapter seven Ṣadrā adds a definition of Iblis and drops most of the chapter. In the dropped portions Bābā Afḍal compares "the folk of the Sunnah and Congregation" (i.e., the true Muslims, the Sunnis) to an earth that gives fruit or fails to give it on the basis of the activity of the angels and satans. He also interprets various Qur'ānic references to Iblis in philosophical and spiritual terms.

Chapter eight is revised and expanded.

Chapter nine has been mostly dropped. The first half of Ṣadrā's chapter is a much expanded version of Bābā Afḍal's first paragraph, and the second half is his own addition.

The first six paragraphs of chapter ten translate and expand upon Bābā Afḍal's points, but most of this chapter is added by Ṣadrā.

### *Part Four*

Only about one-third of the lengthy first chapter is based on Bābā Afḍal. The paragraphs on demonstrations, the unification of the intellecter and the intelligible, the movement of existence toward strength, the final goal of movement, and the blights of the path are all additional.

Chapter two is revised and expanded.

About half of chapter three is additional (from 4.36–41).

In chapter four most of Bābā Afḍal's discussion is dropped, and only the first paragraph represents a revision of one part of it. The dropped sections explain the need for prophets in terms of the earlier discussion of the correspondence between macrocosm and microcosm. Mullā Ṣadrā has already given his own explanation of prophethood in 1.5.

In chapter five Ṣadrā expands on Bābā Afḍal's four paragraphs, but most of the chapter, on the descending order of the cosmos, is taken from Ibn al-ʿArabī.

Chapter six has been revised and expanded.

About half the text in chapter seven is additional, specifically the explanation that prophets do not gain knowledge by following authority or "imitation" *(taqlīd),* and the paragraph explaining the meaning of the "Faithful Spirit" and "John."

The first part of chapter eight and the first subsection are based on Bābā Afḍal, and the second and third subsections are added.

Most of chapter nine is additional; only the third paragraph and part of the fourth are from *Jāwidān-nāma.*

The first half of chapter ten is from Bābā Afḍal, the second half is Mullā Ṣadrā's own conclusion. Most of Bābā Afḍal's final chapter, explaining the usefulness of the book, is dropped.

## The Arabic Text

*Iksīr al-ʿārifīn* was first published in 1302/1885 along with eight other treatises in the *Rasāʾil* of Mullā Ṣadrā. It was given a critical edition, based on the printed edition and two manuscripts, by Shigeru Kamada, who published it along with a Japanese translation in 1984.[39] This is a good edition, but not without defects, such as dropped phrases and sentences. The Ṣadrā Islamic Philosophy Research Institute turned the task of preparing a definitive edition over to Yaḥyā Yathribī, but as of this writing, his edition has not appeared. The Institute sent me a copy of Yathribī's manuscript, which was a thoroughly corrected version of the Kamada edition, employing seven additional manuscripts. It also sent me a copy of one of the manuscripts Yathribī employed (number 10602 from the library of the Majlis-i Shawrā-yi Islāmī), which is said to be an autograph. However, the manuscript lacks several pages of the text and has numerous minor errors and differences with the other manuscripts, so it was not as useful as could have been hoped. If it is in fact in Ṣadrā's hand, it was probably done quickly without being checked carefully against the original.

Despite the great pains that Yathribī has put into collating the manuscripts, his edition in the form I have seen still has a few errors. Some of these will no doubt be corrected by the time it appears in print. For many of them, it is sufficient to know that Ṣadrā was revising *Jāwidān-nāma* and quoting a long passage from the *Futūḥāt*—facts that I have communicated to Yathribī and that he has acknowledged. Even so, his edition will still not be as critical as it might be, because he appears to be using the Qurʾān to correct all Qurʾān citations, despite the fact that the manuscript evidence shows that Ṣadrā sometimes modified the text to make his point—as is commonly done.[40]

My edition, then, is based on the Yathribī manuscript, with a number of minor changes. I have mentioned several of these in the notes, even though some of them will probably coincide with Yathribī's text once it finally appears in print.

## The Translation

My translation follows the Arabic as closely as I could manage without seriously damaging readability. Even though the original words can be checked in the facing text, I assume that a good number of those who read the book will know little more than a smattering of Arabic. For them in particular, consistency and accuracy are important, especially if they want to read the book with some of the care that was traditionally given to works of this sort. Hence I have tried to choose a single English equivalent for each technical term, and I have attempted not to use the same equivalent for other Arabic words. My index of terms includes the Arabic words, thus functioning as a sort of glossary. I have added explanatory notes both to indicate parallel passages in some of Ṣadrā's other works and to clarify references or obscurities. However, I have restrained the impulse to explain the text in detail, or to analyze the manner in which Ṣadrā modifies Bābā Afḍal's *Jāwidān-nāma.*

I have avoided neologisms as far as I could, but on occasion I have adopted terms because the ordinary translations are not adequate. At least the word "soulish" for *nafsānī,* though not especially felicitous, is neither a neologism nor archaic. I use it because the alternatives—such as psychological and psychic—have been preempted by modern usage and obscure the connection with "soul." *Soulish* means simply "pertaining to the soul." The word is needed for the same reason that we need the words *intellective, spiritual,* and *bodily.* Given the central importance of *nafs* in Ṣadrā's philosophy, it seems wrong to dilute attention to the word by translating its adjectival form with a term that does not reflect the derivation.

Some expressions may be unfamiliar to readers who do not know Arabic, and these I try to explain in footnotes. A pair of terms that is especially common is *malakūt* and *mulk,* which designate the world of spirits and the world of bodies and which I translate as "Sovereignty" and "Kingdom." These are Qurʾānic terms that are typically employed as synonyms for two other common Qurʾānic pairs, "Absent" *(ghayb)* and "Witnessed" *(shahāda);* and "Command" *(amr)* and "Creation" *(khalq).* Ṣadrā also mentions the still higher world known as Jabarūt, the world that displays the attributes of God as *al-jabbār,* "the Compeller" or "the Mender." He identifies it with the world of the First Intellect.

I translate *wujūd* as "existence" and *kawn* as "being"; the latter might also be translated as "generation" or "engendered existence." *Wujūd* in the strict sense pertains only to the Necessary Existence *(al-wujūd al-wājibī),* which is God or the First Real *(al-ḥaqq al-awwal).* The existence that is ascribed to the world and all things within it, which are called "existents" *(mawjūdāt),* is ambiguous or gradational. "Being," in contrast to "existence," refers strictly to the world, which comes into existence when God says to it, "Be" *(kun).* Hence the "beings" *(akwān, kāʾināt, mukawwanāt)* are the existents, that is, the created things. God is not called *kawn,* but He is *wujūd* by definition.

Since the introduction is in rhymed prose, I have arranged the first part of the English translation to reflect this fact.

بسم الله الرحمن الرحيم

# The Elixir of the Gnostics

# اكسير العارفين

*In the name of God, the All-Merciful, the Ever-Merciful*

(1) *Glory be to You, O God!*
*O Innovator of the intellects and souls with their gleams and lights,*
*O Deviser of the spheres and planets with their turns and cycles,*
*Gatherer of the scattered elements with their forms and traces,*
*Preserver of the compoundedness of the compound things and progeny with their results and fruits,*
*Life-Giver to the bones of animals with their senses and memories,*
*and Perfecter of the souls of man with their sciences and mysteries!*
*From You to You are glorification and calling holy.*
*Through You for You are laudation and salutation.*
*You are the first of every movement and rest, and their last.*
*You are the inwardness of every thought, and its outwardness.*
*You are the Causer of causes, the First of the seconds and firsts,*
*an Innovator, a Substantiator, an Actor not acted upon;*
*Innovator of the first disposition, Configurer of the last configuration;*
*Uplifter of those who declare His Unity to* the Lote Tree of the Endpoint at which is the Garden of the Home *[53:14–15];*
*Downthrower of all who refuse Him to the depths of the lowest Gehenna and the nethermost hellfire.*

بسم الله الرحمن الرحيم

(١) سبحانك اللّهمّ،
يا مبدع العقول والنفوس بأضوائها وأنوارها،
ويا مخترع الأفلاك والكواكب بأدوارها وأكوارها،
وجامع أشتات العناصر بصورها وآثارها،
وحافظ تركيب المركّبات والمواليد بنتائجها وأثمارها،
ومحيى عظام الحيوان بحواسّها وأذكارها،
ومكمّل نفوس الانسان بعلومها وأسرارها،
لك منك التسبيح والتقديس،
وبك عليك الثناء والتحيّة،
لأنّك أوّل كلّ حركة وسكون وآخره،
وباطن كلّ فكر وظاهره.
أنت معلّل العلل وأَوّل الثوانى والأُولَ،
ومُبدِعُ مجوهرٌ وفاعل غير منفعل،
مبدع الفطرة الأولى ومنشئ النشأة الأخرى،
رافع من وحّده الى سدرة المنتهى،
عنده جنّة المأوى،
ومهبط من جحده الى قعر جهنّم السفلى
وجحيم الأدنى.

(2) And bless the essences whose names were fixed in the tablet inscribed by the pen of the Real before He created the creatures; whose attributes were written in *the book engraved, witnessed by those brought nigh* [83:20–21], *touched by none but the purified* [56:79]. For they are the fruits of workmanship and existence-giving, the leaders of the creatures to the path of the afterworld and Return; or, rather, the storehouses of the treasures of existence, the keys to the gates of effusion and munificence; especially our teacher, our guide, our master, and our leader to our Origin and our Return, Muḥammad the Chosen, the Seal of the prophets and the envoys; and his household, the executors, the purified, the illumined—God's peace be upon them all and upon all the precedent prophets and the subsequent saints!

(3) Now then, thus says the servant taking refuge in the precinct of the Lord of the worlds, Muḥammad al-Shīrāzī, known as Ṣadr al-Dīn: These are a few fine points from the eminent questions of wisdom, and a few choice items from the subtle pearls of knowledge. I have culled them from the books of the folk of God from what is considered beautiful by the tastings of the truthful sages and witnessed to by all the deiform gnostics who have traveled the Real's path. To them I have added showings from tasting and inserted flashes from unveiling. I hope for God's bounty on this poor soul and crave the abode of His generous gifts and nearness, for He is the best success-giver and helper! I have gathered these in a book that I have named *The Elixir of the Gnostics: On the Knowledge of the Path of the Real and Certainty*. I have divided it into parts and chapters that are like pillars and principles.

(4) Its parts are four: First, on the quantity of the sciences and their classification; second, on the locus of knowledge and wisdom, which is the human ipseity; third, on the knowledge of that ipseity's beginnings; and fourth, on the knowledge of its original final goal, which is the furthest final goal.

(٢) وصلّ على الذوات المثبتة أسماؤهم فى اللوح المسطور بقلم الحق قبل أن يخلق الخلق، المكتوبة أوصافهم فى كتاب مرقوم يشهده المقرّبون، لا يمسّه الاّ المطهّرون، لأنّهم ثمرات الصنع والايجاد وقوّاد الخلائق الى سبيل الآخرة والمعاد، بل خزائن كنوز الوجود ومفاتيح أبواب الفيض والجود، خصوصاً معلّمنا وهادينا وسيدنا وقائدنا الى مبدأنا ومعادنا محمّد المصطفى خاتم الأنبياء والمرسلين وآله الأوصياء المطهّرين المنوّرين، سلام الله عليهم أجمعين، وعلى جميع الأنبياء السابقين والأولياء اللاحقين.

(٣) وبعد فيقول العبد الملتجئ الى جناب ربّ العالمين محمّد الشيرازى المعروف بصدر الدين انّ هذه نكت من مسائل شريفة حكمية ونخب من جواهر لطيفة علمية، انتقدتها من كتب اهل الله ممّا استحسنها أذوال الحكماء الصادقين وشهد بها كلّ من سلك سبيل الحقّ من العرفاء المتألّهين مع سوانح ذوقية أضفتُها ولوامع كشفية أردفتها، رجاءً بفضل الله على هذا المسكين وطمعاً فى دار كرامته وقربه، إنّه خير موفّق ومعين. فجمعتها فى كتاب وسمّيته إكسير العارفين فى معرفة طريق الحقّ واليقين وقسمته على أبواب وفصول هى كالدعائم والأصول.

(٤) وأبوابه أربعة، أوّلها فى كمّيّة العلوم وقسمتها، وثانيها فى محلّ المعرفة والحكمة وهى الهويّة الانسانية، وثالثها فى معرفة البدايات لها، ورابعها فى معرفة الغاية الأصلية لها وهى الغاية القصوى.

## PART ONE

*In it are five chapters.*

# Chapter One

*On the division of science in an unqualified sense*

(5) It is of two sorts: this-worldly and afterworldly.

(6) This-worldly sciences are of three sorts: First is the science of words, second the science of acts, and third the science of states. The third is like the line differentiating light from darkness and gathering together the two sides, the isthmus that is intermediary between the two way stations. *Upon the Ramparts are men who know each by their mark* [7:46].[1]

(7) Afterworldly sciences are the sciences of witnessing and unveiling, such as knowledge of God, His angels, His books, His messengers, and the Last Day.[2]

# Chapter Two

*On the divisions of the science of words according to what attaches to it*

(8) It has two divisions: common and elect.[3]

# الباب الأوّل

وفيه خمسة فصول

## الفصل الأوّل

في تقسيم العلم مطلقاً

(٥) وهو قسمان دنيوى وأخروى.

(٦) أمّا العلوم الدنيوية فهى ثلاثة أقسام. الأوّل علم الأقوال، والثانى علم الأفعال، والثالث علم الأحوال، وهو كالخطّ الفاصل بين النور والظلمة الجامع للطرفين البرزخ المتوسّط بين المنزلتين، وعلى الأعراف رجال يعرفون كلا بسيماهم.

(٧) وأما العلوم الأخروية فهى علوم المشاهدة والمكاشفة كالعلم بالله وملائكته وكتبه ورسله واليوم الآخر.

## الفصل الثانى

فى أقسام علم الأقوال بحسب ما يتعلّق به

(٨) وهو قسمان عامّى وخاصّى.

(9) The common has three divisions according to three topics. The first pertains to naked sounds, which are shared by inanimate things and animals, beasts and men, the intelligent and infants.

(10) The second pertains to the solitary letters that come to be from the movements and guises of the sounds.

(11) The third pertains to the vocables signifying meanings that come to be from compounding letters in one of the languages—Arabic, Persian, Hebrew, Syriac, and others. In each language, these vocables are of three sorts—nouns, verbs, and particles—for each signifies either a thing, or its act, or its correlation with another thing. Each of these is a solitary vocable from which are composed compound vocables, whether complete or incomplete. The complete is either a report or an imploration.[4]

(12) The elect science of words pertains to vocables brought by the intelligent—that is, the possessors of astuteness, understanding, and making understood. Through it vowels and consonants are pronounced in the correct and complete manner.

(13) In each of the three mentioned levels, which are the origins of words and narrative, arises one of the three great sciences. From the knowledge of sounds, their numerical quantities, and the melodic relations coming to be within them from levels of sharpness and heaviness is born the science of music, whose topic is the quantity that comes to be in sound.

(14) From the knowledge of heard letters and their declinable and indeclinable vowels and consonants is born the science of declension and prosody.

(15) From the knowledge of the meanings of the vocables is born the science of lexicography and poetry and the technique of meanings, clarification, and the innovated.[5]

(٩) والعامّى ثلاثة أقسام بحسب الموضوعات الثلاثة. الأوّل ما يتعلّق بالأصوات الساذجة المشترك فيها الجماد والحيوان والبهيمة والانسان والعاقل والصبيان.

(١٠) والثانى ما يتعلّق بالحروف المفردة الحاصلة من حركات الأصوات وهيآتها.

(١١) والثالث ما يتعلّق بالألفاظ الدالّة على المعانى الحاصلة من تركيب الحروف فى لغة من اللغات العربية أو الفارسية أو العبرية أو السُريانية أو ما سواها، وهى فى كلّ لغة على ثلاثة أقسام، اسم وكلمة وأداة، لأنّها إمّا أن تدلّ على الشيء أو فعله أو إضافته الى شيء آخر. وكلّ منها لفظ مفرد يتألّف منها لفظ مركّب تامّ وغير تامّ، والتامّ إما خبر أو إنشاء.

(١٢) وأما الخاصى من علم الأقوال فهو ما يتعلّق بألفاظ يتأتّى بها العقلاء من ذوى الفطانة والفهم والأفهام، ويتأدّى بها الحركات والسكنات على وجه الصواب والتمام.

(١٣) ففى كلّ مرتبة من المراتب الثلاث المذكورة التى هى مبادئ القول والحكاية، ينبعث علم من العلوم الثلاثة الكبيرة. فمن معرفة الأصوات وكميتها العددية والنسب النغمية الحاصلة فيها من مراتب الحدّة والثقل يتولّد علم الموسيقى، وموضوعه الكمّية الحاصلة فى الصوت.

(١٤) ومن معرفة الحروف المسموعة وحركاتها وسكناتها الاعرابية والبنائية يتولّد علم الإعراب والعروض.

(١٥) ومن معرفة معانى اللفظ يتولّد علم اللغة والشعر وفنّ المعانى والبيان والبديع.

(16) From the knowledge of the meanings that come to be in thought and the manner in which these are composed to yield the sought conclusion is born the science of logic, which is the upright scale by which reflective thoughts are weighed and theories gauged.

## Chapter Three

*On the divisions of the science of practices*

(17) The sciences of acts have four divisions. The first pertains to the organs and bodily parts, like the crafts and professions of the craftsmen, such as weaving, agriculture, and building. This is the least and meanest division of the sciences of acts.

(18) The second is slightly more elevated than the first. It is the science of writing, the science of devices, the craft of alchemy, magic, physiognomy, and their likes.

(19) The third pertains to the governance of livelihood in a manner connected to the well-being of the affairs of this world so that the individual alone or the species and the communal situation may subsist; or, in a manner connected to the affairs of the religion and the well-being[6] of the afterworld—such as the science of interactions, like marriage, divorce, manumission, and so on; and the science of disciplinary measures, like retaliation, indemnities, fines, penalties, and similar things. This is the science of the Shariʿa.

(20) The fourth pertains to coming to possess beautiful character traits, acquiring habitudes and virtues, and avoiding odious habitudes and vile qualities. This is the science of the Path and the religion.[7]

## Chapter Four

*On the science of thoughts*

(21) It has four divisions. The first division is knowledge of definitions and demonstrations. These are two origins for the coming to be of the things and their realities.[8] One of the two, which is the definition, gives

(١٦) ومن معرفة المعانى الحاصلة فى الفكر وكيفية تأليفها لينتج بها المطلوب يتولّد علم المنطق الذّى هو الميزان المستقيم يوزن به الأفكار ويكال به الأنظار.

## الفصل الثالث
### فى أقسام علم الأعمال

(١٧) العلوم الفعلية على أربعة أقسام. الأوّل ما يتعلّق بالأعضاء والجوارح كصنائع أرباب الصناعات وحرفهم كالحياكة والفلاحة والعمارة، وهو أدون أقسام علوم الأفعال وأخسّها.

(١٨) والثانى ما هو أرفع قليلاً من الأوّل، وهو علم الكتابة وعلم الحيل وصنعة الكيمياء والشعبذة والقيافة وأمثالها.

(١٩) والثالث ما يتعلّق بتدبير المعاش على وجه ينوط بصلاح أمر الدنيا لبقاء الشخص بانفراده أو النوع والهيئة الاجتماعية او على وجه ينوط بأمر الدّين وصلاح الآخرة كعلم المعاملات من النكاح والطلال والعتال وغيرها وكعلم السياسات كالقصاص والديات والجرائم والحدود وما أشبهها، وهو علم الشريعة.

(٢٠) والرابع ما يتعلّق باقتناء الأخلال الجميلة واكتساب الملكات والفضائل والاجتناب عن الملكات الرديّة والرذائل، وهو علم الطريقة والدين.

## الفصل الرابع
### فى علم الأفكار

(٢١) وهو أربعة أقسام. القسم الأوّل معرفة الحدّ والبرهان، وهما مبدآن لحصول الأشياء وحقائقها. فأحدهما وهو الحدّ يؤدّى الى حضور

rise to the presence of the thing's reality and the concept of its whatness. The other gives rise to the presence of its existence and assent to its "whetherness."[9] Each of these shares with the other in the definitions. So, the parts of the definition are identical with the parts of the demonstration, with the difference of arrangement and order that is clarified in the Scale [that is, logic].

(22) The second division is knowledge of arithmetic, number, and the kinds of discontinuous quantities, along with their kinds, levels, and specificities.

(23) The third division is the science of geometry and the continuous quantities that are set up by lines, surfaces, and bodies, and their kinds, guises, and shapes. From this is born the science of the guise [of the cosmos] and the stars, which is the knowledge of the quantities of the spheres, the number of the planets, the measures of their dimensions, the size of their bodies, and the states of their movements in measure and direction. From it is derived the science of the ruling properties [of the stars—that is, astrology] and the science of divination and dream interpretation.

(24) The fourth division is the science of nature, medicine, veterinary medicine, and their like. It is the knowledge of the qualities of the elements, their movements, their passivities, and their comminglings with each other; knowledge of the [bodily] constitution and the generation of complete and incomplete compound things from it; knowledge of the kinds of the three progenies—that is, inanimate things, plants, and animals—and the origins of their movements and stillnesses; the science of animals in all their varieties, and of their perceptual and motor potencies; and the science of man and of his cognitive and practical potencies. The profit and final goal of this science is preserving the constitution, ensuring worthy growth, and making life subsist. When this science is applied to animals other than man it is called "veterinary medicine" and "training," and when it is applied to other than animals it is called "agriculture" and "farming."

## Chapter Five

*On the science of the afterworld*

(25) This is the science that is not corrupted by the corruption of the body or ruined by the ruin of this world. It is knowledge of God, His angels, His books, His messengers, and the Last Day.

حقيقة الشئ وتصوّر ماهيته. وثانيهما يؤدّى الى حضور وجوده والتصديق بهيئته، وكل منهما مشارك للآخر فى الحدود، فأجزاء الحدّ بعينها أجزاء البرهان مع التفاوت فى النظم والترتيب كما بينّ فى الميزان.

(٢٢) والقسم الثانى معرفة الحساب والعدد وأنواع الكميات المنفصلة وأنواعها ومراتبها وخواصّها.

(٢٣) والقسم الثالث علم الهندسة والكميات المتّصلة القارّة من الخطّ والسطح والجسم وأنواعها وهيآتها وأشكالها، ويتولّد منه علم الهيئة والنجوم، وهو معرفة كميات الأفلاك وعدد الكواكب ومقادير أبعادها وعظم أجرامها وأحوال حركاتها قدراً وجهةً، ويتفرّع عليه علم الأحكام وعلم الكهانة والتعبير.

(٢٤) القسم الرابع علم الطبيعة والطبّ والبيطرة ونحوها، وهو معرفة كيفيات العناصر وحركاتها وانفعالاتها وامتزاجات بعضها مع بعض ومعرفة المزاج وتولّد المركّبات التامّة وغيرها منها ومعرفة أنواع المواليد الثلاث من الجمادات والنباتات والحيوانات ومبادئ حركاتها وسكناتها وعلم الحيوان على أصنافه وقواه المدركة والمحرّكة وعلم الانسان وقواه العلمية والعملية. وفائدة هذا العلم وغايته هى حفظ المزاج وإصلاح النماء وإبقاء الحياة. فإذا استعمل هذا العلم فى غير الانسان من الحيوان يسمّى بالبيطرة والرياضة، واذا استعمل فى غير الحيوان يسمّى بالفلاحة والدهقنة.

## الفصل الخامس
### فى علم الآخرة

(٢٥) وهو العلم الذى لا يفسد بفساد البدن ولا يخرب بخراب الدنيا، وهو العلم بالله وملائكته وكتبه ورسله واليوم الآخر.

(26) [§1] Knowledge of God is knowledge of His Essence, His attributes, and His names.

(27) [§2] Knowledge of His angels is knowledge of the existence of spiritual forms hallowed beyond every sort of matter, disengaged from bodies, and perceiving their essences and what is beyond them. They are the residents of the Divine Presence and the veil keepers of the Lordly Courtyard. Their world is the world of power and desire. They are divided into subjugating intellects and governing souls.[10] All are among what God innovated according to the entifications[11] required by His names and His attributes.

(28) For the Necessary Reality demands, as the first of the entifications that It demands, a holy substance named "the First Spirit," "the Most Eminent Intellect," "the Highest Pen," and "the Muḥammadan Reality," according to what has been brought by the prophetic reports and hadiths and spoken of by the divine wisdom. And, by means of it, [It demands] other substances, some spiritual and some soulish. These are the intermediaries of the existences of the heavenly forms and the elemental natures, with their simple and compound sorts of matter and their orbs.[12]

(29) [§3] As for knowledge of His books, it consists of knowledge of His Speech, His Book, and how He gives form to the realities; and knowledge of His Pen, His Tablet, His Decree, and His Measuring Out.

(30) It is necessary to know that His Speech is not similar to the speech of the creatures, His Book not similar to their book, His Pen to their pen, nor His Tablet to their tablet.

(31) His First Pen is an intellective angel brought nigh whose task is to confer realities and give form to the sciences.

(32) His First Tablet is a soulish angel whose task is to acquire the realities and sciences from the right side and to make them manifest and known by giving them shape and form on the left side.[13]

(33) The Decree consists of the fixity of the forms of all things in the intellective world in the universal mode.[14]

(34) The Measuring Out consists of the coming to be of the forms of the things in the soulish world in the particular mode. [These forms] coincide with what is in their external sorts of matter, are ascribed to the occasions and causes, are necessary through them, and are requisite

(٢٦) أما العلم بالله فهو العلم بذاته وصفاته وأسمائه.

(٢٧) وأما العلم بملائكته فهو العلم بوجود صور روحانية مقدّسة عن المواد مجرّدة عن الأجساد مدركة لذاتها ولما عداها، وهم سكّان الحضرة الالهية وحجّاب الساحة الربوبية وعالمها عالم القدرة والارادة، وتنقسم الى العقول القاهرة والنفوس المدبّرة والكلّ ممّا أبدعها الله تعالى بحسب التعيّنات اللازمة لأسمائه وصفاته.

(٢٨) فانّ الحقيقة الواجبية اقتضت أوّل ما اقتضت من تعيّناتها جوهراً قدسياً يُسَمّى بالروح الأوّل والعقل الأشرف والقلم الأعلى والحقيقة المحمّدية على ما وردت به الأخبار والأحاديث النبوية ونطقت به الحكمة الالهية، وبتوسّطه جواهر أخرى روحانية وأخرى نفسانية. وهى وسائط وجودات الصور السماوية والطبائع العنصرية بموادّها وأجرامها البسيطة والمركّبة.

(٢٩) وأمّا العلم بكتبه فهو عبارة عن العلم بكلامه وكتابه وكيفية تصويره الحقائق والعلم بقلمه ولوحه وقضائه وقدره.

(٣٠) فيجب أن يعلم أنّ كلامه لايشبه كلام الخلق وكتابه لا يشبه كتابهم ولا قلمه قلمهم ولا لوحه لوحهم.

(٣١) وانّ قلمه الاوّل ملك مقرّب عقلى شأنه إفادة الحقائق وتصوير العلوم.

(٣٢) ولوحه الاوّل ملك نفسانى شأنه استفادة الحقائق والعلوم من الجانب اليمين وإظهارها وإعلامها بالتشكيل والتصوير على الجانب الشمال.

(٣٣) والقضاء عبارة عن ثبوت صور جميع الأشياء فى العالم العقلى على الوجه الكلى.

(٣٤) والقدر عبارة عن حصول صورها فى العالم النفسى على الوجه الجزئى مطابقة لما فى موادّها الخارجية مستندة الى أسبابها وعللها واجبة

for their moments.[15] The divine solicitude named "God's knowledge" envelops these forms just as the Decree envelops the Measuring Out, and the Measuring Out [envelops] what is in the external realm.

(35) His encompassing knowledge, in the view of the folk of the Real,[16] has no locus, in contrast to the form of the Decree and the form of the Measuring Out, for the Decree's locus is the world of the intellect, and its tablet is the world of the soul, which is the locus of the Measuring Out's form.[17] The [Measuring Out's] tablet is the ledgers of the preparednesses and the tablets of the sorts of matter receptive to the forms of the opposites, which invite each other to obliteration and corruption.[18]

(36) The Decree's locus is named "the Mother of the Book" and "the Tablet Preserved against Erasure and Change," because it belongs to the world of Jabarūt, which is the world of intellects hallowed beyond change and time. But the tablets of the Measuring Out are not preserved against these two, as signified by His words, *God obliterates what He wills and He fixes, and with Him is the Mother of the Book* [13:39]. All the true sciences named "God-given sciences" that He effuses upon us He effuses only from [the Decree's locus]. Thus [He says] in the Wise Qurʾān: *Surely it is in the Mother of the Book with Us, high, wise* [43:4]. He also says, *Recite: And thy Lord is the Most Generous, who taught by the Pen* [96:3–4].

(37) Those intellective substances are the storehouses of His Absent,[19] as He says: *There is nothing whose storehouses are not with Us, so We send it down only with a known measuring out* [15:21]. There is no doubt that the storehouses of His Absent are hallowed beyond change and occurrence, so the Decree is the same.

(38) As for the way stations of His munificence and His mercy—whether these be celestial souls, heavenly or earthly imaginal potencies, or elemental sorts of matter—they are never empty of renewal, elapsing, multiplicity, and division. So, the Measuring Out is the same, and its world is the world of the heavenly and the earthly souls.

(39) In the world of the heavens are found two noble books. One book is soulish and universal, the other imaginal and particular. Each is a clarifying book, a point to which He alludes with His words, *There is not*

بها لازمة لأوقاتها. ويشملها العناية الالهية المسمّاة بعلم الله شمول القضاء للقدر والقدر لما فى الخارج.

(٣٥) ولا محلّ لعلمه المحيط على رأى أهل الحق بخلاف صورة القضاء وصورة القدر، فإنّ محلّ القضاء عالم العقل ولوحها عالم النفس وهو محلّ صورة القدر ولوحه دفاتر الاستعدادات وألواح الموادّ القابلة لصور الأضداد المتداعية الى المحو والفساد.

(٣٦) ومحلّ القضاء هو المسمّى بأمّ الكتاب واللوح المحفوظ عن النسخ والتغيير لكونه من عالم الجبروت وعالم العقول المقدّسة عن التغيّر والزمان، والألواح القدرية غير محفوظة عنهما كما دلّ عليه قوله تعالى يمحو الله ما يشاء ويثبت وعنده أمّ الكتاب. وكلّ ما يفيض علينا من العلوم الحقّة الموسومة بالعلوم اللدنية إنّما يفيض عنه كما فى القرآن الحكيم وإنّه فى أمّ الكتاب لدينا لعلى حكيم، وقال تعالى: اقرأ وربّك الأكرم الذى علّم بالقلم.

(٣٧) وتلك الجواهر العقلية هى خزائن غَيْبِه كما قال تعالى: وإن من شئ الا عندنا خزائنه وما ننزّله الا بقدر معلوم. ولا شكّ أنّ خزائن غيبه مقدّسة عن التغيّر والحدثان، فالقضاء كذلك.

(٣٨) وأمّا منازل جوده ورحمته سواء كانت نفوساً فلكية أو قوى خيالية سماوية أو أرضية أو موادّ عنصرية فهى لا تخلو عن التجدّد والانصرام والتكثّر والانقسام. فالقدر كذلك، وعالمه عالم النفوس السماوية والأرضية.

(٣٩) وفى عالم السموات يوجد كتابان كريمان، أحدهما النفسانى الكلى، والآخر الخيالى الجزئى، وكل منهما كتاب مبين كما أشير اليه

*a grain in the darknesses of the earth, nothing fresh or withered, that is not in a clarifying book* [6:59]. [This comes] after His words, *With Him are the keys to the absent—none knows them but He* [6:59], which are an allusion to His all-encompassing knowledge that is named "the divine solicitude." His words, *He knows what is in the land and the sea; not a leaf falls, but He knows it* [6:59], are an allusion to His differentiated knowledge of the Decree, which encompasses what is in *the land,* or the world of the Kingdom and the Witnessed; *and the sea,* or the world of the Sovereignty and the Absent; and what *falls,* that is, the leaves of the book of the spheres and of the scroll of the heavens' cycles. He stresses this with His words, *There is nothing that crawls . . . whose provision does not rest upon God; He knows its resting-place and its repository; each is in a clarifying book* [11:6]; and His words, *No infliction is inflicted on the earth or in yourselves but it is in a book before We create it* [57:22].

(40) [§4][20] As for knowledge of His messengers and His prophets, it is to know that God has vicegerents in the world of the earth who are intermediaries between God and His servants and who are commanded to ensure the worthiness of the Adamic species by combining the conditions of messengerhood and the specificities of ambassadorship, since they have many excellencies and plentiful virtues. These are excellencies that are comprised of three things:

(41) First and most eminent of all is that the prophet has gained cognizance of the divine sciences, including the Highest Origin and all that follows upon it pertaining to His high and low Sovereignty. He has come to understand the origins and final goals of all. He knows the human soul, its perfections and its degrees, and the levels of its ascent to the Real when it is perfected through knowledge and practice. He takes his sciences and his knowledges from God without the intermediary of a human teacher—as a knowledge derived from Him by way of spiritual unveiling and angelic casting,[21] not by reflective exertion and sense-intuitive[22] contrivance.

(42) Second is that the prophet possesses an inward potency such that the realities become imaginalized to him in the drapery of imaginal apparitions,[23] first in the inward domain and the world of imagination. Then these pervade the world of sensation such that his eminent senses—like his hearing, his eyesight, his taste, his smell, and his touch—are acted upon by them. He witnesses clearly the angel that casts the sciences, and from it he hears clearly God's speech.[24]

بقولـه تعـالى: ولا حبّة فى ظلمـات الأرض ولا رطـب ولا يابس الا فى كتـاب مبين، بعد قوله: وعنـده مفاتح الغيب لا يعلمها الا هو، اشـارةً الى علمه المحيط المسمّى بالعناية الالهية. وقوله: ويعلم ما فى البرّ والبحر وما تسـقط من ورقة الا يعلمها اشـارةٌ الى علمه التفصيلى القضائى المحيط بما فى برّ عالم المُلك والشـهادة وبحر عالم الملكوت والغيب وبما يسـقط من اورال كتاب الافلاك وسجلّ دورات السموات. واكّد ذلك بقوله تعالى: وما من دابّة الا على الله رزقها ويعلم مسـتقرّها ومستودعها كل فى كتاب مبـين، وقوله: ومـا أصاب من مصيبة فى الأرض ولا فى أنفسـكم الا فى كتـابمـن قبـل أن نبرأهـا.

(٤٠) وأمـا العلم برسـله وأنبيائـه فهو أن يعلـم أنّ لله خلفاء فى عالم الأرض متوسّطين بين الله وبين عباده مأمورين بإصلاح هذا النوع الآدمى بواسطة استجماعهم بشرائط الرسـالة وخصائص السفارة لجموم مناقبهم ووفور فضائلهم. وهى المناقب التّى يشملها أمور ثلاثة.

(٤١) امـا الأوّل وهو أشرف الجميع فكون النبـى مطّلعاً على العلوم الالهيـة من المبدأ الأعلى وما يليه من ملكوته العلوى والسـفلى واقفاً على المبـادئ والغايات للجميـع عارفاً بالنفس الانسـانية وكمالاتها ودرجاتها ومراتـب عروجهـا الى الحقّ اذا اسـتكملت بالعلم والعمـل، آخذاً علومه ومعارفه من الله بلاتوسّـط معلّم بشرى علماً مسـتفاداً منه بطريق الكشف الروحى والإلقاء السبّوحى لا بالتعمّل الفكرى والاحتيال الوهمى.

(٤٢) وامـا الثانـى فكونـه ذا قوّة باطنيـة يتمثّل له الحقائق بكسـوة الأشـباح المثاليـة أوّلاً فى الباطـن وعالم الخيال ثم تـسرى الى عالم الحسّ، فينفعل عنها حواسّـه الشريفة كسـمعه وبصره وذوقه وشمّه ولمسه فيشاهد المَلَك المُلقى للعلوم عياناً ويسمع منه كلام الله عياناً.

(43) The Prophet (God bless him and his household) has reported about the unveiling of his illumined eyesight with his words, "The earth was gathered together for me, so I was shown its easts and its wests."[25] About his hearing he said, "The heaven groans, and it has a right to groan. Within it there is not the space of a foot that does not have an angel brought nigh, bowing or prostrating."[26] About his eminent sense of smell he said, "Surely I find the breath of the All-Merciful from the side of Yemen."[27] About his taste he said, "I spend the night with my Lord—He gives me to eat and to drink."[28] About his touch he said, "God placed His hand upon my shoulder, and I found the cold of His fingers between my breasts."[29]

(44) Third is that the prophet possesses a strong potency and an intense capacity to subjugate God's enemies and the satans'[30] friends and to exert mastery over those who deny God's right—that is, the unbelievers, the refusers, and the ungodly; and he possesses perseverance in trials and adversities, power and ability in acts of resistance, and firmness in battles and combats.

(45) The totality of these three descriptions is among the specificities of the messenger. However, each of them may be found in other than messengers, since the first is realized in the saints, one sort of the second is found in the folk of divination and monks, and the third may come to be in kings who are intense in aspiration and force.

(46) *A Branching Off from the Throne.* It is as if the prophet were compounded of three magnificent individuals, each of whom is a chieftain and is obeyed among his species. Through his spirit and intellect, he is one of the angels brought nigh; through the mirror of his soul and his heart, he is a celestial sphere elevated beyond the defilements of elemental things and a tablet preserved from the touch of the satans; and through his body and his nature, he is a king among the magnificent kings and sultans.

(47) The verification of this is that the configurations are three and the worlds three—the configuration of the intellect, the configuration of the soul, and the configuration of sensation and nature.[31] These parallel the world of this world, the world of the afterworld, and the world of the Command. Man, according to the predominance of each configuration, has entered into what corresponds to him, either potentially or actually. Through his sensation he is one of the folk of this world and belongs to the animals chastised in *the lowest reach* [of hell, 4:145]; through his soul he is one of the folk of the afterworld and belongs to the Lower Sovereignty, and through his spirit he is one of the folk of God and

(٤٣) وقد أخبر النبى صلى الله عليه وآله عن مكاشفة بصره المنوّر بقوله زويت لى الأرض فأريت مشارقها ومغاربها؛ وعن سمعه بقوله أطّت السماء وحق لها أن تئطّ ليس فيها موضع قدم الا وفيه مَلَك مقرّب راكع أو ساجد؛ وعن شمّه الشريف بقوله إنّى لأجد نَفَس الرحمن من جانب اليمن؛ وعن ذوقه بقوله أبيتُ عند ربّى يطعمنى ويسقينى؛ وعن لمسه بقوله وضع الله على كتفيّ يده فوجدت برد أنامله بين ثديىّ.

(٤٤) واما الثالث فكونه ذا قوّة قوية وبسطة شديدة يقهر على أعداء الله تعالى وأولياء الشياطين ويسلّط على منكرى حقّ الله من الكافرين والجاحدين والفاسقين، وكونه ذا مصابرة على المحن والشدائد واقتدار وتمكّن على المقاومات وتثبّت فى المحاربات والمبارزات.

(٤٥) ومجموع هذه الأوصاف الثلاثة من خصائص الرسول. وأمّا آحادها فقد يوجد فى غير الرسل، فإنّ الأولى متحقّق فى الأولياء، وضرب من الثانية يوجد فى أهل الكهانة والرهابين، والثالثة قد يكون فى الملوك الشديدة الهمّة والبأس.

(٤٦) تفريع عرشى. فالنبى كأنّه مركّب من ثلاثة اشخاص عظيمة كلّ منهم رئيس مطاع فى نوعه، فبروحه وعقله يكون مَلَكاً من المقرّبين، وبمرآة نفسه وقلبه يكون فلكاً مرفوعاً عن ادناس العنصريين ولوحاً محفوظاً من مسّ الشياطين، وبجسمه وطبعه يكون مَلكاً من عظماء الملوك والسلاطين.

(٤٧) وتحقيق ذلك ان النشآت ثلاث والعوالم ثلاثة، نشأة العقل ونشأة النفس ونشأة الطبع والحسّ بإزاء عالم الدنيا وعالم الآخرة وعالم الأمر. والانسان بحسب غلبة كل نشأة داخل فيما يناسبه إمّا بالقوّة أو بالفعل، فبحسّه من أهل الدنيا وجملة الحيوانات المعذّبة فى الدرك الأسفل، وبنفسه من أهل الآخرة وجملة الملكوت الأسفل، وبروحه من

belongs to the Higher Sovereignty. However, what overcomes most creatures is the configuration of sensation and the homestead of this world, and their final return in the afterworld is to hellfire.

(48) As for the substance of prophecy, it has the gathering together of the configurations and the perfection and employment of all the potencies. Hence he (God's blessing be upon him and his household) has the most magnificent mastership, the greatest chieftainship, and the divine vicegerency in all the worlds. So he is a lawgiver, a messenger, and a prophet. Through the first he rules like a king, through the second he reports like the spheres, and through the third he knows like the angel. So understand, and take the booty!

(49) [§ 5] As for knowledge of the Last Day, it is faith in the resurrection, the grave, the Uprising, the Mustering, the Reckoning, the Scales, the outspreading of the pages, and the omens given by the books. This is the final goal of the sciences of unveiling, but this is not the place for details. We have spoken extensively concerning it in some of our compositions, according to what God conferred upon us and designated as our portion and provision from His bounty and His mercy. To allude to it here, we say:

(50) It is necessary for you to know that *you are laboring unto your Lord laboriously, and you shall encounter Him* [84:6] through death, which is the severance of the spirit's attachment to the body by means of an unconditional ailment in all its organs. Thereby the body leaves off obeying the spirit through the nullification of its potencies and tools. Through death, everything absent from the spirit in the state of its life is unveiled for it—that is, what was inscribed in the book, that *He will disclose* only at *its moment* [7:187]. For, the deep-rootedness of guises and the consolidation of attributes—named "habitude" by the folk of wisdom and "angel and satan" by the folk of unveiling and prophecy—necessitate the everlastingness of reward and punishment and the perpetuity of beautiful and ugly forms, and these necessitate giving bliss to the folk of the Gardens and chastising the companions of hellfire with the fires. So, everyone who has done *an atom's weight of good* and *evil* [99:7–8] shall see its trace written in the page of his essence, or in an even more elevated page, at the outspreading of the pages and the laying open of the books.

(51) As the moment approaches when his eyesight is to fall on the face of his essence—at the removal of the covering[32] and of the distractions of this nethermost domain and everything brought in by the senses—he pays regard to the page of his inwardness and the page of his heart.

أهل الله وجملة الملكوت الأعلى، لكن الغالب على أكثر الخلق نشأة الحسّ وموطن الدنيا ومآلهم فى الآخرة الى الجحيم.

(٤٨) وأما جوهر النبوّة فله جامعية النشآت واستكمال واستعمال القوى كلّها، فله صلوات الله عليه وآله السيادة العظمى والرياسة الكبرى والخلافة الالهية فى جميع العوالم. فهو شارع ورسول ونبىّ، يحكم بالأوّل كالمَلِك ويخبر بالثانى كالفلك ويعلم بالثالث كالمَلَك. فافهم واغتنم.

(٤٩) وأما العلم باليوم الآخر فهو الايمان بالقيامة والقبر والبعث والحشر والحساب والميزان ونشر الصحائف وتطائر الكتب. وهذه غاية العلوم الكشفية، ليس هذا الموضع محلّ تفاصيلها، وقد بسطنا فيها القول فى بعض تآليفنا حسب ما أفادنا الله وجعل قسطنا ورزقنا من فضله ورحمته. وللاشارة اليه هنا نقول:

(٥٠) يجب عليك أن تعلم أنّك كادح الى ربّك كدحاً فملاقيه بالموت، وهو قطع تعلّق الروح عن البدن بواسطة زمانة مطلقة فى جميع أعضائه يخرج بها عن طاعة الروح ببطلان قواه وآلاته. فيكشف له بالموت ما يغيب عنه فى حال حياته ممّا كان مسطوراً فى كتاب لا يجلّيها الا بوقتها، فإنّ رسوخ الهيآت وتأكّد الصفات وهو المسمّى عند أهل الحكمة بالملكة وعند أهل الكشف والنبوّة بالملك والشيطان توجب خلود الثواب والعقاب ودوام الصور الحسنة والقبيحة الموجبتان لتنعيم اهل الجنان وتعذيب أصحاب الجحيم بالنيران. فكلّ من فعل مثقال ذرّة من خير وشرّ يرى أثره مكتوباً فى صحيفة ذاته أوصحيفة أرفع منها عند نشر الصحائف وبسط الكتب.

(٥١) واذا حان وقت أن يقع بصره الى وجه ذاته عند كشف الغطاء وشواغل هذا الأدنى وما يورده الحواسّ فيلتفت الى صفحة باطنه وصحيفة

This is expressed in His words, *When the pages are spread out* [81:10]. Those heedless of their essence and the reckoning of their secret heart will then say, *"How is it with this book, that it leaves nothing behind, small or great, but it has numbered it?" And they shall find present what they had done, and thy Lord shall not wrong anyone* [18:49].

(52) The source of this is that the abode of the afterworld is the abode of life and perception, according to His words, *Surely the afterworld's abode is life, did they but know* [29:64]. The sorts of matter of that abode's individuals are reflective cogitations and concepts of the heart. When man is severed from this world and becomes disengaged from the body's means of awareness, and when the covering is removed from him, then the Absent becomes for him the Witnessed, the secret the open, knowledge the eye, and the report clear-sightedness.[33] He will have piercing eyesight and read his book, according to His words, *We have removed from you your covering, so your eyesight today is piercing* [50:22], and His words, *Each man—We have fastened to him his bird of omen on his neck; and We shall bring forth for him, on the day of resurrection, a book he shall meet wide open: "Read your book! Your soul suffices you this day as a reckoner against you"* [17:13–14].

(53) Everyone among the folk of felicity and the Companions of the Right Hand will be *given his book in his right hand* [69:19] from the direction of Illiyyūn.[34] *Surely the book of the pious is in Illiyyūn* [83:18]. But, if he is one of the wretched and rejected, he will be *given his book in his left hand* [69:25] from the direction of Sijjīn. *Surely the book of the depraved is in Sijjīn* [83:7], for he is one of the guilty, those with hanging heads, according to His words, *If you could see the guilty, hanging their heads at their Lord* [32:12].

(54) These forms will become either tight graves, within which are "serpents and scorpions" according to ugly guises [of the soul], or garden plots of good pleasure, within which flow the "rivers" of endless life that accord with true beliefs. So, the graves are either "one of the garden plots of the Garden or one of the pits of the Fires."[35] Thus it has come in the prophetic hadith:

> He—bless him and his household—said, "In his grave the believer has a verdant garden; his grave is made seventy cubits wide for him and is brightened until it is like the moon on the night when it is full.

قلبه، وهو المعبّر عنه بقوله تعالى: واذا الصحف نشرت، فمن كان فى غفلة عن ذاته وحساب سرّه يقول عند ذلك: ما لهذا الكتاب لا يغادر صغيرة ولا كبيرة الا أحصاها ووجدوا ما عملوا حاضراً ولا يظلم ربّك أحداً.

(٥٢) ومنشأ ذلك أنّ دار الآخرة هى دار الحياة والإدراك، لقوله تعالى: وإنّ الدار الآخرة لهى الحيوان لو كانوا يعلمون. وموادّ أشخاص تلك الدار هى التأمّلات الفكرية والتصوّرات القلبية. فاذا انقطع الانسان عن الدنيا وتجرّد عن مشاعر البدن وكشف عنه الغطاء، يكون الغيب له شهادة والسرّ علانية والعلم عيناً والخبر عياناً. فيكون حديد البصر قارئاً لكتابه لقوله تعالى: فكشفنا عنك غطاءك فبصرك اليوم حديد، وقوله تعالى: وكلّ انسان ألزمناه طائره فى عنقه ويخرج له يوم القيامة كتاباً يَلقاه منشوراً اقرأ كتابك كفى بنفسك اليوم عليك حسيباً.

(٥٣) فمن كان من أهل السعادة وأصحاب اليمين فقد أوتى كتابه بيمينه من جنة علّيين. إنّ كتاب الأبرار لفى علّيين. ومن كان من الأشقياء المردودين فقد أوتى كتابه بشماله من جهة سجّين. إنّ كتاب الفجّار لفى سجّين؛ لأنّه من المجرمين المنكوسين لقوله تعالى: ولو ترى اذ المجرمون ناكسوا رؤوسهم عند ربّهم.

(٥٤) فهذه الصور ستصير إمّا قبوراً ضيّقةً فيها حيّات وعقارب بحسب الهيآت السوئ وإمّا رياضاً رضوانيةً فيها تجرى أنهار الحياة الأبدية بحسب العقائد الحقّة. فهذه القبور إما روضة من رياض الجنّة او حفرة من حفر النيران، كما ورد فى الحديث النبوى:

> أنّه صلى الله عليه وآله قال للمؤمن فى قبره روضة خضراء ويوسع له قبره سبعين ذراعاً ويضيئ حتى يكون

Do you know concerning what the verse *His life shall be a life of narrowness* [20:124] was sent down?"

They said, "God and His messenger know best."

He said, "The chastisement of the unbeliever in his grave: Ninety-nine *tinnīns* will be given mastery over him. Do you know what a *tinnīn* is? Ninety-nine serpents, each of which has nine heads: They will be gnawing, devouring, and blowing into his body until the day of resurrection."[36]

(55) One should not wonder at these numbers, for in the afterworld blameworthy character traits themselves are turned into serpents and scorpions. To this is the allusion in the Prophet's words, "They are only your deeds given back to you."[37]

(56) Know also that we have two resurrections—a smaller and a greater. The greater belongs to all creatures, and plain texts have given witness to its details: the blowing of the Trumpet, the earth of the Mustering Place, the gathering of the creatures, the length of the day of resurrection, the interrogation in the grave, the Scales, the Reckoning, the Narrow Path, the Pool, the intercession, the attributes of Gehenna, and the attributes of the Garden. But this brief work cannot recount these.[38]

(57) The Smaller Resurrection is death, because of the Prophet's words, "When someone dies, his resurrection has stood forth."[39] Everything in the Greater Resurrection has an equivalent in the Smaller, as has been detailed in its place. The key to knowledge of the day of resurrection is knowledge of the human soul and her levels in the degrees [of paradise] and the reaches [of hell] and the knowledge that man is a microcosm, within which is everything in the macrocosm.

(58) So, everything in the Greater Resurrection—which is the death of all the individuals of the cosmos—has an equivalent in the Smaller Resurrection.[40] When your body—which is your earth specific to you—is

كالقمر ليلة البدر، وهل تدرون فيماذا أنزلت: فإنّ له معيشة ضنكاً.

قالوا الله ورسوله اعلم.

قال: عذاب الكافر فى قبره؛ يسلّط عليه تسعة وتسعون تنّيناً. هل تدرون ما التنّين؟ تسعة وتسعون حيّة؛ لكل حيّة تسعة رؤوس ينهشون ويلحسون وينفخون فى جسمه الى يوم القيامة.

(٥٥) ولا ينبغى أن يتعجّب من هذا العدد، فإنّ الأخلال المذمومة تنقلب بعينها فى الآخرة حيّات وعقارب، واليه الاشارة بقوله صلى الله عليه وآله انمّا هى أعمالكم تردّ اليكم.

(٥٦) واعلم أنّ لنا قيامتين صغرى وكبرى. أمّا الكبرى فهى لجميع الخلائق وقد شهدت النصوص بتفاصيلها من نفخة الصور وأرض المحشر وجمع الخلائق وطول يوم القيامة ومساءَلة القبر والميزان والمحاسبة والصراط والحوض والشفاعة وصفة جهنّم وصفة الجنّة ولا يحتمل هذا المختصر ذكرها.

(٥٧) والقيامة الصغرى هى الموت لقوله صلى الله عليه وآله: من مات فقد قامت قيامته. وكلّ ما فى القيامة الكبرى له نظير فى الصغرى كما فصّل فى موضعه. ومفتاح العلم بيوم القيامة هو معرفة النفس الانسانية ومراتبها فى الدرجات والدركات ومعرفة أنّ الانسان عالم صغير فيه جميع ما فى العالم الكبير.

(٥٨) فكلّ ما فى القيامة الكبرى وهو موت أفراد العالم جميعاً له نظير فى القيامة الصغرى. فاذا انهدم بالموت بدنك، وهو أرضك الخاصّ بك،

destroyed through death, then *the earth will have been shaken with a mighty shaking* [99:1]. When your bones—which are the mountains of your earth—decay, then *[the earth and the mountains will have been lifted up] and crushed with a single blow* [69:14], so your *mountains will be scattered like ashes* [20:105]. When your heart—which is the sun of your world—is darkened at the [soul's] extraction, then your *sun* will have been *folded up* [81:1]. When your senses are nullified, then your *stars* will have become *opaque* [81:2]. When your brain is split apart, then your *heaven will have been split apart* [55:37]. When your eyes burst from the terror of death, then your *seas will have been made to burst open* [82:3]. When your potencies are dispersed and your troops are scattered, then your *wild animals will have been mustered* [81:5]. And when your spirit and your potencies depart from the body, then your *earth will have been stretched, and it will cast forth what is within it and become empty* [84:3–4].

(59) The equivalent of the Narrow Path is your walking straight on the path of *tawḥīd* without falsifying, declaring ineffectual,[41] or turning aside toward blameworthy character traits. The equivalent of the chastisement of the grave is your suffering pain through separation from things you love. The equivalent of the disgrace on the day of resurrection is the disgrace of ugly character traits and deeds that are unveiled for an informed knower who is cognizant of what is in the inmost thoughts. The equivalent of the constant chastisement in the Fire is the pain of your being held back from things you love and the partition between you and the bliss of the Gardens and gazing upon the All-Merciful, such that your heart is constantly severed from all good. We seek refuge in God!

(60) Death is like birth. So, after the this-worldly being, the Smaller Resurrection is related to the Greater Resurrection just as coming forth from the loins' tightness into the space of the womb is related to birth, which is coming forth from the womb's tightness into the space of this world. The days of pregnancy are like the time in the grave and the *barzakh*.[42] The time and location of the afterworld are related to the time and location of this world just as these are related to the time of pregnancy and the location of the womb. So gauge the afterworld by the first world, for *your creation and your uprising are as but one soul* [31:28].

فقد زلزلت الأرض زلزالها. واذا رمّت عظامك، وهى جبال أرضك، فقد دكّتا دكّة واحدة فقد نسفت جبالك نسفاً. واذا أظلم قلبك عند النزع، وهو شمس عالمك، فقد كوّرت شمسك. واذا بطلت حواسّك فقد انكدرت نجومك. واذا انشقّ دماغك فقد انشقّت سماؤك. واذا انفجرت من هول الموت عيناك فقد فجّرت بحارك. واذا تفرّقت قواك وانتشرت جنودك فقد حشرت وحوشك. واذا فارقت روحك وقواك عن البدن فمدّت أرضك وألقت ما فيها وتخلّت.

(٥٩) ونظير الصراط استقامتك على طريق التوحيد من غير إبطال وتعطيل وعدول الى ذمائم الأخلال. ونظير عذاب القبر تألّمك بمفارقة المحبوبات. ونظير الافتضاح يوم القيامة الافتضاح بما ينكشف عن قبائح الأخلال والأعمال عند عارف خبير مطّلع على ما فى الضمير. ونظير العذاب الدائم فى النار التألّم بمنعك عن المحبوبات والحيلولة بينك وبين نعيم الجنان والنظر الى الرحمن، فينقطع قلبك عن الخيرات على الدوام. نعوذ بالله.

(٦٠) والموت كالولادة، فنسبة القيامة الصغرى بعد الكون الدنياوى الى الكبرى كنسبة الخروج من مضيق الصلب الى فضاء الرحم الى الولادة التى هى الخروج من مضيق الرحم الى فضاء الدنيا. وأيّام الحمل كزمان القبر والبرزخ. وزمان الآخرة ومكانها بالنسبة الى زمان الدنيا ومكانها كهما بالنسبة الى زمان الحمل ومكان الرحم. فقس الآخرة بالأولى، فما خلقكم ولا بعثكم الا كنفس واحدة.

*PART TWO*

*On the Knowledge of the Soul, which is a Receptacle for the Sciences*

*In it are ten chapters.*

## Chapter One

*Explaining the cause of her being impeded from reaching the final goal*

(1) Know that the disagreements[1] among the schools and paths cannot be numbered, but despite their multiplicity, they grow up from dispute over four roots. The first root is knowledge of *tawḥīd,* like the dispute among the Embodiers, the Ineffectualists, the Heretics, and the Aeonists.[2] [The dispute] grows up only from ignorance of the state of the Origin and Return of existent things.

(2) The second root is knowledge of prophecy and warning. Dispute in it is like the disagreement among the Jews, the Christians, and the Sabeans. [This disagreement] grows up only from ignorance of the state of the Messenger.

(3) The third root is knowledge of imamate and caliphate, like the disagreement among the Shiʿites, the Sunnis, the Ghulāt, and the Nawāṣib.[3] It grows up only from lack of knowledge of the state of the Imam and his level in knowledge and rulership.

(4) The fourth root is knowledge of *fatwā*s and judgments, like the disagreement of the mujtahids. [This disagreement] grows up only from ignorance of the Book, Hadith, transmission, and consensus.[4]

# الباب الثانى

## فى معرفة النفس التى هى قابلة للعلوم

## وفيه عشرة فصول

### الفصل الأوّل

### فى بيان سبب تعوّقها عن البلوغ الى الغاية

(١) اعلم ان الاختلاف فى المذاهب والطرل غير محصورة فى عدد الا أنّها مع كثرتها إنّما نشأت من الخلاف فى أصول أربعة. الأصل الأوّل علم التوحيد كخلاف المجسّمة والمعطّلة والملاحدة والدهرية، وهو إنّما نشأ من الجهل بحال مبدأ الموجودات ومعادها.

(٢) والأصل الثانى علم النبوّة والإنذار والخلاف فيه كاختلاف اليهود والنصارى والصابئين فيه، وهو إنّما نشأ من الجهل بحال الرسول.

(٣) والأصل الثالث علم الإمامة والخلافة كاختلاف بين الشيعة والسنّية والغلاة والنواصب، وهو إنّما نشأ من عدم المعرفة بحال الامام ومرتبته فى العلم والسياسة.

(٤) والأصل الرابع علم الفتاوى والأقضية كاختلاف المجتهدين، وهو إنّما ينشأ من الجهل بالكتاب والحديث والرواية والإجماع.

(5) Given that these disagreements are in the branches, they rise up only from disagreement in the science of *tawḥīd* and the knowledge of the soul. These two are the sciences of the Origin and the Return, and from them all sciences grow up. When the root is unknown, it is even more appropriate that the branch be unknown.

## Chapter Two

*On the knowledge that is individually incumbent*[5] *on man and must be learned for his subsistent existence*

(6) This is certain knowledge of the encounter with God, of His unity, His attributes, and His acts, then knowledge of the human world and the manner of its first and second configurations.[6] Anyone ignorant of these two sciences will fall short in the establishment of his existence and the perfection of his reality, even if he is proficient in the other sciences. He is like an infant, or like a sleeper who sees diverse forms in his sleeping and then, waking up from his sleep, finds no trace of them. So also is the property of the forms that man sees with his outward senses in this world or that he imagines with his inward senses. All these are unreal affairs and vanishing properties and dreams that have no subsistence in the wakefulness of the world of the afterworld—except for the true sciences, which are afterworldly forms and have entities fixed at God. *And what is with God is better for the pious* [3:198].

(7) The profit in God's sending forth the prophets and sending down the books is the arousal of souls from the sleep of nature and the drowsiness of heedlessness and ignorance, their recovery from the drunkenness of inadequacy and deficiency, their standing at the resurrection before God, their gaining cognizance of the forms of the afterworldly realities, and their coming to understand the Reckoning, the Narrow Path, and the Scales.

(8) So, man must first obtain the knowledge of *tawḥīd* and the knowledge of the soul. Then he may gradually climb up to deep-rootedness in knowledge until he joins with the folk of clear-sighted witnessing. Then, through the light of contemplative *tawḥīd,* he will gaze upon the worlds of Creation and Command and the horizons and the souls.[7] He will be mustered to God and take up residence in His neighborhood *in a seat of truthfulness with an All-Powerful King* [54:55], thereby verifying His words,

(٥) وهـذه الاختلافات لكونها فى الفروع إنّما تنبعث من الاختلاف فى علم التوحيد وعلم النفس، وهما علما المبدأ والمعاد ومنهما ينشأ جميع العلوم. فمتى كان الأصل مجهولاً كان الفرع أحرى بأن يكون مجهولاً.

## الفصل الثانى

### فى العلم الذى هو فرض عين على الانسان ولا بدّ لوجوده البقائى من تعلّمه

(٦) وهـو العلـم اليقينى بلقـاء الله ووحدانيته وصفاتـه وأفعاله، ثم معرفة العالم الانسـانى وكيفية نشأته الأولى والثانية. وكلّ من جهل هذين العلمين فهو ناقص فى قوام وجوده وكمال حقيقته وإن أحكم سائر العلوم؛ كالطفل أو النائم الذى يرى فى نومه صوراً مختلفة ثم اذا استيقظ من نومه لايجـد منها أثـراً. فهكذا حكم الصور التى يراها الانسـان فى هذا العالم بحواسّه الظاهرة او يتخيّلها بحواسّـه الباطنة. فكلّها أمور باطلة وأحكام وأحـلام زائلة لا بقـاء لها فى يقظة عالم الآخرة الا العلوم الحقيقية التى هى الصور الأخروية ولها أعيان ثابتة عند الله وما عند الله خير للأبرار.

(٧) وإنّمـا الفايـدة فى بعثـة الأنبياء عليهم السـلام وإنزال الكتب من الله هـى انتباه النفوس من نوم الطبيعة وسـنة الغفلة والجهالة، وإفاقتهم عن سكر القصور والنقصان وقيامهم فى القيامة عند الله واطّلاعهم على صور الحقائق الأخروية ووقوفهم على الحساب والصراط والميزان.

(٨) فـلا بدّ أن يحصّل الانسـان أوّلاً علم التوحيـد وعلم النفس، ثم يتـدرّج فى الرسـوخ فـى المعرفة الى أن يصـير من أهل المشـاهدة العيانية، ثـم ينظر بنور التوحيد الشـهودى عالمى الخلق والأمـر والآفال والأنفس. فيحشر الى الله ويسكن الى جواره فى مقعد صدل عند مليك مقتدر، تحقيقاً

*We shall show them Our signs in the horizons and in their souls until it becomes clear to them that He is the Real; suffices it not as to thy Lord, that He is witness over everything?* [41:53].

# Chapter Three

## *On that through which is attained the afterworld's felicity and through which is perceived the encounter with God*

(9) Know that no substance or accident upon which the name *being* falls possesses an independent ipseity such that it would be possible to regard its essence in its essence while ignoring its Establisher and its Existence-Giver, for there is no atom of being that is not encompassed by the light of the Real and contemplated by it.

(10) So, everyone should contemplate his own essence and its Establisher and Existence-Giver with a contemplation hallowed beyond the bodily parts and the senses. *However, most people do not know* [7:187]; *rather, they disbelieve in the encounter with their Lord* [32:10], not because some external preventer is realized, but rather because of the lack of inward eyesight, intellective hearing, and a heart dilated by the light of faith. For the veil between the servants and their object of worship is neither heaven nor earth, land nor sea. The veil is only ignorance and incapacity, or appetite, wrath, and caprice.[8]

(11) All those who are delivered and saved from the captivity of nature and the illness of the soul and caprice, whose eyesights and hearings are opened, and whose hearts are dilated by the light of knowledge and guidance will be conjoined with the world of the Absent and the Higher Plenum and mustered among the ranks of the angels, *the prophets, [ . . . ] the witnesses, and the worthy*[9]*—beautiful are they as companions!* [4:69]. They will be secure from God's chastisement in the abode of punishment, hellfire's reaches, and the lowest pit among the serpents, scorpions, swarmers, satans, and the *worst comrade* [43:38]. Those whose insights are opened to reading the Divine Book and their ears to hearing God's signs [that is, verses] and understanding the mysteries of the afterworld and those whose breasts and hearts are dilated to the remembrance of God, *for them are good tidings in the life of this world and [ . . . ] the afterworld. There is no altering the words of God; that is the mighty triumph* [10:64].

لقوله تعالى: سَنُرِيهم آياتنا فى الآفال وفى أنفسهم حتّى يتبينّ لهم أنّه الحقّ، أوَ لم يكفِ بربّك أنّه على كلّ شئ شهيد.

## الفصل الثالث

### فى أنّه بأىّ شىْء ينال سعادة الآخرة ويدرك لقاء الله تعالى

(٩) اعلم أنّ كلّ ما يقع عليه اسم الكون من الجواهر والأعراض فليس هو ذا هويّة مستقلّة يمكن اعتبار ذاتها بذاتها مع قطع النظر عن مقوّمها وموجدها، فلا ذرّة من ذرات الكون الا ونور الحقّ محيط بها شاهد عليها.

(١٠) فلكلّ أحد أن يشهد ذاته ومقوّمها وموجدها شهوداً مقدّساً عن الجوارح والحواسّ، ولكنّ أكثر الناس لا يعلمون بل هم بلقاء ربّهم كافرون، لا لتحقّق مانع خارجى بل لعدم البصر الباطنى والسمع العقلى والقلب المنشرح بنور الايمان، فإنّ الحجاب بين العبد ومعبوده ليس سماء ولا أرضاً ولا برّاً ولا بحراً، وإنّما الحجاب إمّا الجهل والقصور وإمّا الشهوة والغضب والهوى.

(١١) فكلّ من خلص ونجى عن أسر الطبيعة ومرض النفس والهوى وانفتح بصره وسمعه وانشرح قلبه بنور المعرفة والهدى اتّصل بعالم الغيب والملأ الأعلى وحشر فى زمرة الملائكة والنبييّن والشهداء والصالحين وحسن أولئك رفيقاً، ويكون آمناً من عذاب الله فى دار العقوبة والدرك الجحيم والهاوية السفلى مع الحيّات والعقارب والحشرات والشياطين وبئس القرين. ومن فتحت بصائرهم لقرائة الكتاب الالهى وأسماعهم لسماع آيات الله وفهم أسرار الآخرة وانشرحت صدورهم وقلوبهم لذكر الله فأولئك لهم البُشْرى فى الحياة الدنيا والآخرة. لا تبديل لكلمات الله. ذلك هو الفوز العظيم.

## Chapter Four

*On that through which recourse is had to the knowledge of the horizons and the souls*

(12) Know that the divine levels of Kingdom and Sovereignty that come to be in the two worlds of the horizons and the souls are like a treasure whose door is locked. The door is opened only with the key of the knowledge of the Adamic soul,[10] her world, her empire, and the parts of her essence. This is because knowledge of a thing comes only after knowledge of the knowing essence, and man does not know anything save by means of that [equivalent] of it which is found in his own essence and witnessed in his own world. Thus, for example, knowledge of heaven consists of the presence of a form equal to heaven in the knower's essence.

(13) It belongs to man to know everything, and his essence has the receptivity for every form, since there is nothing without an equivalent within him. So, all existent things are parts of his essence and, despite his oneness, he is all things, because his essence is a macrocosm, his body is a microcosm, and his ruling property flows in all things through subjection. There is nothing that is not under his subjection in reality. This is because of a divine secret that He conferred by His words, *And He subjected to you what is in the heavens and what is in the earth, all together* [45:13].

(14) Know that subjection is of two sorts—true and not true. The not true is of three sorts. The lowest is the situational, accidental sort, like His subjecting the face of the earth and what is in it to man for tilling, planting, and other things. *He subjected to you what is in the earth* [22:65]. Part of it is the subjection of the mountains and the minerals: *And He has appointed for you of the mountains refuges* [16:81]. Part of it is the subjection of the seas: *He subjected the sea, that you may eat of it fresh flesh, and bring forth [from it] ornaments for you to wear* [16:14]. Part of it is the subjection of ships: *He subjected to you the ships* [14:32] *to run upon the sea by the blessing of God* [31:31].[11] Part of it is the subjection of the trees for planting and taking fruits and other things: *Eat of the fruits* [6:141] and His words *Eat, and pasture your cattle* [20:54]. Part of it is the subjection

## الفصل الرابع

### فيما به يتوسّل الى معرفة الآفال والأنفس

(١٢) اعلم أنّ مراتب المُلك والملكوت الالهية الحاصلة فى عالمى الآفال والأنفس بمثابة كنز يُغلق بابه، وإنّما يفتح ذلك الباب بمفتاح معرفة النفس الآدمّية وعالمها ومملكتها وأجزاء ذاتها، لأنّ معرفة كلّ شئ إنّما يكون بعد معرفة الذات العالمة، ولا يعرف الانسان شيئاً الا بواسطة ما يوجد منه فى ذاته ويشاهد فى عالمه. فمعرفة السماء مثلاً عبارة عن حضور صورة مساوية للسماء فى ذات العارف.

(١٣) وللانسان أن يعرف كلّ شئ ولذاته قابلية كل صورة، اذ ما من شئ الا وله نظير فيه. فجميع الموجودات أجزاء ذاته وهو مع وحدته جميع الأشياء لأنّ ذاته عالم كبير وبدنه عالم صغير وحكمه جار فى الأشياء بالتسخير. وما من شئ الا ويكون تحت تسخيره بالحقيقة. وذلك لسرّ الهى أفاده تعالى بقوله: وسخّر لكم ما فى السموات وما فى الأرض جميعاً.

(١٤) واعلم أنّ التسخير على ضربين حقيقى وغير حقيقى. اما الغير الحقيقى فهو على ثلاثة أقسام. أدناها الوضعى العرضى كتسخيره تعالى وجه الأرض وما فيها للانسان للحرث والزرع وغير ذلك، وسخّر لكم ما فى الأرض جميعاً. ومن ذلك تسخير الجبال والمعادن وجعل لكم من الجبال أكناناً. ومنه تسخير البحار، وسخّر لكم البحر لتأكلوا منه لحماً طرياً وتستخرجون حلية تلبسونها. ومنه تسخير الفُلْك، وسخّر لكم الفلك لتجرى فى البحر بنعمة الله. ومنه تسخير الأشجار للغرس وأخذ الثمار وغيرها، كلوا من الثمرات، وقوله: كلوا وارعوا أنعامكم. ومنه

of the beasts and the cattle for riding, ornaments, and carrying loads, according to His words: *And the cattle—He created them for you* [16:5]; His words, *Have they not seen how We created for them of what Our hands wrought cattle that they own? We have abased them to them, and some of them they ride and some they eat* [36:71–72]; and His words, *And there is beauty in them for you, when you bring them home to rest and when you drive them abroad to pasture; and they carry your loads unto a land that you would never reach, except with hardship of souls* [16:6–7]. Part of it is subjection of women and slave girls for descendants and procreation: *Your women are a tillage for you* [2:223].

(15) The middle sort is natural subjection. It is the subjection of the troops of the vegetal potencies and their sites to man for nourishment, growth, procreation, attraction, retention, digestion, expulsion, form-giving, and shaping.

(16) The highest sort is soulish subjection. It is the subjection of the Sovereignty of the senses and the Kingdom of their organs to the human soul. These troops subjected to man are of two varieties—a variety from the world of the Witnessed (that is, the organs and the outward senses); and a variety from the world of the Absent (that is, the potencies and the means of awareness). With respect to their innate dispositions, all of them are subjected to the human spirit and innately inclined to obey it. It turns affairs over to them with its two fingers—the intellective and the practical.[12]

(17) The first troop are not able to dispute with the spirit or rebel against it. When it commands the eye to open, it opens. When it commands the leg to move, it moves. When it commands the tongue to speak and resolves to rule it, it speaks. So also are all the other outward organs.

(18) As for the other troop, they are the same, except that sense-intuition has a certain satanity with respect to innate disposition.[13] It accepts leading astray by Satan, so it resists the intellect in its goals of demonstration and faith. Hence the intellect needs a new, afterworldly confirmation[14] from the side of God to subjugate [sense-intuition], overcome it, and drive away its darknesses.

تسخير الدوابّ والأنعام للركوب والزينة وحمل الأثقال لقوله تعالى: والأنعام خلقها لكم، وقوله: أو لم يروا أنّا خلقنا لهم ممّا عملت أيدينا أنعاماً فهم لها مالكون، وذلّلناها لهم فمنها ركوبهم ومنها يأكلون، وقوله تعالى: ولكم فيها جمال حين تريحون وحين تسرحون وتحمل أثقالكم الى بلد لم تكونوا بالغيه الا بشقّ الأنفس. ومنه تسخير النسوان والجوارئ للنسل والتوليد، نساؤكم حرث لكم.

(١٥) وأوسطها التسخير الطبيعى، وهو تسخير جنود القوى النباتية ومواضعها للانسان للتغذية والتنمية والتوليد والجذب والإمساك والهضم والدفع والتصوير والتشكيل.

(١٦) وأعلاها التسخير النفسانى، وهو تسخير ملكوت الحواسّ ومُلْك أعضائها للنفس الانسانية. وهذه الجنود المسخّرة للانسان على صنفين، صنف من عالم الشهادة وهو الأعضاء والحواسّ الظاهرة، وصنف من عالم الغيب وهى القوى والمشاعر. وجميعها مسخّرةٌ للروح الانسانى بحسب فطرتها مجبولةٌ على طاعته. وهو المحوّل لها بأصبعيه العاقلة والعاملة.

(١٧) واما الجند الأوّل فلا يستطيعون له خلافاً ولا عليه تمرّداً. فاذا أمر العين للانفتاح انفتحت، واذا أمر الرِجل للحركة تحرّكت، واذا أمر اللسان للكلام وجزم الحكم به تكلّم. وكذا سائر الأعضاء الظاهرة.

(١٨) واما الجند الآخر فكذلك الا أنّ الوهم له شيطنة بحسب الفطرة، يقبل إغواء الشيطان فيعارض العقل فى مقاصده البرهانية الايمانية، فيحتاج الى تأييد جديد أخروى من جانب الله ليقهره ويغلب عليه ويطرد ظلماته.

(19) As for true subjection, it consists of God's subjecting the intellective, divine meanings[15] to the perfect man and arrived saint who, through his inward strength over them, makes them spiritual forms or absent images existent in his intellective world or his afterworldly configuration. He transfers things from the world of the Witnessed to the world of the Absent by extracting[16] universals from particulars and by grasping the spirits from the matter of the bodies and apparitions with God's aid by way of His name "the Grasper." [He does all this] while returning from this world to the afterworld and turning back from the state of dispersion and separation to the state of gathering and encounter; from the mine of sorrow, sickness, and fear to the fountainhead of joy, health, and security; and from the locus of ignorance and doubt to the seat of truthfulness and certainty. *So he turns back to his folk joyfully* [84:9]. That is *the Day of Encounter* [40:15], and that is *the Day of Gathering, wherein there is no doubt* [42:7]. *Enter into them in peace and security!* [15:46].

(20) Once what we have mentioned becomes settled and what we have illumined becomes manifest, it will be unveiled for the intelligent and the seeing that all things in the cosmos are potentially among the parts of man, and that it belongs to him to bring them forth from potency to act with the confirmation of God, the Originator, the One who makes return.[17] Then he will have encompassment of and mastery over everything, through configuring and devising within his own world—*he will do what he wills* [3:40] and *he will rule as he desires* [5:1][18] through the potency of the Exalted, the Praiseworthy.[19]

(21) *An Insightful Confirmation.* Consider how the elemental beings walk the path of the human world and turn toward the Kaᶜba of [the human] heart, within which are the signs of the Real. Thereby the elemental bodies, which are far from similar to him, become a subtle food after their subtilization little by little, their transformation from state to state, their crossing over the degrees of plant and animal, their traversing the far roadways, and their entrance into the city of his frame and his world,[20] obedient and submitted *[muslim]* to him, just as the people *enter God's religion in droves* [110:2]. This is because they are innately disposed to the service of man and to prostration before Adam, moving toward him in search, worship, and yearning for God's religion, *willingly or unwillingly.*[21]

(١٩) واما التسخير الحقيقى فهو عبارة عن تسخير الله المعانى العقلية الالهية للانسان الكامل والولى الواصل، وجعله بقوّته الباطنية إيّاها صوراً روحانية او أمثلة غيبية موجودة فى عالمه العقلى او نشأته الأخروية؛ ونقله الأشياء من عالم الشهادة الى عالم الغيب بانتزاعه الكليات من الجزئيات، وقبضه الأرواح من موادّ الأجسام والأشباح بإمداد الله من اسمه القابض، راجعاً من عالم الدنيا الى الآخرة، ومنقلباً من حال التفرقة والافترال الى حالة الجمع والتلال، ومن معدن الحزن والسقم والخوف الى منبع السرور والصّحة والأمن، ومن محلّ الجهل والشكّ الى مقعد الصدل واليقين. وينقلب الى أهله مسروراً. وذلك يوم التلال وذلك يوم الجمع لا ريب فيه ادخلوها بسلام آمنين.

(٢٠) فاذا تقرّر ما ذكرنا وظهر ما نوّرناه انكشف لدى العاقل البصير أنّ جميع ما فى العالم من أجزاء الانسان بالقوّة، وله أن يخرج بها من القوّة الى الفعل بتأييد الله المُبدء المعيد. فيكون له الإحاطة والتسلّط على الكل بالإنشاء والاختراع فى عالمه، يفعل ما يشاء ويحكم ما يريد بقوّة العزيز الحميد.

(٢١) تأييد استبصارى. انظر الى الكائنات العنصرية كيف سلكت سبيل العالم الانسانى وتوجّهت شطر كعبة قلبه التى فيها آيات الحقّ فى صيرورة الأجسام الأسطقسية البعيدة الشبه له غذاءً لطيفاً بعد تلطّفها يسيراً يسيراً وتحوّلها من حال الى حال وطيّها درجات النبات والحيوان وقطع مسالكها البعيدة ودخولها فى بلدة قالبه وعالمه طائعة مسلمة له دخول الناس فى دين الله أفواجًا. وذلك لكونها مفطورةً فى خدمة الانسان وسجدة آدم حركةً اليه طلباً وشوقاً وتعبّداً لدين الله طوعاً أو كرهاً. فعلم

Thus is it known that all beings are a ransom for man and are transformed into him, but within him is no altering into anything else.[22] *There is no altering the words of God* [10:64]. *So set thy face to the religion as one of pure faith—God's innate disposition according to which He disposed people. There is no altering God's creation. That is the right religion* [30:30].

(22) Hence the returning place of the cosmos is the essence of man, and his returning place is to the Divine Ipseity. With his world's openers and his empire's keys are opened the locked gates of heaven and earth through mercy, forgiveness, wisdom, and knowledge.

# Chapter Five

(23) Everything man needs with which to achieve perfection and climb to the world of holiness—that is, the realities of the existent things, the configurations of this world and the afterworld, and the worlds of Creation and Command—is written in the Adamic tablet and engraved on the human page with an inimitable script and a divine engraving. In the same way, the imprint of all is found in the tablets of the beings and the animal pages. However, the book of man is more complete, more truthful, and higher. *Surely the book of the pious is in Illiyyūn; and what shall teach you what Illiyyūn is? A book engraved, witnessed by those brought nigh* [83:18–21]. And *surely the book of the depraved is in Sijjīn; and what shall teach you what Sijjīn is? [A book engraved.] Woe on that day to those who cry lies* [83:7–10].

(24) Each of these high and low books speaks and bears witness in truth to the existence of the Writer, His knowledge, and His power. *This is Our book that speaks against you in truth* [45:29]. This speaking book is identical with the book that shall be hung on man's neck and shall be brought forth from him on the day of resurrection. Thus each man must read his book with understanding and realization and act according to what it demands. Otherwise, [this hanging of the book] will come under the heading of hanging pearls on the necks of swine. God says, *Every man—We have fastened to him his bird of omen on his neck; and We shall bring forth for him, on the day of resurrection, a book he shall meet wide open. "Read your book. Your soul suffices you this day as a reckoner against you." Whoever is guided is guided only for his soul, and whoever is misguided is misguided only against it* [17:13–15].

أنّ جميع الكائنات فداء الانسان متحوّل اليه، وليس فيه تبديل الى غيره. لا تبديل لكلمات الله. فأقم وجهك للدين حنيفاً فطرةَ الله التى فطر الناس عليها لا تبديل لخلق الله ذلك الدين القيّم.

(٢٢) فمعاد العالم هو ذات الانسان ومعاده الى الهويّة الالهية. وبمفاتيح عالمه ومقاليد مملكته ينفتح مغاليق أبواب السماء والأرض بالرحمة والمغفرة والحكمة والمعرفة.

## الفصل الخامس

(٢٣) كلّ ما يحتاج اليه الانسان فى أن يستكمل به ويرتقى الى عالم القدس من حقائق الموجودات ونشأتى الدنيا والآخرة وعالمى الخلق والامر فهو مكتوب فى اللوح الآدمى ومرقوم فى الصحيفة الانسانية بخط معجز ورقم الهى. وكذلك يوجد نقش الكل فى الألواح الكونية والصحائف الحيوانية، الا أنّ كتاب الانسان أتمّ وأصدل وأعلى، إنّ كتاب الأبرار لفى علّيين وما أدراك ما علّيون كتاب مرقوم يشهده المقرّبون، وإنّ كتاب الفجّار لفى سجّين وما أدراك ما سجّين، ويل يومئذ للمكذّبين.

(٢٤) وكل واحد من هذه الكتب العلوية والسفلية ينطق ويشهد بوجود الكاتب بالحقّ وعلمه وقدرته، هذا كتابنا ينطق عليكم بالحق. وهذا الكتاب الناطق هو بعينه الكتاب الذى يعلّق فى عنق الانسان ويستخرج يوم القيامة منه، فيجب على كل انسان أن يقرأ كتابه قراءةَ فهمٍ وتحقيقٍ ويعمل بمقتضاه لئلا يكون من باب تعليق الدرّ فى أعنال الخنازير. قال الله تعالى: وكلّ انسان ألزمناه طائرَه فى عنقه، ونخرج له يوم القيامة كتاباً يَلقاه منشوراً اقرأْ كتابك كفى بنفسك اليوم عليك حسيباً من اهتدى فإنّما يهتدى لنفسه ومن ضلّ فإنّما يضلّ عليها.

# Chapter Six

*On the knowledge of the divine vicegerency in the earthly world*

(25) Everyone who desires to know Him who governs and orders the cosmos with a divine governance and a wise order should first be intent upon knowledge of the human soul, her governance of the human microcosm, her ordering and arranging this Adamic empire, the purpose to which she applies herself and toward which she leans, and the final cause that calls her to this arranging and ordering, lest her acts be futile and her existence nullified.

(26) Knowledge of an empire's governor and the manner in which he governs his empire will only come to be by means of knowledge of his servitors and his troops. So also is the property of the human configuration, for the administrator of this empire and his governing of his province can only be known by knowing his servitors and his potencies, which are sent forth from his heart to his frame. The chieftains of these troops are restricted to nine in number. *And We gave Moses nine signs* [17:101], which include hearing, eyesight, smell, taste, and touch. Each of these [five] chieftains has one specific site in this nethermost world that is the abode of its lodging for an appointed period, and they also have gatherings in a common meeting place near their abodes and dwellings. After these, there are [four more] chieftains—conception, imagination, sense-intuition, and intellect. Of these four the first two pertain to the clime of the middle world, and the other two to the last clime.

(27) The troops of the five senses are obedient in service, without any disobedience, and compelled in their act without freely choosing, because they are imprisoned in the jail of this cosmos. Each of them has a limited boundary that it does not transgress. It is not for eyesight to secede from seeing colors and lights or to be deficient in its act, nor will it see white as black. So also are hearing, taste, and the others. Each is incapable of the other's act, and each *has a known station* [37:164].[23] Eyesight does not hear, and hearing does not see. The two of them do not taste or smell, nor conversely. And so it goes.

## الفصل السادس

### فی معرفة الخلافة الالهیة فی العالم الأرضی

(۲۵) كلّ من یرید أن یعلم مدّبر العالم ومرتّبه بالتدبیر الالهی والترتیب الحکمی فلیعمد أولاً الی معرفة النفس الانسانیة وتدبیرها للعالم الصغیر الانسانی وترتیبها ونظمها لهذه المملکة الآدمیة والغرض الذی تؤمّه وتنحو نحوه والسبب الغائی الذی یدعوها الی هذا النظم والترتیب کیلا یکون فعلها عبثاً ووجودها باطلاً.

(۲۶) ثمّ إنّ العلم بمدبّر مملكة وكيفية تدبير مملكته لا يحصلان الا بوسيلة العلم بخدّامه وجنوده. فكذا حكمُ النشأة الانسانية، فإنّما يعرف والى هذه المملكة وتدبيره فی ولايته من جهة معرفة خدّامه وقواه المنبعثة من قلبه فی قالبه. ورؤساء هذه الجنود منحصرة فی تسعة أعداد، ولقد آتينا موسى تسع آيات، منها السمع والبصر والشمّ والذول واللمس. ولكلّ من هذه الرؤساء موضع خاصّ من مواضع هذا العالم الأدنى، وهو دار إقامته مدّةً مضروبة، ولهم أيضاً اجتماعات فی مجمع مشترك بقرب دورهم ومنازلهم. ثمّ بعدهم رؤساء التصوّر والتخيّل والوهم والعقل. فالأوّلان من هذه الأربعة من إقليم العالم الأوسط، والآخران من الاقليم الآخر.

(۲۷) فجنود الحواسّ الخمس مطيعة فی الخدمة من غير عصيان مجبورة فی فعلها غير مختارة لكونها محبوسة فی سجن هذا العالم. فلكلّ منها حدّ محدود لا يتعدّاه. فليس للبصر خروج عن رؤية الألوان والأضواء ونقص عن فعله ولا له أن يرى الأبيض أسود، وكذا السمع والذول وغيرها. وكلّ منها يعجز عن فعل الآخر، وكلٌّ له مقام معلوم. فالبصر لا يسمع والسمع لا يبصر وهما لا يذوقان ولا يشمّان ولا بالعكس وهكذا.

(28) As for the remaining four, each is like one that freely chooses in its act and is versatile in its workmanship. *It does what it desires* [2:253] whenever it desires because it undergoes transition from form to form. So, imagination conceives of any form there may be, and it records it in its storehouse. Sense-intuition intuits any meaning and form there may be and retains both, and it dominates over them whenever it wills.

(29) In addition, each of the five informants comes with reports from the districts and gives the information to the empire's administrator without understanding the response or taking it back. Rather, each is like a messenger who hands over his message without knowing anything about his message. Eyesight bears the message of colors but does not perceive the meaning of color, nor of the delivery and the message, because it is unable to perceive its own essence; nor can it perceive its perception of colors and its delivery to the governor, in contrast to the inward troops: each of them informs of the report, understands it, and returns with the response. The intellect, which is the last, is the speaker, responder, listener, and ruler.

(30) Moreover, the acts of these five troops do not become conjoined with each other, nor does any one of them deliver its act over to another. Hearing does not deliver heard things over to eyesight, nor does eyesight deliver seen things over to hearing, and so also should the rest be gauged. So, the one that hears is blind, the one that sees is deaf, the one that tastes does not smell, and the one that smells has no touch.

(31) All of them are of this sort, in contrast to the entities of the four inward troops. Reflective thought delivers the forms that it cogitates over to sense-intuition, sense-intuition [delivers them] over to memory, and the remembering [potency] recalls them to the intellective potency. The whole is like one individual that reflects, conceptualizes, remembers, and is wise. Disparity and distinction among them are in terms of viewpoint, not difference and separation, as in the case of the outward senses.

(32) Indeed, the governor of this human empire and this abode of lordly vicegerency can know and dominate over all of these outward and inward troops, and it can act with their acts, because it takes illumination from the light of God, the Exalted, the Kindly. So, the lights of these beings obey it, because it is ruler, subjugator, governor, dominating. Its rule

(٢٨) وامّـا الأربعـة الباقية فكلّ منهـا بمنزلة المختار فـى فعله المتفنّن فـى صنعه يفعل ما يريـد متى يريد، اذ لها الانتقال مـن صورة الى صورة. فالخيال يتصـوّر أىّ صورة كانت ويضبطها فى خزانته، والوهم يتوهّم أىّ معنى وصورة كانا ويضبطهما ويتصرّف فيهما متى شاء.

(٢٩) وأيضـاً كلّ من المنهيات الخمسـة يأتى بالأخبـار عن النواحى وينهيهـا الى والى المملكة من دون فهم الجـواب والمراجعة به، بل كل منها بمنزلة رسـول مبلّغ رسـالته من غـير أن يكون له خبر عن رسـالته. فالبصر يتحمّل رسالة الألوان ولا يدرك معنى اللون ولا التأدية والرسالة، اذ ليس له أن يدرك ذاته ولا أن يدرك إدراكه الألوان وتأديته الى المدبّر بخلاف الجنود الباطنة، فإنّ كلاً منها ينهى بالخبر ويفهمه ويرجع بالجواب. والعقل الأخير هو القائل والمجيب والسامع والحاكم.

(٣٠) وأيضاً أفعال هذه الجنود الخمسـة لا يتّصل بعضها ببعض، ولا يؤدّى واحد منها فعله الى الآخر. فالسـمع لا يؤدّى مسموعاته الى البصر، ولا البـصر يؤدّى مبصراته اليـه، وكذا القياس فى البواقى. فالسـامع منها أعمى والبصير منها أصمّ والذائق منها أزكم والشامّ منها أجذم.

(٣١) وهكـذا كلّـه بخلاف أعيـان الجنود الأربعـة الباطنة. فالفكر يـؤدّى الصـور التـى تأمّلت الى الوهـم، والوهـم الى الحفـظ، والحافظة تسـترجعها الى القوّة العاقلة. والكلّ كشخص واحد مفكّر متصوّر حافظ حكيـم. والتفـاوت والتمايز بينها بالاعتبار لا بالمباينـة والافتراق كما بين الحواسّ الظاهرة.

(٣٢) نعم للمدبّر فى هذه المملكة الانسـانية ودار الخلافة الربّانية أن يعلم ويتصرّف فى كلّ من هذه الجنود الظاهرة والباطنة ويفعل فعلها لكونه مسـتشرقاً بنـور الله العزيز المنّـان. فتطيعه أنوار هذه الأكـوان لأنّه الحاكم

pervades each of them and its command penetrates into them. Furthermore, it is that which descends from its essence's highness and its degree's heaven to the earths of their receptivities. It performs its acts in the loci of their preparednesses, and its reality's face discloses itself in the mirrors of their entities. So, it itself is the touching, smelling, tasting, hearing, seeing, reflecting, remembering, rational, wise, and deiform, despite the unity of its essence and the plurality of these essences, because, despite their multiplicity, they are absorbed in its oneness; and it is the owner, the governor.

(33) These nine are signs that are witnessed in [man's] Kingdom and his Sovereignty according to the outward aspects of their created nature and the inward aspects of their innate disposition. In the same way, through what he has of the two configurations, he is a witness of Him to *whom belong the Creation and the Command* [7:54]—high indeed is His majesty! So, from this book read God's wisdom in creating the heavens and the earth, and ponder the magnificence of the Innovator of all, the God of the worlds.

## Chapter Seven

*That man has another world*

(34) The nine human way stations are exactly like nine celestial spheres in the world of human Sovereignty. With respect to each, the soul has one of the designated levels of Sovereignty. These nine signs are those brought by "Moses," the human spirit. They are alluded to in His words, *Insert thy hand in thy bosom and it will come out white without any evil—among nine signs [to Pharaoh and his people]* [27:12]. Thus God commanded him to insert his "hand," which is that which dominates through reflective thought, into his inwardness, so as to bring forth and make manifest these signs "to Pharaoh," who is the motor potency, the one that *commands to evil* [12:53], "and his people," who are the wrathful and appetitive potencies. Thereby they may come to obey God's command and not employ the "children of Israel," who are the perceptual potencies, in the unreal, pharaonic purposes and the sense-intuitive, this-worldly wishes.

(35) For the soulish "hand" possesses nine Sovereigntarial signs that came to her from the rays of God's Sovereigntarial fire, which is seen on the *right side of the watercourse* [28:30] in the world of holiness. When someone

القاهر المدبّر المتصرّف يسرى حكمه الى كلّ منها وينفذ أمره فيها، بل هو الذى ينزل من علوّ ذاته وسماء درجته الى أراضى قابلياتها ويفعل فعله فى محالّ استعداداتها ويتجلّى وجه حقيقته فى مرائى أعيانها. فهو بعينه اللامس الشامّ الذائق السميع البصير المفكّر الحافظ الناطق الحكيم المتألّه مع أحدية ذاته وتعدّد هذه الذوات، لأنّها مع كثرتها مستهلكة فى وحدته، وهو المالك المدبّر.

(٣٣) وهذه التسع آيات مشاهدة فى ملكه وملكوته بحسب ظواهر خلقتها وبواطن فطرتها، كما أنّه بماله من النشأتين شاهد على من له الخلق والأمر تعالى جدّه. فاقرأ من هذا الكتاب حكمة الله فى خلق السموات والأرض وتدبّر فى عظمة مبدع الكلّ اله العالمين.

## الفصل السابع
### فى أن للانسان عالماً آخر

(٣٤) إنّ المنازل التسعة الانسانية هى بعينها كالأفلاك التسعة فى عالم الملكوت الانسانى. وللنفس باعتبار كلّ منها مرتبة معيّنة من مراتب الملكوت. وهذه الآيات التسع هى التى أتى بها موسى الروح الانسانى المشار اليها فى قوله تعالى: أدخل يدك فى جيبك تَخْرُج بيضاءَ من غير سوءٍ فى تسع آيات. فأمر الله له أن يدخل يده المتصرّفة بالفكر فى باطنه لإخراج هذه الآيات وإظهارها الى فرعون القوّة المحرّكة الأمّارة بالسوء وقومه من القوى الغضبية والشهوية ليطيعوا أمر الله ولا يستخدموا بنى اسرائيل القوى المدركة فى الأغراض الباطلة الفرعونية والأمانى الوهمية الدنياوية.

(٣٥) فانّ اليد النفسانية هى ذات تسع آيات ملكوتية حصلت لها من أشعّة نار الله الملكوتية التى رؤيت فى الواد الأيمن فى عالم القدس. فمن علم

knows these nine signs that he witnesses in the book of his soul, it is time for him to read the Qurʾān, recite God's speech, and witness *the greatest signs of his Lord* [53:18]—I mean, the seven inward levels, which are nature, soul, intellect, spirit, secret heart, hidden, and most hidden.[24] Thereby he realizes the "doubled seven" *and the magnificent Qurʾān* [15:87][25] sent down upon Muḥammad (God's blessing be upon him and his household). When he witnesses the outwardness of the book of the cosmos and examines God's signs in it with the outward eyesight, and when he examines *the greatest signs of his Lord* with the inward insight of the heart, then he is the arrived servant and the perfect saint, and his heart is at peace, residing with God through perpetual certainty, without doubt or surmise.

## Chapter Eight

*That the book of the soul signifies the Book of God, and her speech His Speech*

(36) Know first that "speech" is other than "book," and neither is the same as the other, because speech is perceived only through hearing and book is perceived only through eyesight. So, the Real's Speech is perceived through inward hearing, and His Book is perceived through inward eyesight. As for the soul's speech and book, they are perceived only through outward hearing and eyesight.

(37) Now that this has been settled, we say that once the human soul has been awakened and aroused from the state of inanimate sleep, vegetal drowsiness, and animal heedlessness, and once she has been transformed into the state of human uprightness and the cognitive, afterworldly configuration; then the first of the degrees that she attains is the degree of counting and arithmetic. This degree is found only in man, because the intellective angels are elevated beyond it and the mute animals are sunk below attaining it. So, the human soul is "the numberer, the measurer," as was settled in its own place.[26] At the beginning of her affair, the soul comes to know the science of number and arithmetic, so that she may know through it the levels of the inward Sovereignty.

(38) From the levels of the numbers are born their names. However, speech comes only with respect to hearing, so letters and sounds have priority over the names, just as the simple has priority over the compound.

هذه الآيات التسع التى شاهدها فى كتاب نفسه فقد حان له أن يقرأ القرآن ويتلو كلام الله ويشاهد آيات ربّه الكبرى، أعنى المراتب السبع الباطنية، وهى الطبيعة والنفس والعقل والروح والسرّ والخفى والأخفى. فيتحقّق بالسبع المثانى والقرآن العظيم المنزل على محمّد صلى الله عليه وآله. فاذا شاهد ظاهر كتاب العالم وطالع آيات الله التى فيه بالبصر الظاهرى وطالع آيات ربّه الكبرى بالبصيرة القلبية الباطنية فهو العبد الواصل والولى الكامل والمطمئنّ الساكن قلبه عند الله باليقين الدائم من غير شكّ وتخمين.

## الفصل الثامن

### فى دلالة كتاب النفس على كتاب الله وكلامها على كلامه

(٣٦) اعلم أوّلًا أنّ الكلام غير الكتاب وليس أحدهما عين الآخر، لأنّ الكلام لا يدرك الا بالسمع والكتاب لا يدرك الا بالبصر. فكلام الحق يدرك بالسمع الباطنى وكتابه بالبصر الباطنى. وامّا كلام النفس وكتابها فانّما يدركان بهذا السمع وهذا البصر الظاهريين.

(٣٧) اذا تقرّر هذا فنقول إنّ النفس الانسانية اذا استيقظت وانتبهت من حالة النوم الجمادى والسِّنَة النباتية والغفلة الحيوانية وتحوّلت الى حالة القيام الانسانى والنشأة العلمية الأخروية، فأوّل درجة نالتها من الدرجات هى درجة العدّ والحساب. ولا يوجد هذه الدرجة الا فى الانسان لارتفاع الملائكة العقلية عنها وانحطاط الحيوانات العجمية عن نيلها. فالنفس الانسانية هى العادّة الماسحة كما تقرّر فى مقامه. فالنفس فى بداية أمرها عرفت علم العدد والحساب لتعلم به مراتب الملكوت الباطنية.

(٣٨) ومن مراتب العدد يتولّد أساميها. لكن بحكم أنّ الكلام إنّما يتأتّى من جهة السمع، فالحروف والأصوات تتقدّم على تلك الأسامى

The most precedent of the letters are the letters of prolongation, because they come into being merely by the lengthening of the vowel, whether upwards like *alif,* downwards like *yāʾ,* or toward the middle like *wāw.* This is why *alif* is the name of the first of the solitary numbers from one to one thousand, to which correspond the *abjad* letters from *alif* to *ghayn.*[27]

(39) Then the compounds come to be from these solitary letters. Their names are composed from the names of the solitaries, and their figures, from the figures of the solitaries, by compounding some of the solitaries of these worlds with others. So, the numbers signify the existence of the world of the intellect; the letters along with their sounds and tones signify the world of the *barzakh* and images, and the figures pertain to the world of the witnessed. Thus the numbers' existence is in the tablet of the soul, and the letters' existence is in the page of air—the breath that moves because of the potency of speech—and only hearing perceives them. Eyesight perceives the imprints of the writing of the names, and these signify the names and what is in the soul.

(40) Hence the things have [1] an existence in the soul, [2] an existence in the human breath, which is the subtle air that comes forth from his inwardness and corresponds to the All-Merciful Breath, which is the effusion of His existence deployed over the levels of the possible things, and [3] an existence in writing.[28] The first is not through positioning or exertion, in contrast to the latter two. The first is the soul's word, the second her speech, and the third her book. The soul's word signifies His words, *When We desire it, Our word to it is "Be!" and it comes to be* [2:117]; her speech His speech, *Grant him protection until he hears the Speech of God* [9:6]; and her book His Book, *Alif Lām Mīm. That is the Book in which there is no doubt, a guidance to the god-wary* [2:1–2].

(41) Know also that "one" is the imam of all the numbers, their actor, and their source, because, as long as "one" does not exist, none of them has any existence whatsoever. It is independent of all, because they come to be only by "one's" repetition and diversification in diverse sorts of transformations and its unfoldment within the stages of itself. In the

تقدّم البسيط على المركّب. وأسبق الحروف هى حروف المدّ لتكونّها من مجرّد إشباع الحركة إمّا الى الفول كالألف او الى التحت كالياء او الى الوسط كالواو. ولهذا كانت الألف اسم أوّل مراتب العدد المفردة من الواحد الى الألف التى بإزائها حروف الجُمَّل من الألف الى الغين.

(٣٩) ثم يحصل المركّبات من هذه الحروف المفردات ويتالّف أساميها من أسامى المفردات وأرقامها من أرقام المفردات بتركيب مفردات من هذه العوالم بعضها مع بعض. فالأعداد دليل على وجود عالم العقل، والحروف بأصواتها ونغماتها دليل على عالم البرزخ والمثال والأرقام من عالم الشهادة. فالعدد وجوده فى لوح النفس، والحروف وجودها فى صحيفة الهواء النفسى المتحرّك بسبب قوّة التكلّم، وانّما يدركها السمع. والبصر يدرك نقوش كتابة الأسامى الدالّة عليها وعلى ما فى النفس.

(٤٠) فللأشياء وجودٌ فى النفس، ووجودٌ فى النَفَس الانسانى وهو الهواء اللطيف الخارج من باطنه الذى هو بإزاء النفس الرحمانى الذى هو فيض وجوده المنبسط على مراتب الممكنات، ووجودٌ فى الكتابة. فالأوّل ليس بوضع وتعمّل بخلاف الأخيرين. والأوّل قول النفس والثانى كلامها والثالث كتابها. وقول النفس دليل على قوله تعالى: اذا أردناه أن نقول له كن فيكون، وكلامها على كلامه تعالى: فأجِره حتّى يسمع كلامَ الله، وكتابها على كتابه تعالى: ألم، ذلك الكتاب لا ريب فيه هدى للمتّقين.

(٤١) واعلم أنّ الواحد إمام الأعداد كلّها وفاعلها ومنشأها، اذ ما لم يوجد الواحد لم يكن لشئ منها وجود أصلاً، وهو غنى عن الكل لأنّها إنّما تحصل من تكرار الواحد وتفنّنه بفنون التحوّلات وتطوّره فى أطوار

same way, the reflecting soul is the imam that dominates over the levels of the soulish sciences and unfolds in the stages of reflective cogitations. So it is up to the traveler to make her into a straight path by which he may be guided to the precinct of the Real. *Say: This is my path; I call to God upon insight—I and whoso follows me* [12:108].

## Chapter Nine

*That the world of Sovereignty, which is the inwardness of this cosmos, is to be gauged against the Sovereignty of the world of man, which is his inwardness and the absent of what is witnessed of him*

(42) It has now been settled and clarified that in everything witnessed there is something absent, that with respect to everything outward and witnessed there is something inward and curtained, and that every bodily sign is linked to a spiritual sign—just as the Kingdom is attached to the Sovereignty, writing to meaning, and body to spirit. Hence it has become manifest that no bodily outwardness becomes established save through a supraformal[29] inwardness. So also is the state of the cosmos, its magnificent [celestial] bodies, and its noble angels.[30]

(43) The body becomes established through the spirit such that, when the linkage is severed, it disintegrates and falls away. The ear becomes established through the potency of hearing; the eye becomes established through the potency of eyesight, and so also the others. So much is this so that, when the spirits and potencies are nullified and made ineffectual in their act, the organs become corrupted, rot, and fall away. So also, were the bodies of the celestial spheres and the elements not preserved by the fact that the spiritual things, their writing, and their preserving are attached to the Real's command and speech, no trace of existence would remain for them.

(44) In the same way, words are combined in the world of the soul only so that the forms of deeds may emerge. This is because a command comes to be from a fully active commander only so that the deed may occur by way of acquiescence on the part of the commanded one. Then the trace of this goes back to the commander's self. Were there no rationality

نفســه. فهكذا النفس المتفكّرة هى الامام الذى يتصرّف فى مراتب العلوم النفسـانية ويتطوّر فـى أطوار التأمّـلات الفكرية. فللسـالك أن يجعلها صراطاً مسـتقيماً يهتدى به الى جناب الحقّ، قل هذه سـبيلى أدعو الى الله على بصيرة أنا ومن اتّبعنى.

## الفصل التاسع

### فى أنّ عالم الملكوت الذى هو باطن هذا العالم على قياس ملكوت عالم الانسان الذى هو باطنه وغيب شهادته

(٤٢) لّما تقرّر وتبينّ أنّ فى كلّ شـهادة غيباً وبحسـب كل ظاهر مشـهود باطناً مسـتوراً، وأنّ كلّ آية جسـمانيةً ترتبط بآيـة روحانية تعلّقَ المُلْك بالملكوت والكتابة بالمعنى والجسـد بالـروح، فظهر أن لا قوام لكل ظاهر جسـمى الا بباطن معنوى. فكذلك حال العالم وأجسـامها العظام وملائكتها الكرام.

(٤٣) فكمـا أنّ قـوام البدن بالـروح بحيث اذا انقطـع ارتباطها منه انفسـخ وسـقط؛ وكذا قوام الأذن بقوّة السـمع وقوام العـين بقوّة البصر، وهكـذا غيرهما، حتـى اذا بطلت أرواحهـا وقواها وتعطّلـت عن فعلها فسـدت هذه الأعضاء ورمّت وسقطت؛ فكذلك أجساد الفلك والعناصر لو لم ينحفظ بتعلّق الروحانيات وكتابتها وحفظها بأمر الحق وكلامه لم يبق لها أثر الوجود.

(٤٤) كمـا أن فى عالم النفس تأليف الأقوال انّما يكون لصدور صور الأعمـال، لأنّ حصول الأمر مـن الآمر الفعّال انّما يكـون لحصول العمل مـن المأمور علـى وجه الامتثال ليعود أثر ذلك الى نفس الآمر. فلو لم يكن

and speech in this world [of the soul], the forms of writing and diverse figures would not be generated in the documental earths,[31] nor would they climb up with respect to eyesight, or rather, with respect to hearing, to their place of return, which is the perceiving, fully active intellect.

(45) The same is so in the divine world. Whenever something is first determined in its guise and time in the world of the Precedent Decree, it then comes to exist, through the intermediary of the spheres and their movements, on the page, which is the earth's face. It may be the form of an inanimate thing, a plant, or an animal; it is worked by the hands of the All-Merciful for the purpose of the knowledge that yields the true felicity that comes at the return to Him who is the returning place and final goal of everything, and the life and utmost end of everything alive.

(46) Do you not see that whenever the fully knowing, fully active soul combines the form of word or writing by means of outward sensation, this is first weighed and gauged by the scale of reflective thought and the gauge of consideration? Then it comes to exist in the external realm in accordance with what the soul first determined and decreed. Finally, it returns to the world of the soul, either proportioned and balanced in the mode of truthfulness and correctness or inverted and twisted in the mode of error, mistake, and falsehood, which necessitate cursing and chastisement.

(47) So also is the state of the forms of the beings, which are first determined in the World of the Precedent Decree and [then] return by way of the human soul to the world of the afterworld. When the day of resurrection comes and the Scales are set up—as in His words, *And We shall set up the just scales for the day of resurrection* [21:47]—then *God will recompense every soul for what it has earned* [14:51]. *Woe on that day to those who cry lies* [77:15].

(48) *A Remark.* Now, it should not be hidden from you that the senses, which are subjected to the soul and compelled in their act and in their obedience to her, are like the tools of the crafts for craftsmen, for no tool can be aware of the measure of the work and the gauge of the workmanship. Do you not see that when a hand is at work, it becomes

النطق والكلام فى هذا العالم لم يتولّد صورة الكتابة والأرقام المختلفة فى الأراضى القرطاسية ولا ترتقى من جهة البصر بل من جهة السمع الى معادها التى هى العقل الدرّاك الفعّال.

(٤٥) فكذلك فى العالم الالهى كلّما يقدّر أوّلاً بهيئته وزمانه فى عالم القضاء السابق فهى توجد بواسطة الأفلاك وحركاتها على صحيفة وجه الأرض من صور الجماد والنبات والحيوان ممّا عملته أيدى الرحمن لغرض العرفان المثمر للسعادة الحقيقية الحاصلة عند العود الى من اليه مرجع كلّ شئ وغايته وحياة كلّ حىّ ونهايته.

(٤٦) أوَلا ترى أنّ كلّما تؤلّف النفس العلّامة الفعّالة من صورة القول والكتابة بوسيلة الحسّ الظاهر، فيوزن ويقاس أوّلاً بميزان الفكر ومقياس النظر، ثمّ يوجد فى الخارج على طبق ماقدّرت وقضيت أوّلاً، ثم يعود الى عالم النفس أخيراً إمّا مستوياً موزوناً على وجه الصدل والصواب أو منتكساً معوجّاً على وجه الغلط والخطأ والكذب الموجب للّعن والعذاب.

(٤٧) فكذلك حال صور الكائنات المقدرّة أوّلاً فى عالم القضاء السابق العائدة من طريق النفس الانسانية الى عالم الآخرة. فاذا جاء يوم القيامة ووضع الميزان كما فى قوله تعالى: ونضع الموازين القسط ليوم القيامة فحينئذ يجزى الله كلَّ نفسٍ ما كسبت. ويل يومئذ للمكذّبين.

(٤٨) تنبيه. ثم لا يخفى عليك أنّ هذه الحواسّ مسخّرة للنفس مجبورة فى فعلها وطاعتها لها بمنزلة آلات الصنائع لذوى الصنائع، اذ ليس للآلة أن يشعر بمقدار العمل ومقياس الصنع. أوَلا ترى أنّ اليد اذا كانت

ineffectual or makes mistakes as soon as the soul becomes occupied with and absorbed in her reflective thought? So also is the property in the macrocosm relative to the Governor of the heavens and the earth, He who is *the Living, the Ever-Established; drowsiness takes Him not, neither sleep* [2:255].

(49) For, the heaven's world turns by the effusion of His munificence, just as a mill turns by water. It is not for the water to know the scale of the mill's movement, since it is a tool subjected to the governor, the miller. The water does not act to move the mill save through the desire of the miller and the determination of his reflective thought. Were it not for the governor and his governance, its structure would quickly go to ruin. So also, were it not for God's command, His word, and His desire, the structure that is the spheres would be destroyed and end up in ruination and perishment.

(50) Hence, the Real, the Ever-Established, established the cosmos in obedience to Him, inwardly and outwardly, in one well-established manner. *There is nothing that crawls but He takes it by the forelock; surely my Lord is on a well-established path*[32] [11:56], so *He is the first and the last and the outward and the inward, and He is knower of everything* [57:3].

(51) *Another Remark.* Now, it should not be hidden from you that every sign in the world of the soul has a specific locus of manifestation, which has specific confines. This is like eyesight, for its locus of manifestation, which is the eye, has a designated site, but the potency of eyesight has no location and confines, as verification has shown. For, the color of the seen objects is not a location for the perception of color, nor does their represented form have a location or a position that accepts sensory pointing. Given that the form present with the perceiver has no position and does not accept sensory pointing, the potency that perceives it is likewise. Such also is the state of the rest of the senses, their loci of witnessing, and their configurations in the Sovereignty. So what do you suppose about what is above them?

(52) Hence, all the outward signs of the soul are locational affairs, and all her inward signs are nonlocational affairs. So, through the hole of this *niche,* consider the *lamp* of *the Light of the heavens and the earth* [24:35]. The fully knowing, governing soul that perceives these signs and their Sovereignty has no need to attain them by dwelling in one location rather than another location, nor to become absent and disappear from

فى عمل فتعطّل او تغلط عند اشتغال النفس بفكرها واستغراقها فيه. فكذا الحكم فى العالم الكبير بالاضافة الى مدبّر السموات والأرض وهو الحىّ القيّوم لا تأخذه سنة ولا نوم.

(٤٩) فإنّ بفيض جوده يدور عالم السماء دوران الرحى من الماء، وليس للماء أن يعلم ميزان حركة الرحى من حيث هو آلة مسخّرة للمدبّر الرحوى. فلا فعل للماء فى تحريك الرحى الا بموجب إرادة الرحوى وتقدير فكره. ولو لم يكن المدبّر وتدبيره لخرب بناؤه سريعاً، فكذلك لو لم يكن أمر الله وقوله وإرادته لانهدم بناء الأفلاك وانجرّ الى البوار والهلاك.

(٥٠) فالحق القيّوم تعالى أقام العالم فى طاعته ظاهراً وباطناً على نهج واحد مستقيم، ما من دابّة الا وهو آخذ بناصيتها إنّ ربّى على صراط مستقيم، فهو الاوّل والآخر والظاهر والباطن وهو بكلّ شئ عليم.

(٥١) تنبيه آخر. ثم لا يخفى عليك أنّ لكلّ آية فى عالم النفس مظهراً خاصّاً له حيّز خاصّ كالبصر، فإنّ لمظهره وهو العين موضعاً معيّناً وليس للقوّة الباصرة مكان وحيّز كما هو التحقيق، فإنّ لون المبصرات ليس مكاناً لإدراكه، ولا لصورتها الارتسامية مكان ووضع تقبل الاشارة الحسّيّة. فاذ لم يكن للصورة الحاضرة عند المدرك وضع وقبول للاشارة الحسّيّة وكذلك القوّة المدركة لها، وهكذا حال سائر الحواسّ ومشاهدها ونشأتها الملكوتية. فما ظنّك بما فوقها.

(٥٢) فكلّ من ظواهر آيات النفس أمور مكانية وبواطنها أمور لا مكانية. فانظر من ثقب هذه المشكاة مصباح نور السموات والأرض. فالنفس العلامة المدبّرة التى تدرك هذه الآيات وملكوتها ليست تحتاج فى نيلها الى أن تنزل فى مكان دون مكان ولا أيضاً ممّا يغيب ويزول عن

one location for another location. Her existence does not pertain specifically to the inward rather than the outward, nor to the witnessed rather than the absent. So, [her existence] is the witnesser, the absent, the high, the low, and she is *the knower of the absent and the witnessed* [6:73], *the hearing, the seeing* [17:1].

(53) Thus the soul can hear the speech of the supplicator in hearing's heaven[33] and respond to its supplication in tasting's earth, which makes the plant of the body grow. Despite all this, she has no site to which she pertains specifically, whether in the highest heaven of the body and its brain or in the lowest earth of its feet.[34]

(54) Also, she can read with the light of eyesight a writing whose answer is written by way of the hand, without moving from one site to another. Rather, all the sites and locations in her world, both the high and the low, are established through her, and all the tools and the means of awareness, both outward and inward, act through her act.

(55) So, the heavens of the means of awareness and the earths of the organs, in both the absent and the witnessed, are illumined by her light. Her troops accept her commands and her prohibitions, [which are issued] without speaking in sounds and letters, without movement and weariness, but simply with a desire and a command that descends from the High Presence, which is the "absent of absents"[35] of her essence; first to the "sitting place of the Throne," which is her heart, and then to the "Footstool," which is her breast, by means of the "carriers"[36] that are the potencies and spirits. The body and tools are all passive toward her exercise of effects. They come to life with her essential life and are illumined by her holy light, which arrives upon her from the right side and falls from her as rays and shadows on the empire of the body and its perceptual and motor potencies.

(56) So also should one gauge the greatest divine signs in the outward and inward aspects of the macrocosm. The Divine Ipseity that employs these in His tasks and His activities is more rightfully and properly declared incomparable with and hallowed beyond being delimited by a specific limit or restricted to a location or position in His Essence or in other than He, such as the body's states. Rather, it is He through whom are established heaven, earth, and what is within and with the two, and

مكان الى مكان. فلا يختصّ وجودها بالباطن دون الظاهر ولا بالشهادة دون الغيب، فهو الشاهد الغائب العالى الداني، وهو عالم الغيب والشهادة السميع البصير.

(٥٣) فلها أن تسمع كلام الداعى فى سماء السمع وتستجيب عن دعائه فى أرض الذول التى تُنبت نبات البدن. ومع ذلك ليس لها موضع تختصّ به لا فى أعلى سماء البدن ودماغه ولا فى أسفل أرض قدمه.

(٥٤) ولها أيضاً أن تقرأ بنور البصر كتاباً كتب جوابه من طريق اليد من غير أن تتحرّك من موضع الى موضع، بل جميع المواضع والأماكن فى عالمها يقوم بها عالية وسافلة، ويفعل بفعلها كلّ الآلات و المشاعر ظاهرة وباطنة.

(٥٥) فتتنوّر بنورها سموات المشاعر وأراضى الأعضاء غيباً وشهادةً، ويقبل جنودها أوامرها ونواهيها من غير تكلّم بأصوات وحروف ولا حركة وتعب، بل بمجرّد إرادة وأمر نازل من عالى حضرة غيب غيوب ذاتها الى مستوى عرش قلبها أوّلاً ثم الى كرسى صدرها بواسطة حملة القوى والأرواح. فينفعل منها جميع البدن والآلات بتأثيرها، يحيى بحياتها الذاتية ويتنوّر بنورها القدسى الوارد عليها من الجانب الأيمن الواقع منها أشعّة وأظلال على مملكة البدن وقواه المدركة والمحرّكة.

(٥٦) فكذلك قياس الآيات الكبرى الالهية فى ظواهر العالم الكبير وبواطنه. فالهويّة الالهية المستعملة إيّاها فى شؤونها وأفاعيلها أحقّ وأحرى بأن يكون منزهاً مقدّساً عن التقيّد بقيد مخصوص والانحصار بمكان او وضع بذاته او بغيره كأحوال الجسم، بل هو الذى به يقوم السماء والأرض وما

He is the Existence-Giver, the Mover of all, through a beginningless will and a divine strength, without change, transition, movement, or departure. So *He is the Living, there is no god but He* [40:65]. There is no task in which His task is not.[37] *It is God who created seven heavens, and of the earth their like; between them the command descends, that you may know that God is powerful over everything and that God has encompassed everything in knowledge* [65:12].

# Chapter Ten

*On the consolidation of the discussion of how one arrives at the lordly world and witnesses His greater signs and the Sovereignty of the highest heavens by means of the key that is knowledge of the human soul, and examination of her smaller signs and the Sovereignty of the senses and the potencies*

(57) You have come to know from the past chapters that none of these bodies comes to be established save through attachment to its Sovereignty and its inwardness, for the ear's outwardness is established only through the Sovereignty that is the auditory potency, and the mouth's outwardness and bodiment is completed only through the Sovereignty that is the sense of taste—lest speech not come forth from the gate of tasting. Were hearing not realized, it would be impossible for reflective thought to be determined and sent forth by way of hearing and eyesight, and no speech would occur from the outlet that is tasting.

(58) By this gauge, if, in the macrocosm, the outward Kingdom of heaven were not linked to the inward Sovereignty of God's majestic Throne, and the outward bodiment of the earth were not linked to the inward Sovereignty of His Gardens, *the words of God* that do *not run out* [31:27] or cease could not be generated on the face of the earth through the ink of hyle, which is like the saliva that aids in configuring speech and the ink for writing figures.[38]

فيهمـا ومعهما، وهو الموجد المحرّك للكلّ بمشـيئة أزلية وقوّة الهية من غير تغـيّر وانتقال وحركة وارتحال. فهو الحىّ لا اله الاهو، ليس شـأن ليس فيه شـأنه، الله الذى خلق سبع سـموات ومن الأرض مثلهنّ يتنزّل الأمر بينهنّ لتعلموا أنّ الله على كل شئ قدير وأنّ الله قد أحاط بكل شئ علماً.

## الفصل العاشر

فى تأكّد القول فى كيفية الوصول الى العالم الربوبى ومشاهدة آياته الكبرى وملكوت السموات العُلى بمفتاح معرفة النفس الانسانية ومطالعة آياتها الصغرى وملكوت الحواسّ والقوى

(٥٧) لمّا علمت فى الفصول الماضية أن لا قوام لشئ من هذه الأجسام الا بالتعلّـق بملكوتها وباطنها، فإنّ ظاهـر الأذن لا يقوم الا بملكوت القوّة السـمعية، وظاهر الفم وجسـميته لا يتمّ الا بملكوت الحـسّ الذوقى كيلا يخرج الكلام من باب الذول؛ ولو لم يتحقّق السماع لم يمكن تقدير الفكر وانبعاثه من طريق السمع والبصر و لم يحدث الكلام من مخرج الذول.

(٥٨) فعلـى هـذا القياس لو لم يكن فى هـذا العالم الكبير ظاهر ملك السـماء مرتبطاً بباطـن ملكوت عرش الله المجيد وظاهر جسـمية الأرض مرتبطـاً بباطـن ملكوت جنانه، لم يمكن أن يتولّد كلمـات الله التى لا تنفد ولا تبيد فى وجه الأرض بمداد الهيولى التى هى بمنزلة ريق الفم الممدّ لإنشاء الكلام والحبر لكتابة الأرقام.

(59) Next, know that in the world of man, the establishment of the body's tools and the life of their apparitions is connected to the life of their spirits. In the same way, the life of all these spirits is established through the inwardness of the fully knowing, fully active soul. So much is this so that relative to the spirits' inwardness, the fully knowing, fully active soul is like the spirits' inwardness in relation to the apparitions' outwardness.

(60) Thus the soul is the spirit of the spirits and the heart of the hearts. *The likeness of* her *light* in her world, her levels, her spirits, and her apparitions *is as* the likeness of *a lamp in a glass.* The property of her outward body is the property of the *niche.* Her glass, which is like a *glittering star,* is lit up from the branched *olive tree* of reflective thought, which is neither from the *east* of the spirits nor the *west* of the bodies. Rather, it has two directions and is an intermediary between the two worlds. When reflective thought becomes limpid and undefiled, from it comes to be the *oil* of the Actual Intellect, which *would well nigh shine* in the world of the Return, *even if no fire* of the Fully Active Intellect and the Greatest Spirit *touched it.* So, when it takes on brightness through God's light, it is a *light upon a light* [24:35].

(61) Hence the fully knowing soul that is fully active through her outward and inward levels is among that which is illumined and brought to life by the Real, Divine Ipseity, through which things are alive and established. So much is this so that, if the aid of life and establishment did not reach her from the Living, the Ever-Established, the chain of causes would be severed, the heavens would be destroyed, the planets would be effaced, the stars would fall, and the elements would cease to exist.

(62) He is *Independent* in His Essence *of the worlds* [3:97]. No knowledge encompasses Him and no thought masters Him. *He is the subjugating over His servants* [6:18], and He *encompasses everything* [41:54]. He is described by

(٥٩) ثـمّ اعلـم أنّ فى عا لم الانسـان ينوط قـوام آلات البدن وحياة أشـباحها بحيـاة أرواحها. وكذا تكـون حياة كلّ تلـك الأرواح متقوّمة بباطـن النفـس العلّامة الفعّالة حتـى أنّ النفس العلامة الفعّالة بالنسـبة الى باطن الأرواح كباطن الأرواح بالقياس الى ظاهر الأشباح.

(٦٠) فتكون النفـس روح الأرواح وقلب القلوب، ومَثَل نورها فى عالمها ومراتبها وأرواحها وأشـباحها كمثـل مصباح فى زجاجة. وحكم ظاهر جسدها حكم المشكاة. يتوقّد زجاجتها التى بمثابة الكوكب الدرّى مـن زيتونة الفكرة المنشـعبة التى ليسـت مـن شرل الأرواح ولا من غرب الأجسـاد، بـل ذات جهتين وواسـطة بـين العالمين. واذا صفـت الفكرة ونقيـت، حصلت منها زيت العقـل بالفعل الذى يكاد يضئ فى عا لم المعاد وإن لم تمسسه نار العقل الفعّال والروح الأعظم. فاذا استضاء بنور الله كان نوراً على نور.

(٦١) فالنفس العلّامة الفعّالة بمراتبها الظاهرة والباطنة ممّا يتنوّر ويحيى بالهوية الحقّة الالهية التى بها حياة الأشياء وقوامها بحيث لو لم يصل اليها مدد الحياة والقوام من الحىّ القيّوم لتقطّعت سلسلة الأسباب وانهدمت السموات وانطمست الكواكب وتساقطت النجوم وعدمت الأسطقسات.

(٦٢) وهـو غنى فى ذاته عن العالمين لا يحيط به علم ولا تسـلّط عليه فكـرة وهو القاهر فول عباده وبكلّ شـئ محيط. فـلا يوصف بوصف ولا

no description, depicted by no depiction, defined by no definition, known by no demonstration, and gauged by no scale. Rather, He is the demonstration of everything; through His life everything alive comes to life, and through His light every light, shadow, and shade becomes manifest.

(63) What is intended by the folk of gnosis in beholding the mirror of the souls and the horizons is only to turn their gaze from it toward beholding the Light of lights and to obliterate the form of the others from the page of their insight so that the face of *the One, the All-Subjugating* [40:16] may disclose itself.

(64) So you, O traveler, *turn your face toward* [2:144] the intended Kaᶜba, *sacrifice* [108:2] your animality so as to seek nearness to God, and remove from your road to Him the harm of your existence.[39] Sever your gaze from the mirror of your own ipseity lest you be an associator having two faces.[40] Climb and rise up from witnessing the signs of the horizons and the souls and from seeing the Sovereignty of the heavens and earth to the level of true *tawḥīd* and witnessing the encounter with God, the Subsistent. Follow the religion of your father Abraham and say, as he said, *I have turned my face to Him who originated the heavens and the earth, unswerving,* submitted,[41] *and I am not of the associators* [6:79], that you may see every power drowned in His power, every knowledge and desire drowned in His knowledge and His desire, every hearing and seeing absorbed in His hearing and His seeing, and every life dissolved in His life.[42] You will be a follower of the Shariᶜa of your master and your leader, God's beloved, and then the Real will love you.[43] He will come near to you through the nearness of obligatory works, and you will come near to Him through the nearness of supererogatory works, with respect to His words, *And when My servants question thee concerning Me, surely I am near; I respond to the supplication of the supplicator* [2:186] and His words, "The servant never ceases coming near to Me through supererogatory works until I love him. Then, when I love him, I am the hearing through which he hears," and so on.[44]

ينعت بنعت ولا يحدّ بحدّ ولا يعرف ببرهان ولا يقاس بميزان، بل هو البرهان على كلّ شئ وبحياته يحيى كلّ حيّ وبنوره يظهر كلّ نور وظلّ وفئ.

(٦٣) وإنّما مقصود أهل المعرفة من ملاحظة مرآة الأنفس والآفال انعطاف النظر منها الى ملاحظة نور الأنوار وانمحاء صورة الاغيار عن صفحة بصيرتهم ليتجلّى وجه الواحد القهّار.

(٦٤) فأنت أيّها السالك ولّ وجهك شطر كعبة المقصود وانحر تقرّباً الى الله حيوانيّتك وازل عن طريقتك اليه أذى وجودك واقطع النظر عن مرآة هويتك لئلا تكون مشركاً ذا الوجهين. فارتق واصعد من مشاهدة آيات الآفال والأنفس ورؤية ملكوت السموات والأرض الى مرتبة التوحيد الحقيقى ومشاهدة لقاء الله الباقى. واتّبع ملّة أبيك ابرهيم وقل كما قال: وجّهتُ وجهى للذى فطر السموات والأرض حنيفاً مسلماً وما أنا من المشركين، لترى كلّ قدرة مستغرقة فى قدرته وكلّ علم وإرادة مستغرقاً فى علمه وإرادته وكلّ سمع وبصر مستهلكاً فى سمعه وبصره وكلّ حياة مضمحلاً فى حياته، فتكون متّبعاً لشريعة سيّدك وقائدك حبيب الله. فيحبّك الحقّ ويقرب منك قرب الفرائض وتقرب منه قرب النوافل لقوله تعالى: وإذا سألك عبادى عنى فإنّى قريب أُجيب دعوةَ الداع، وقوله تعالى: لا يزال العبد يتقرّب الىّ بالنوافل حتّى أُحبَّه فإذا أحببته كنت سمعه الذى به يسمع الحديث.

# PART THREE
## *On the States of the Beginnings*

*In it are ten chapters.*

## Chapter One

### *On the divisions of beginning and firstness*

(1) Know that "priority" in things has two divisions. First is that which accords with the quantity of something that has continuous extent or discontinuous number, such as a single line or a single series; one of the extremities will be prior and the other posterior. That which accords with time with respect to undergoing renewal[1] and passing away is named "temporal priority." That which accords with location with respect to its position and order is named "precedence in order." So, undergoing renewal is to time as position is to location.

(2) Second is that which accords with existence, because existence is something that by essence demands unneedingness and need—with respect to perfection and deficiency, necessity and possibility. A thing's priority with respect to its necessity by its essence, or by other than itself as required by the necessity of another thing's existence, is named "causal precedence." With respect to the root of existence, without regard to necessity, this is named "priority through nature," like the priority of occurrences put into order either according to essence or according to time.

(3) The criterion of priority in the latter two is the root of existence or the consolidation of existence, but in the first two, it is either time or location.

# الباب الثالث

## فى أحوال البدايات
## وفيه عشرة فصول

### الفصل الأوّل
### فى أقسام البداية والأوّلية

(١) اعلم أنّ التقدّم للشئ على قسمين. الأوّل ما بحسب الكمّية للشئ الذى له مقدار متّصل او عدد منفصل كخطّ واحد او صفّ واحد، فيكون أحد طرفيه متقدّماً والآخر متأخّراً. فما بحسب الزمان من جهة ما له من التجدّد والتقضّى يسمّى بالتقدّم الزمانى، وما بحسب المكان من جهة ما له من الوضع والترتيب يسمّى بالسبق الرتبى. فالتجدّد للزمان كالوضع للمكان.

(٢) والثانى ما بحسب الوجود لأنّ الوجود ممّا يقتضى لذاته الغنى والحاجة بحسب الكمال والنقص والوجوب والامكان. فتقدّمه من جهة وجوبه بذاته او بغيره المستلزم لوجوب وجود آخر يسمّى بالسبق العلّى، ومن جهة أصل الوجود من غير اعتبار الوجوب يسمّى بالتقدّم بالطبع كتقدّم الحوادث المترتّبة إمّا بحسب الذات وإمّا بحسب الزمان.

(٣) فملاك التقدّم فى هذين أصل الوجود او تأكّد الوجود وفى الاوّلين إمّا الزمان او المكان.

(4) Just as time is the cause of renewal and change in an unqualified sense, so location is the cause of the lack of presence and absence. These two [time and location] are the two sources of death and ignorance, because what is attached to the two is qualified by their specificity—that is, the absence of each part from others and the absence of the whole from the parts, for the whole is nothing but all the parts.

(5) As long as the form is not disengaged from embodiment and renewal, it will not exist by its essence, nor will it perceive itself. Hence, being a knower hinges on disengagement. So, the gnostic who gazes at things through the light of inspiration sees the high and the low at once, and he also witnesses the past and the future all at once, with a gauge that he finds from his own world in his essence. For he encompasses in knowledge what is in his hand and his domination, from the highest peak of his head to the lowest part of his foot, all through one knowledge, like the knowledge of one point. So also he encompasses the times that are the measure of his knowledge and his movement from the first of his life span to its utmost end, all at once, like the instant. Through this scale, he recognizes the "withness" of the First Real with all things, which are put into order and given priority some over others through a withness that is neither temporal nor locational.[2] He recognizes the First's encompassment of all precedent and subsequent things through an encompassment that is hallowed beyond multiplicity and change. He knows that the Author has subjected the human empire along with everything within it—outward and inward, absent and witnessed—to the soulish ipseity, so that she may know the scale of things and the reckoning of beings. This is why she is made to stand up at the resurrection—so that her deeds and acts may be weighed with justice on the day of reckoning. Were the guideposts and scales of things not implanted in the innate Adamic disposition, no one would be recompensed by them on the day of resurrection, nor would the soul be taken to task at God for her neglect and be punished by her castigation and going astray.[3]

(6) Do you not see that the human ipseity is innately inclined toward knowing things, scrutinizing them, and penetrating deeply into them? Man cannot restrain himself from striving to understand things that are

(٤) فكما أنّ الزمــان علّة التجدّد والتغيرّ على الاطلال، فكذا المكان علّــة عدم الحضور والغيبة، وهما منشــآن للموت والجهل لأنّ المتعلّق بهما يكــون متّصفــاً بخاصّيتهمــا من غيبة كلّ جــزء عن آخر وغيبــة الكلّ عن الأجزاء على أنّ الكل ليس غير جميع الأجزاء.

(٥) فمــا لم يتجــرّد الصورة عن التجسّــم والتجــدّد لم يكن موجوداً لذاتــه ولا مدركاً لنفســه. فمدار العالميــة على التجــرّد. فالعارف الناظر للأشياء بنور الإلهام يرى العالى والسافل مرّةً واحدةً، وكذا يشاهد الماضى والمستقبل دفعةً بمقياس يجده من عالمه فى ذاته حيث أحاط علماً بما فى يده وتصرّفه من أعلى قلّة رأسه الى أسفل قدمه جميعاً بعلم واحد كالعلم بنقطة واحدة، وكذا أحاط بالأزمنة التى هى مقدار علمه وحركته من أوّل عمره الى منتهــاه فــى دفعة واحدة كالآن. فبهذا الميزان يعــرف معيّة الحقّ الأوّل مع جميع الأشــياء المترتّبــة المتقدّمة بعضها على بعــض معيةً غير زمانية ولا مكانيــة، ويعرف إحاطة الأوّل بجميع الأشــياء الســابقة واللاحقة إحاطةً مقدّســة عن التكثّر والتغيّر. ويعلم أنّ البارئ إنّما ســخّر المملكة الانســانية بجميع ما فيها ظاهراً وباطناً وغيباً وشــهادةً للهوية النفســانية لتعلم ميزان الأشياء وحســاب الكائنات، وبهذا السبب تقام فى القيامة ليوزن أعمالها وأفعالهــا بالقســط ليوم الحســاب. ولو لم يكــن معالم الأشــياء وموازينها مرتكــزة فى الفطرة الآدمية لم يكــن مجزياً بها يوم القيامة و لم تكن مؤاخذةً عند الله تعالى بإهمالها معاقبةً بنكالها وضلالها.

(٦) ألا تــرى كيف تكون الهوية الانســانية مجبولة فى معرفة الأشــياء والتفتيــش عنها والتعمّــق فيها بحيث لا يصبر عن التطلّع الى فهم الأشــياء المرتفعــة عــن فهمه ولا يقف عن البحث عن سرّ القــدر وما فول ذلك عند

elevated beyond his understanding. He does not stop short of investigating the mystery of the Measuring Out or what lies beyond it, at some limit beyond which he cannot pass on to something else.[4] On the contrary, the more he increases[5] in knowledge and cognizance, the more he increases in seeking and yearning, without any rest—except for the one who is weak in humanness, or diverted to this-worldly appetites and distractions, or ill in soul through soulish impairments.

(7) Once you have come to know this, know that the soul recognizes universal realities only from the numbers of the particulars by the perception of the senses, because, at the first of her configuration, the soul has the degree of the senses. Then she is elevated to the degree of imagination, then intellection. This is why it is said, "Whoever lacks a sense lacks a knowledge."[6] When it happens that she senses one of the parts of the cosmos, and when a number of sense objects actually come to be within her by means of their parts that she has in her essence—parts that are, as it were, those sense objects in potentiality, for a thing perceives something only through the potentiality that it has in its essence—then, when the soul perceives them, she deposits them in the storehouse of her perceived objects. The remembering potency retains their number. Then she cogitates with the reflective potency concerning her deposited objects of perception. She recalls them time after time, and she undergoes transition from one to another. From this the knowledge of number and measurement come to be for her. Hence it is said, "Number is a moving intellect," for number is the quantity of all the knowledge that comes to be from each part of the soul.

(8) So, we say: When man considers the locational dimensions, he finds that some parts of the cosmos are encompassing and other parts encompassed—like the layers of the elements and the spheres. He knows that the end point of the encompassing part is the location of the part that is within it. Then, from the location of a part, he falls to seeking and probing after the location of the part that is above it, until, in probing after the locations, he ends up seeking the location of the part that is the last of the parts—in which location is it?

(9) In the same way, when he considers the temporal dimensions and finds parts of the cosmos prior and parts of it posterior, like ordered and concatenated occurrences, some of which prepare for the existence of others—such as the parent before the child, the sperm drop before the

حـدّ لا يتعدّاه الى ما هو وراءه. بـل كلّما ازدادت معرفةً واطّلاعاً ازدادت طلباً وشوقاً من غير سكون، اللّهمّ الا فى ضعيف الانسانية أوالمنحرف الى الشهوات والشواغل الدنيوية أوالمريض النفس بالآفات النفسانية.

(٧) اذا علمـت هـذا، فاعلم أنّ النفس إنّما تعـرف الحقائق الكلّيّة من أعداد الجزئيات بوسيلة إدراك الحواسّ لأنّ النفس فى أوّل نشأتها فى درجة الحواسّ ثم ترتفع الى درجة التخيّل ثم التعقّل. ولهذا قيل من فقد حسّاً فقد فقد علماً. فاذا وقع لها إحساس بجزء من أجزاء العالم وحصل عندها عدد من المحسوسـات بالفعل بوسـيلة ما فى ذاتها من أجزائهـا التى هى كأنّها تلك المحسوسـات بالقوّة اذا الشـئ لا يدرك شيئاً الا بقوّة ما فى ذاته، فاذا أدركتهـا النفس أودعتها فـي خزانة مدركاتها. فأمسـكت القوّة الحافظة عددها ثم تأمّلت بالقوّة المفكّرة مدركاتها المستودعة واسترجعتها مرّة بعد أخـرى وانتقلت مـن واحد الى واحـد. فحصل لها من ذلـك علم العدد والمسـاحة، ومن هذا قيل العدد عقل متحرّك، اذ العدد هو كمية مجموع ما حصل من العلم بجزء جزء من النفس.

(٨) فنقـول اذا نظر الانسـان الى الأبعاد المكانية، وجـد أجزاء العالم بعضها محيطاً وبعضها محاطاً به كطبقات العناصر والأفلاك، فعلم أنّ منتهى الجـزء المحيط مكان الجزء الذى فـى جوفه. فيقع فى الطلب والفحص من مكان جزء الى مكان الجزء الذى فوقه حتى ينتهى فى الفحص عن الأمكنة الى طلب مكان الجزء الذى هو آخر الأجزاء أنّه فى اىّ مكان هو.

(٩) وكذلـك اذا نظر الى الأبعاد الزمانية ووجـد أجزاء العالم بعضها متقدّمـاً وبعضها متأخّراً كالحوادث المترتّبة المتسلسـلة التـى بعضها معدّة لوجـود البعـض كالوالـد قبل الولـد والنطفة قبـل العلقة والمفـردات قبل

blood clot, and the simples before the compounds—he falls to seeking and probing after the beginning of this chain. We will mention the origin of the knowledge of location and time, and of order according to them, in the two coming chapters.

## Chapter Two

*On the quiddity of location*[7]

(10) Know that, according to the majority of the sages, the location of each body is the inside surface of the body that surrounds it, such that no part of it is outside that surface.[8] This state is only in the parts of the cosmos, like the units that are the elements and the spheres. When the totality of all the locations and localized things in the cosmos is taken as one thing named by one name, then nothing remains outside of it with a positional externality that could be the location of the totality. Otherwise, the totality would not be a totality.

(11) From this it becomes manifest that the cosmos, taken altogether, has no location, just as numbers and numbered things, taken altogether, have no number of their own kind. This is because, were the mind to postulate them such that no number or numbered thing were outside of them, in this regard [the totality] could never be divided, nor could there be someone to number or something numbered. So also is the property of the totality of the bodily things and the locational quantities. When all are taken together as if they were one thing, no body or measure is external to them, so [the totality] is not divided in any respect. Its property is that of the point, or rather, more elevated than it beyond spatial confinement, because the point, in contrast to it, has position in one sense.

(12) From this it is known that the cosmos is one, and the "after-abode" is not of the same kind as this abode, nor is it strung along with it on one string. On the contrary, it has a second configuration, because it is within the veils of the heavens and the earth, just as we have verified in the questions on the Return.[9]

المركّبات، فيقع فى الطلب والفحص عن بدو هذه السلسلة. فلنذكر مبدأ معرفة المكان والزمان وما بحسبهما من الترتيب فى الفصلين الآتيين.

## الفصل الثانى

### فى ماهية المكان

(١٠) اعلم أنّ مكان كل جسم كما عليه الجمهور من الحكماء هو السطح الباطن من الجسم الحاوى له بحيث لم يكن جزء منه خارجاً عن ذلك السطح. وهذه الحال لا تكون الا فى أجزاء العالم كآحاد العناصر والأفلاك. فاذا أخذ مجموع ما فى العالم من الأمكنة والمتمكّنات كلّها بما هو شئ واحد مسمّى باسم واحد فلم يبق شئ خارجاً منه خروجاً وضعياً حتى يكون مكان المجموع، والا لم يكن المجموع مجموعاً.

(١١) وظهر من ههنا أن لامكان للعالم جميعاً كما لاعدد لجميع الأعداد والمعدودات من جنسها، وذلك لأنّها اذا فرضها الذهن بحيث لا يشذّ عنها عدد ولا معدود فلا يكون بهذا الاعتبار مقسوماً أبداً ولا عادّاً ولا معدوداً. فكذلك حكم مجموع الأجسام والكميات المكانية اذا أخذت بأجمعها كأنّها شئ واحد، فلا يخرج عنها جسم ولا مقدار فلم يكن منقسماً بوجه من الوجوه، فيكون حكمه حكم النقطة بل أرفع منها عن التحيّز لكونها ذات وضع بوجه بخلافه.

(١٢) ومن ههنا علم أنّ العالم واحد وأنّ الدار الآخرة ليست من جنس هذه الدار ولا منسلكة معها فى سلك واحد. بل لها نشأة ثانية لكونها داخلة فى حجب السموات والأرض كما حقّقنا فى المسائل المعادية.

# Chapter Three

*On the quiddity of time*

(13) Time is the scale of movement and the gauge of moving things inasmuch as they are moving things. It is not, as has been supposed, the measure of existence in an unqualified sense. Rather, it is the measure of weak, gradual existence and the yardstick of its extension according to what comes forth from potency to act not all at once. So, movement is the thing's coming forth from potency to act not all at once. There is no movement in the thing's substance, because in movement there must be something that is fixed in entity and altering in attribute, and the thing's attribute is external to its essence.[10] Time is the measure of this change. The "instant" is its extremity, just as the "point" is the extremity of the line.

(14) Movement is something that is changing and occurring,[11] so it needs an active mover through which to be established and a receptive locus in which to dwell. Just as the measure of movement is established through movement, so also movement is established through something that precedes it, external to movement and time. Otherwise, there would be concatenation without end.[12] Hence, before time and movement there is no time and movement whatsoever. Thus it is known that the Mover of the whole is something unitary in essence, encompassing all that is beginningless and endless, not undergoing renewal through leaving the past and entering the future, not delimited by locations and states, and not having movement and transition.

(15) Considering the quiddity of movement will guide you to the knowledge that "With your Lord there is neither morning nor evening"[13] and that His courtyard is elevated beyond the fantasy of change and annihilation. So, rise up to the peak of gnosis from the falling place of the ignorance of the low, and say, *I love not those that set* [6:76].

(16) *Another Remark.* Movement has two divisions. One is continuous, like the movement of the spheres and what is within them; the other is discontinuous, like the movement of the elements and what is derived from them, which have a temporal beginning and a temporal end.

## الفصل الثالث

### فى ماهية الزمان

(١٣) الزمان ميزان الحركة ومقياس المتحرّكات من حيث هى متحرّكات. وليس كما ظنّ انّه مقدار الوجود مطلقاً، بل مقدار الوجود الضعيف التدريجى ومعيار امتداده بحسب ما يخرج من القوّة الى الفعل لا دفعة. فالحركة خروج الشئ من القوّة الى الفعل لا دفعة. فلا حركة فى جوهر الشئ اذ لا بد فى الحركة من شئ ثابت العين متبدّل الصفة وصفة الشئ خارجة عن ذاته. والزمان مقدار هذا التغيّر، والآن طرفه كما أنّ النقطة طرف الخطّ.

(١٤) والحركة لكونها أمراً متغيّراً حادثاً تحتاج الى محرّك فاعل تقوم به وإلى محلّ قابل تحلّ فيه. فكما أنّ مقدار الحركة يقوم بالحركة فهى أيضاً ممّا يقوم بأمر سابق عليها خارج عن الحركة والزمان، والا لتسلسل الأمر الى لا نهاية. فليس قبل الزمان والحركة زمان وحركة أصلاً. فعلم أنّ محرّك الكلّ أمر وحدانى الذات محيط بالآباد والآزال غير متجدّد بالمضى والاستقبال ولا متحدّد بالأمكنة والأحوال ولا له الحركة والانتقال.

(١٥) فالنظر الى ماهية الحركة يرشدك الى العلم بأن ليس عند ربّك صباح ولا مساء وأنّ ساحته أرفع من توهّم التغيّر والفناء فاصعد الى ذروة العرفان من مهبط جهالة السافلين وقل إنّى لا أحبّ الآفلين.

(١٦) تنبيه آخر. الحركة على قسمين. إحداهما متّصلة كحركة الأفلاك وما فيها، والأخرى منفصلة كحركة العناصر وما منها التى لها ابتداء زمانى وانتهاء زمانى.

(17) So also, in one sense, time has two divisions. One is continuous time, which is the measure of the movement of the cosmos—namely days, nights, months, years, and centuries. The other is interrupted time, like the time of the growth of plants, the maturation of animals, and the seasons of the year.

(18) Just as the life span of the individual and the period of his being cannot be realized before him, so also the life span of the cosmos and the period of its being cannot have come to be before it.

## Chapter Four

*On beginning and end with respect to existence and ipseity*

(19) Priority and posteriority in existence consist in there being two things such that one is existent through itself even if the other is ignored, but it is not possible for the other to have existence unless the first is existent. This is like the state of a writer and writing. It is said that the first is "prior" and the second "posterior" to it by essence, even if the two be together in time—if the two are temporal. For example, whiteness is prior to the white thing with this sort of priority, but the two are together in time. One of the specificities of this priority is that the thing prior in this regard is not nullified at the presence of the posterior thing, in contrast to temporal and locational priority.

(20) So, when the folk of consideration probe the cosmos, it is not permissible for them to seek a temporal beginning for it, or else the seeking will deliver them over to disquiet. Rather, it is necessary for them to take time as one of the parts of the cosmos, just as the divine ones[14] did, for they took the cosmos and everything within it and with it as one whole, as if it were one individual. Then they investigated the cause of its beginning.

(21) It has already been remarked that the existence of time comes from changing things, since it consists of a standard by which is gauged the measure of movements and changing things. Neither the existence of substance qua substance nor the subsistence of realities and essences has a time, since these have no quantity or change in their essences. Rather, the relation of fixed essences to fixed essences is called "sempiternity," and their relation to changing essences "aeon." Their beginning

(١٧) فالزمان أيضاً على قسمين بوجه. أحدهما الزمان المتّصل، وهو مقدار حركة العالم من الايّام والليالى والشهور والسنين والقرون، وثانيهما الزمان المنقطع كزمان نموّ النبات وبلوغ الحيوان وفصول السنة.

(١٨) فكما أنّ عمر الشخص ومدّة تكوّنه لا يمكن أن يكون متحقّقاً قبله، فكذلك عمر العالم ومدّة تكوّنه لا يمكن أن يكون حاصلاً قبله.

## الفصل الرابع

### فى البداية والنهاية بحسب الوجود والهوية

(١٩) التقدّم والتأخّر فى الوجود هو أن يكون شيئان بحيث يكون أحدهما موجوداً بنفسه وإن قطع النظر عن الآخر، ولا يمكن للآخر وجود الا ويكون هو موجوداً كالحال بين الكاتب والكتابة. فيقال للأوّل متقدّم وللآخر متأخّر عنه بالذات وإن كانا معاً فى الزمان إن كانا زمانيين. فالبياض مثلاً متقدّم على الأبيض هذا النحو من التقدّم وهما معاً فى الزمان، ومن خصائص هذا التقدّم أنّ المقدّم بحسبه لا يبطل عند حضور المتأخّر بخلاف التقدّم الزمانى والمكانى.

(٢٠) فأهل النظر اذا فحصوا عن هذا العالم فلم يجز لهم أن يطلبوا له بدواً زمانياً، والا لتأدّى بهم الطلب الى الوسواس؛ بل يجب لهم أن يأخذوا الزمان جزءاً من أجزاء العالم كما فعله الالهيون حيث أخذوا العالم بما فيه ومعه جملة واحدة كأنّها شخص واحد، فبحثوا عن علّة بدوه.

(٢١) وقد وقع التنبيه على أنّ الزمان وجوده من المتغيّرات لأنّه عبارة عن مكيال يكال به قدر الحركات والمتغيّرات. وليس لوجود الجوهر بما هو جوهر ولا لبقاء الحقائق والذوات زمان، اذ لا كمّية لها ولا تغيّر لذواتها، بل يقال لنسبة الذوات الثابتة الى الذوات الثابتة سرمد، ولنسبتها

[is called] "beginninglessness" and their end "endlessness," since they have no temporal beginning or temporal end. The cause of the existence, establishment, and subsistence of substantial realities is called the "Divine Ipseity."

(22) There is no temporal intermediary between God and the soulish Sovereignty. Rather, the soulish Sovereignty is an intermediary between God and His servants, who are changing substances. Thus the existence of changing substances subsists and continues in the attribute of change along with the scale of change, which is "time." In the same way, the soulish Sovereignty's withness pertaining to the changing substances is the "aeon," and the Divine Ipseity's withness with all is "sempiternity."[15]

# Chapter Five

*On the beginning of human existence*

(23) The origins of man with respect to his reality and his last domain, like his origins with respect to his bodiment and his first domain, are four affairs deriving from the origins of the world of the soulish Sovereignty. One of them is the highest soul, whose name is Seraphiel, the owner of the Trumpet.[16] His specific act is blowing the spirits into the molds of the bodies and bestowing life and the potency of sensation and movement so that yearning and seeking may be sent forth.

(24) The second is the soul whose name is Michael. His specific act is bestowing provisions by nourishing and giving growth according to an appropriate measure and a known scale.

(25) The third is the soul whose name is Gabriel. His act is revelation, teaching, and delivering speech from God over to His servants.

(26) The fourth is the soul whose name is Azrael. His act is extracting forms from the sorts of matter, disengaging spirits from bodies, and bringing forth the rational soul from the body and transferring her from this world to the afterworld.

الى الـذوات المتغيّرة دهر، ولبدوهـا أزل ولانتهائها أبد، اذ لم يكن لها بدو زمانـى ولا نهايـة زمانية. ويقال لعلّـة وجود الحقائـق الجوهرية وقوامها وبقائها الهوية الالهية.

(٢٢) فليس بـين الله وبـين الملكـوت النفسـانى واسـطة زمانية بل الملكوت النفسـانى واسـطة بين الله وبين عباده من الجواهر المتغيّرة ليكون وجـود الجواهر المتغـيّرة باقية مسـتمرّة بنعت التغيّر مع ميـزان التغيّر وهو الزمان، كما أنّ معية الملكوت النفسـانى للجواهر المتغيّرة هى الدهر ومعية الهوية الالهية مع الكل هى السرمد.

## الفصل الخامس

### فى بدو وجود الانسان

(٢٣) إنّ مبادئ الانسـان بحسـب حقيقته وأخراه كمبادئه بحسب جسميته وأولاه أمور أربعة هى من مبادئ عالم الملكوت النفسانى. أحدها النفس العليا اسـمها إسرافيل صاحب الصُور، وفعلها الخاصّ نفخ الأرواح فى قوالب الأجسـاد وإعطاء الحياة وقوّة الحسّ والحركة لانبعاث الشـول والطلب.

(٢٤) وثانيهـا النفـس التى اسـمها ميكائيل، وفعلها الخـاصّ إعطاء الأرزال بالتغذية والتنمية على قدر لائق وميزان معلوم.

(٢٥) وثالثهـا النفس التى اسـمها جبرئيل، وفعلهـا الوحى والتعليم وتأدية الكلام من الله الى عباده.

(٢٦) ورابعها النفس التى اسـمها عزرائيـل، وفعلها نزع الصُوَر من المـوادّ وتجريد الأرواح من الأجسـاد وإخـراج النفس الناطقـة من البدن ونقلها من الدنيا الى الآخرة.

(27) By the "rational" potency we do not mean this partial potency through which man goes about speaking sounds and letters with the tool of the tongue. Rather, we mean by it the imam of the other inward and outward potencies in the soulish world. Its specificity is the representation of meanings and cognitive forms on the pages of the Sovereignty. In terms of analogy, it is like the hand in representing written figures on the pages of the sorts of matter, because it records cognitive meanings and intellective forms on the page of the heart. Through it human activities take place, and from it derive the potency of the movements of nourishment, giving growth, and procreation.

(28) For, these four souls have linkages with four potencies of the human soul—Seraphiel with reflection, Michael with memory and retention, Gabriel with rationality, and Azrael with form. Were it not for the Seraphielic potency, the potency of yearning, seeking, and movement would not be sent forth to obtain perfection. Were it not for the Michaelic potency, bodies would not sprout up and grow and spirits would not unfold in the stages of the Sovereignty; the bodily creation would not obtain sensory provisions, nor the innate soulish disposition sciences in great number. Were it not for the Gabrielic potency, no one would acquire any of the meanings from clarification and words, and no one's heart would receive the Real's inspiration or His casting into the inmost mind. Were it not for the Azraelic potency, there could be no transmutations and vicissitudes in bodies, no reflective achievement of perfection and no transitions in souls, and no coming forth from this world and standing before God for spirits. Rather, all things would halt in a single dwelling place and a first station, and the seeds of the spirits would not come forth from the hiding places of the bodies and the bellies of the wombs.

(29) When the Author deposits the sperm drops of the souls in the wombs of the bodies and then, through right guidance and teaching, perfects them and makes them reach the degree of supraformal adulthood and configures them in the configuration of the afterworld, this is just like the farmer who deposits seeds in the soil and irrigates them with water so that they may grow and increase in measure and reach utmost perfection. To this He alludes with His words, *Do you see the sperm that you spill? Do you*

(٢٧) ونحـن لا نريد بالقوّة الناطقة هـذه القوّة الجزئية التى يتأتّى بها للانســان أن يتكلّم بالأصوات والحروف بآلة اللســان، بـل نروم بها إمام ســائر القوى الباطنة والظاهرة فى العالم النفســانى وخاصّتها رسم المعانى والصـور العلمية فـى صحائف الملكـوت. وهى بحسـب التمثيل كاليد فى رسـم الأرقـام الكتابية فى صحائف الموادّ لأنّهـا تضبط المعانى العلمية والصور العقلية فى صحيفة القلب، وبها ايضاً الأفاعيل البشرية ومنها قوّة حركات التغذية والتنمية والتوليد.

(٢٨) اذ لتلـك النفوس الأربـع ارتباطات بقوى أربع من هذه النفس الانســانية، فلاسرافيل مع الفكرة ولميكائيل مع الحفظ والإمساك ولجبرئيل مع النطق ولعزرائيل مع الصورة. فلو لم تكن القوّة الاسرافيلية لم تنبعث قوة الشول والطلب والحركة لتحصيل الكمال. ولو لم تكن القوّة الميكائيلية لم يحصل النشوء والنماء فى الأبدان والتطوّر فى أطوار الملكوت فى الأرواح ولا يحصل الأرزال الحسّية للخلقة البدنية ولا العلوم الجمّة الغفيرة للفطرة النفســانية. ولـو لم تكن القوّة الجبرئيلية لم يسـتفد أحـد معنى من المعانى بالبيــان والقــول ولا يقبل قلب أحد إلهام الحق وإلقــاءه فى الروع. ولو لم تكن القوّة العزرائيلية لم تمكن الاســتحالات والانقلابات فى الأجسام ولا الاستكمالات والانتقالات الفكرية فى النفوس والخروج من الدنيا والقيام عند الله للأرواح، بل كانت الأشياء كلّها واقفة فى منزل واحد ومقام أوّل، ولم يكن لبذور الأرواح خروج عن مكامن الأجسام وبطون الأرحام.

(٢٩) فـإنّ إيـداع البـارئ نطـف النفوس فـى أرحام الأجســام ثم تكميلهــا وتبليغها بالإرشــاد والتعليم الى درجة البلوغ المعنوى وإنشــائها فى نشــأة الآخرة بمنزلة إيداع الدهقان البذور فى الأراضى وسـقيها المياه لتنمو وتزيد فى المقدار وتبلغ غاية الكمال. واليه أشار بقوله تعالى: أفرأيتم

*yourselves create it, or are We the creators?* [56:58–59]. And His words, *Do you see what you are you tilling? Do you sow it, or are We the sowers?* [56:63–64].

(30) *An Allusion.* How similar is the state of the human soul—in her vicissitudes in the stages of creation, her coming down from the world of the innate disposition to the dunghills of the ignorant, and her forgetfulness of her world when she fell to the dwelling places of the vile, until finally she reaches the degree of the Fully Active Intellect—to the state of the seed in the vicissitudes of the stages until it reaches the level of the fruit! It first begins as a seed whose kernel undergoes corruption in the earth and is annihilated from its essence in alien locations. Then it is transmuted by the potency of growth from state to state until it finally reaches what it was at first and arrives at the degree of the kernel that it had at the beginning of its affair, along with a large number of individuals of its kind, and many profits and gains that come to be from the leaves, the trees, and the lights during the journey. It comes forth from the midst of those husks and weeds—by God's leave—as a limpid kernel and a worthy fruit that is the result of those prior steps and the end of those transitions. It[17] comes to be an existent that subsists through the subsistence of its Existence-Giver, despite the disintegration and disappearance of those affairs.

(31) It has become manifest to you through what we mentioned that the limpid core and what was originally intended[18] from the beings' coming to be was the rational spirit and the human Sovereignty. Animals and plants were created only from its leftover, just as leaves, firewood, and straw are born from seeds as uninvited guests. Do you not see that the farmer does not deposit seeds in the soil for the sake of the branches and the leaves? Rather, he deposits the seeds only for the sake of the seeds and for the bounty, increase, and plentifulness of good and perfection that come to be along with them.

(32) So also, the purpose of the Craftsman who sows the spirit-seeds in the soil of the apparitions' receptivities and who waters them with the buckets of the celestial spheres' waterwheel—which is turned by the motor, animate, celestial potency and governed by the soul that drives the heavenly beast in its eight-fold journey (like the journey of the seconds)[19] in obedience to an intellective governor and a divine commander—is only the

ما تمنون أأنتم تخلقونه أم نحن الخالقون، وقوله: أفرأيتم ما تحرثون أأنتم تزرعونه أم نحن الزارعون.

(٣٠) إشارة. ما أشبه حال النفس الانسانية فى تقلّبها فى أطوار الخلقة ووقوعها من عالم الفطرة فى مزابل الجّهال ونسيانها عالمها عند الهبوط الى منازل الأرذال الى أن يصل الى درجة العقل الفعّال بحال البذر فى تقاليب الأطوار الى أن يبلغ مرتبة الثمار. فيبتدئ اوّله وهو بذر يفسد لبّه فى الأرض ويفنى عن ذاته فى الأماكن الغريبة، ثم يستحيل بقوّة نامية من حال الى حال حتى ينتهى الى ما كان أوّلاً ويصل الى درجة اللبّ الذى كان عليها فى بدو أمره مع عدد كثير من أفراد نوعه وفوائد وأرباح كثيرة حاصلة من سفره من الأورال والأشجار والأنوار فيخرج من بين تلك القشور والحشائش لبّاً صافياً باذن الله وثمرة صالحة هى نتيجة تلك المقدّمات ونهاية تلك الانتقالات، تكون موجودة باقية ببقاء موجدها مع انفساخ تلك الأمور وزوالها.

(٣١) فظهر لك بما ذكرنا أنّ اللباب الصافى والمقصود الأصلى من حصول الكائنات هو الروح النطقى والملكوت الانسانى، وإنّما خلقت الحيوانات والنباتات من فضالته كتولّد الأورال والحطب والتبن من البذور تطفّلاً. ألا ترى أنّ الدهقان لا يودع البذور فى الأراضى للأغصان والأورال، بل إنّما يودع البذور للبذور مع ما يحصل لها من الفضل والزيادة والوفور فى الخير والكمال.

(٣٢) فكذلك غرض الصانع الزارع لبذور الأرواح فى أراضى قابليات الأشباح وسقيها من دوالى دولاب الأفلاك التى تديرها القوّة المحرّكة الحيوانية الفلكية، وتدبّرها النفس السئسة للدابّة السماوية بسيرها الثمانى كسير الثوانى طاعةً لمدبّر عقلى وآمر الهى إنّما هو فطرة الانسان.

innate disposition of man. Then, from his leftover and refuse, He created the other beings with all the states and the sorts of good that are consequent upon their existence while they are still in the world of corruption, the house of opposites, ill state, and dissolution.[20]

(33) When the moment approaches for him to depart from this dark pit, that is the moment of coming to be for the fruit of the contemplations,[21] which come to be from the trees of reflective thoughts; [it is the moment] of coming forth from the vegetal and animal husks and skins into the almond's kernel, which is the innate human disposition, lit up in the world of lights and the mine of all good, and [the moment] of being aroused and standing up from the slumber of ignorance and the sleep of heedlessness into the level of the divine wisdom that comes to be for *the possessors of hands and eyes* [38:45].

(34) In reality, this is the secret of Adam's offense, his fall from the garden of knowledge to the place where feet stumble and to the dunghills where souls undergo transformations, his distance from his home, and the stumble of his foot. So, when he arises from his fall and gets up from his foot's stumbling in this period and in the six divine days,[22] when he repents and turns again to his Lord in the abode of reward, and when he returns to the Lord of lords and reaches his original innate disposition, then he will sit up straight, seated in the sphere of knowledge, embarked on the ship of salvation, delivered from perishment and drowning in the sea of nature, and saying *In the name of God shall be its course and berthing* [11:41]. He will report about what he sees of the signs of his Lord, the Highest, *who created the heavens and the earth in six days, then sat [upon the Throne]* [10:3].

# Chapter Six

*On the angels' prostration to Adam—upon him be peace*

(35) Know that the Author (majestic is His mention) set up the Adamic soul on four columns so that Adam might stand with these columns on the platform of speaking and address the folk of the cosmos. The first leg is in earth, and its name is "nature"; the second is in water, and its name is "the growth potency"; the third is in air, and its name is "the animal potency"; and the fourth is in fire, and its name is "the soulish potency." So understand!

فخلق من فضالته وحشوه سائر الأكوان على هذه الأحوال والخيرات التى يترتّب على وجودها وهى بعدُ فى عالم الفساد ومنزل الأضداد وسوء الحال والاضمحلال.

(٣٣) فاذا حان وقت أن يرتحل من هذه الهاوية المظلمة فذلك وقت حصول ثمرة الأنظار الحاصلة من أشجار الأفكار والخروج من القشور والجلود النباتية والحيوانية الى لباب لوز الفطرة الانسانية المستضيئة فى عالم الأنوار ومعدن الأخيار والانتباه والقيام من رقدة الجهالة ونوم الغفلة الى رتبة الحكمة الالهية الحاصلة لأولى الأيدى والأبصار.

(٣٤) وهذا بالحقيقة سرّ خطيئة آدم عليه السلام وسقوطه عن جنّة المعرفة الى مزلّة الأقدام ومزابل تحاويل النفوس وبعده عن مأواه وزلّة قدمه. فاذا قام من سقوطه ونهض من مزلّة قدمه فى هذه المدّة والأيام الستّة الالهية وتاب وأناب الى ربّه فى دار الثواب ورجع الى ربّ الأرباب وبلغ الى فطرته الأصلية، فاستوى جالساً فى فلك المعرفة راكباً على سفينة النجاة ناجياً عن الهلاك والغرل فى بحر الطبيعة قائلاً بسم الله مَجراها ومُرساها. فأخبر بما رآه من آيات ربّه الأعلى الذى خلق السموات والأرض فى ستّة أيّام ثمّ استوى.

## الفصل السادس

### فى سجود الملائكة لآدم عليه السلام

(٣٥) اعلم أنّ البارئ جلّ ذكره أقام النفس الآدمية على أربع قوائم ليقوم بهذه القوائم على مسند التكلّم والخطاب مع أهل العالم. فالقدم الأولى فى الأرض واسمها الطبيعة، والثانية فى الماء واسمها القوّة النامية، والثالثة فى الهواء واسمها القوّة الحيوانية، والرابعة فى النار واسمها القوّة النفسانية، فافهم.

(36) The human spirit is like an eloquent tongue addressing all the tribes of the cosmos. The leg that it has in earth is dead; the leg in plants asleep; the leg in animals perplexed, astonished, and seeking; and the leg in man awake and rational. Among these legs, one is broken, one inverted, one midway between inversion and standing straight, and one standing up.

(37) At the beginning of her configuration, the soul's leg is broken. When the brokenness disappears and her leg extends, she comes forth inverted among the plants. When she inclines away from inversion toward the level of the dumb beasts, she is midway between inversion and standing straight. When in her movement she reaches the degree of humanness, her stature has stood up straight, and her "resurrection has stood forth"[23] so that she may stand before the Author.

(38) Of these four columns, *three*[24] are *darknesses, one above another* [24:40]. No one obtains standing and alertness save him[25] who has *the leg of truthfulness at* his *Lord* [10:2].

# Chapter Seven

*On the quiddity of Iblīs and the satans*

(39) The Iblīs of every man is his soul when following caprice and traveling on the path of disquiet, refusal, recalcitrance, and arrogance. However, the first to travel the road of straying and misguidance and to be driven by the Real away from the world of His mercy came to be named "Iblīs." He is an evil, rational substance that comes to be from the world of the soulish Sovereignty in a dark and odious aspect, such as possibility and the like.[26] His task is leading astray and his road is misguidance, as in His words, in quoting from the accursed one, *By Thy exaltation, I shall lead them all astray, except Thy servants among them who are sincere* [38:82–83]. *For Thy leading me astray, I shall surely sit in ambush for them on Thy straight path* [7:16].

(40) At the beginning, the human reflective potency is like a flame of the Sovereignty that has the light of inspiration and the darkness of disquiet, since the soul was brought into being from the sorts of matter of this cosmos and the smoke[27] of the elements that had been struck by the light of the Real's effusion, as has come in the words of the Prophet,

(٣٦) فالروح الانسانى كلسان فصيح يخاطب جميع طوائف العالم. فالقدم التى منه فى الأرض مائتة والتى فى النبات نائمة والتى فى الحيوان هائمة مدهوشة طالبة والتى فى الانسان يقظانة ناطقة. وهذه الأرجل منها منكسرة ومنها منكوسة ومنها متوسّطة بين الانتكاس والاستقامة ومنها قائمة.

(٣٧) فالنفس فى أوّل نشأتها مكسورة القدم، فاذا زال الانكسار وامتدّت قدمها خرجت الى النبات منكوسة، واذا مالت عن الانتكاس الى رتبة البهائم توسّطت فى الانتكاس والاستقامة، واذا وصلت فى حركتها الى درجة الانسانية استقامت قامتها وقامت قيامتها لتقوم عند البارئ.

(٣٨) وهذه القوائم الأربع ثلاث منها ظلمات بعضها فول بعض. ولا يحصل القيام والانتباه الا لمن له قدم صدل عند ربّه.

## االفصل السابع

### فى ماهية ابليس والشياطين

(٣٩) ابليس كلّ انسان هو نفسه عند متابعة الهوى وسلوك طريق الوسواس والجحود والعتو والاستكبار، لكن أوّل من سلك سبيل الغواية والضلالة وطرده الحقّ من عالم رحمته وقع عليه اسم ابليس. وهو الجوهر النطقى الشرير الحاصل من عالم الملكوت النفسانى بجهة ظلمانية رديئة كالإمكان ونحوه. وشأنه الإغواء وسبيله الإضلال كما فى قوله تعالى حكاية عن اللعين: فبعزّتك لأُغوينّهم أجمعين، الا عبادك منهم المخلصين، وقوله: فبما أغويتنى لَأقعدنّ لهم صراطك المستقيم.

(٤٠) والقوّة الفكرية الانسانية فى الابتداء كشعلة ملكوتية لها نور الإلهام وظلمة الوسواس، لأنّ تكوين النفس من موادّ هذا العالم وأدخنة العناصر أصابها نور إفاضة الحق كما ورد عن النبى صلى الله عليه وآله إنّ

"Surely God created the creatures in darkness, then He sprinkled upon them some of His light."[28] So these souls, at the first of their innate disposition, are mixed light and darkness. Within them are inspiration and disquietening, guidance and leading astray.

(41) In everyone, the ruling property[29] belongs to the outcome. When someone is overcome by satanity, which is cunning, deception, rebellion against obeying God, seeking egoism, and pride; when tranquillity and serenity disappear from him; and when the inspiration of the angels and the Real's effusion of the true sciences of faith are severed from his heart, then he belongs to the party of Satan, and his final return will be to the abode of ruination and the dwelling of the evil ones. But when someone is overcome by the seeking of knowledge; when the earth of his soul is pure[30] of the foulnesses of vile attributes and soulish evils, such as pursuing appetites, disobedient acts, sophistry in beliefs, disquiet in acts of worship, and cunning in interactions; and when his heart is illumined by faith in God and the Last Day, then he is one of God's saints. Those *are the party of God; surely God's party, they are the prosperers*[31] [58:22]. *As for him who was insolent and preferred the life of this world, surely hellfire shall be the refuge. But as for him who feared the station of his Lord, and forbade the soul its caprice, surely the Garden shall be the refuge* [79:37–41].

(42) Know also that disquiet gains access to the soul because of her fall from her original innate disposition and her dispositional station, just as illness gains access to the body through its being stricken because its constitution deviates from proper equilibrium. When someone's nature is sound, his [observance of the] Shari$^{c}$a is sound.

## Chapter Eight

*That the inspiration of the angel and the disquietening of the satan[32] come down on the souls according to four manners and marks*

(43) One of [the marks] is like the knowledge and certainty that come to be from the right side of the soul (that is, the intellective potency) which is counter to the caprice and appetite that come to be from the soul's left side (that is, the sense-intuitive potency).

الله خلق الخلق فى ظلمة ثم رشّ عليهم من نوره الحديث. فهذه النفوس فى أوّل فطرتها ممتزجة من النور والظلمة، ففيها الإلهام والوسوسة والهداية والغواية.

(٤١) فالحكم للعاقبة فى كلّ واحد. فمن غلب عليه الشيطنة من الحيلة والمكر والتمرّد عن طاعة الله وطلب الأنانية والافتخار وزال عنه السكينة والطمأنينة وانقطع عن قلبه إلهام الملائكة وإفاضة الحق عليه بالعلوم الحقّة الايمانية، فهو من حزب الشيطان فيكون مآله الى دار البوار ومنزل الأشرار. ومن غلب عليه طلب المعرفة وطهر أرض نفسه من خبائث الصفات الرذيلة والشرور النفسانية من طلب الشهوات والمعاصى والسفسطة فى العقائد والوسواس فى العبادات والحيلة فى المعاملات وتنوّر قلبه بالايمان بالله واليوم الآخر، فهو من أولياء الله أولئك حزب الله ألا إنّ حزب الله هم المفلحون. فأمّا من طغى وآثر الحياة الدنيا فإنّ الجحيم هى المأوى وأما من خاف مقام ربّه ونهى النفس عن الهوى فإنّ الجنّة هى المأوى.

(٤٢) واعلم أنّ تطرّل الوسوسة فى النفس إنّما يكون لأجل سقوطها عن فطرتها الأصلية ومقامها الفطرى كتطرّل المرض الى البدن بالاعتلال لأجل انحراف مزاجه عن صوب الاعتدال. من صحّت طبيعته صحّت شريعته.

## الفصل الثامن

### فى أنّ إلهام الملك ووسوسة الشيطان يقع فى النفوس على وجوه وعلامات أربع

(٤٣) أحدها كالعلم واليقين الحاصلين من جانب يمين النفس أعنى القوّة العاقلة فى مقابلة الهوى والشهوة الحاصلين من جانب شمال النفس أعنى القوّة الوهمية.

(44) The second is that the form of the human world, which coincides with the form of this cosmos, is like a steep pathway between the disquietening of the satan and the inspiration of the angel. Whenever you consider the signs of the souls and the horizons by way of doubtfulness, heedlessness, and turning away from them—as happens to the commoners, the imitators,[33] and the disputatious—from them will grow up for you doubt and disquiet in sense-intuition and imagination, which are on the left side of the rational potency. Thus are His words, *How many a sign there is in the heavens and in the earth that they pass by, turning away from it!* [12:105]. So also a hadith says, "Woe upon him who recites this verse"—alluding to His words, *Surely in the creation of the heavens and the earth [and the alternation of night and day and the ship that runs in the sea with profit to men . . . surely there are signs for a people having intellect]* [2:164]—"and then wipes his mustache with it."[34]

(45) However, when you consider those signs in terms of sound arrangement and unambiguousness, doubts and sense-intuitions will disappear from you and you will obtain gnosis and wisdom in the intellective potency, which is on the right side of the soul. Thus the "unambiguous signs" are like holy angels—that is, intellects and universal souls—because they are the origins of the sciences of certainty; but those that are "ambiguous" and rooted in sense-intuition correspond to the satans and the sense-intuiting souls, because they are the origins of the sophistic premises.[35]

(46) The third of [the marks] is following the folk of refusal and denial, the folk of declaring ineffectual and declaring similar,[36] and the unbelievers. This is counter to obeying the chosen Messenger, the pure Imams, and the choice sages—upon them be peace and good pleasure from the King, the Compeller! Everyone who travels the road of misguidance is like the satans, and whoever follows caprice has followed the accursed Satan. Everyone who travels the road of guidance is one of the folk of God and the possessors of true inspirations—that is, the prophets and the saints, whose degree is the degree of angels brought nigh, the enraptured ones, those who inspire with the Book and Wisdom. These are the party of God, and the other group are the party of Satan.

(٤٤) وثانيها أنّ صورة العالم الانسانى المطابقة لصورة هذا العالم هى بمنزلة عقبة بين وسوسة الشيطان وإلهام الملك، فإنّك مهما نظرت الى آيات الآفال والأنفس على سبيل الاشتباه والغفلة والإعراض عنها كما وقع للعوامّ والمقلّدين والمجادلين، نشأت لك منها الشبهة والوسواس فى الواهمة والمتخيّلة، وهى على الجانب الأيسر من القوّة النطقية كما فى قوله تعالى: وكأيّن من آية فى السموات والأرض يمرّون عليها وَهُم عنها مُعرضون، وفى الحديث: ويل لمن تلا هذه الآية، إشارة الى قوله تعالى: إنّ فى خلق السموات والأرض الآية، ثم مسح بها سبلته.

(٤٥) واذا نظرت الى تلك الآيات على سبيل النظام والإحكام، زالت عنك الشكوك والأوهام وحصلت لك المعرفة والحكمة فى القوّة العاقلة، وهى على الجانب الأيمن منها. فالآيات المحكمات بمنزلة الملائكة المقدّسة من العقول والنفوس الكلية لأنّها هى مبادئ العلوم اليقينية، والمتشابهات الوهميات بمنزلة الشياطين والنفوس الوهمانية لأنّها مبادئ المقدّمات السفسطية.

(٤٦) وثالثها متابعة أهل الجحود والإنكار وأهل التعطيل والتشبيه والكفّار فى مقابلة طاعة الرسول المختار والأئمّة الأطهار والحكماء الأخيار عليهم السلام والرضوان من الله المَلِك الجبّار. فكلّ من سلك سبيل الضلال فهو بمنزلة الشياطين ومن اتّبع الهوى فقد تابع الشيطان اللعين وكلّ من سلك سبيل الهداية فهو من جملة أهل الله وذوى الإلهامات الحقّة من الأنبياء والأولياء الذين درجتهم درجة الملائكة المقرّبين المهيّمين الملهمين للكتاب والحكمة. فأولئك حزب الله، والفرقة الأخرى حزب الشيطان.

(47) The fourth is that the spiritual angels, who are the inhabitants of the world of the heavenly Sovereignty, are counter to the Iblīses, who are driven from God's gate, veiled from the precinct of holiness, prevented from entering the heavens, and imprisoned in the darknesses. Someone whose sciences and perceptions are of high topics and eminent entities—like faith in God, His intellective angels, His heavenly books, His messengers, the Last Day, the Uprising, the standing of the Hour, the creatures' standing respectfully before God, and the presence of the angels, *the prophets, [ . . . ] the witnesses, and the worthy* [4:69]—is similar to the angels and the All-Merciful's troops. But someone whose sciences and perceptions come under the heading of cunning, cleverness, sophistry, and cogitation concerning this-worldly affairs, and whose understanding does not come forth from the abode of sense objects, is similar to the satans, who are imprisoned in the layers of hellfire, deprived in this world of climbing to the Sovereignty of heaven, and veiled in the afterworld from the Abode of Bliss. Hence he is mustered along with them and present in their ranks.

(48) Know also that a class of the jinn and a sort of the rebellious satans—those who are stripped of the innate disposition such that their degree falls beneath the degree of the Sovereigntarials—have no power over acting to harm any of the folk of traveling, because they are *deaf, dumb, blind* [2:18], bound in chains and fetters, chastised by the fire of hellfire, the chastisement, and the painful castigation.

(49) *An Influx by Unveiling.*[37] It has been unveiled that the root of misguidance, blindness, and ignorance comes from the satan, and the root of guidance, insight, and certainty comes from the angel. The name *Iblīs* is like the name of *a foul tree* [14:26], and the satans are like the branches of this *accursed tree* [17:60]. Its leaves and its fruits are the particular reflective thoughts attached to immediate, animal appetites and this-worldly pleasures. It is alluded to in His words, *It is a tree that comes forth from the root of hellfire; its spathes are as the heads of satans, and they eat of it, and of it they fill their bellies* [37:64–65].

(٤٧) ورابعهـا ان الملائكة الروحانية التى هى سـكّان عالم الملكوت السـماوى فى مقابلة الأبالسة المطرودة عن باب الله، المحجوبة عن جناب القـدس، الممنوعة عن ولوج السـموات، المحبوسـة فـى الظلمات. فمن كان علومـه وإدراكاته فى الموضوعات العالية والأعيـان الشريفة كالايمان بالله وملائكته العقلية وكتبه السـماوية ورسله واليوم الآخر والبعث وقيام السـاعة ومثول الخلائق بين يدى الله وحضور الملائكة والنبيين والشـهداء والصالحين فقد شابه الملائكة وجنود الرحمن. ومن كان علومه وإدراكاته مـن باب الحيـل والحذيقة والسفسـطة والتأمّـل فى الأمـور الدنياوية ولم يخرج فهمه عن دار المحسوسات فقد شابه الشياطين المحبوسة فى طبقات الجحيم المحرومة فى الدنيا عن الارتقاء الى ملكوت السـماء، المحجوبة فى الآخرة عن دار النعيم، فهو محشور معهم حاضر فى زمرتهم.

(٤٨) واعلم أنّ طبقةً من الجنّ وضرباً من مردة الشـياطين المنسـلخة عن الفطرة حيث سقطت درجتهم عن درجة الملكوتيين لا اقتدار لهم على فعل الضرر على أحد من أهل السـلوك، لأنّهم صمّ بكم عمى مقيّدون فى السلاسل والأغلال معذّبون بنار الجحيم والعذاب والنكال الأليم.

(٤٩) وارد كشـفى. قد انكشـف أنّ أصل الضلال والعمى والجهل من الشيطان وأصل الهدى والبصيرة واليقين من الملك. واسم ابليس كاسم شجرة خبيثة، والشـياطين بمنزلة أغصان هذه الشـجرة الملعونة، وأوراقها وأثمارها هى الأفكار الجزئية المتعلّقة بالشهوات العاجلة الحيوانية واللذّات الدنياوية. وأشـير اليه فى قوله تعالى: إنّها شـجرةٌ تخرجُ فى أصل الجحيم طلعُها كأنّه رؤوس الشياطين فإنّهم لآكلون منها فمالئون منها البطون.

(50) The names "angel" and "intellect" are like the name of *a pleasant tree: Its root is fixed and its branch is in heaven; it gives its food at every moment by the leave of its Lord* [14:24–25]—as the Qurʾān has made allusion. The fruits that come from it are the universal sciences and the divine knowledges. This is also the tree of Ṭūbā that was planted by the hand of the All-Merciful.[38] It is also *a blessed tree, an olive neither of the east nor the west* [24:35], because it is disengaged from the world's east and west and it is not specific to a location or a time. So, it is not found on one side rather than another, just as it is not found at one moment rather than another.

# Chapter Nine

*On the aspect of wisdom in the creation of the satans*

(51) Just as man benefits from the angel's inspiration, so also he benefits from the satan's disquietening in a certain respect, for the latter's existence inevitably comes from God for the sake of a wisdom and an advantage.[39] Otherwise, he would not exist, since futility and ineffectuality are absurd for Him.

(52) For the followers of the satans are all followers of sense-intuition and imagination. Were it not for the sense-intuitions of those who declare Him ineffectual and the imaginings of the pseudophilosophers, the Aeonists, and the other friends[40] of false gods, and [were it not for] their impostures and the diverse sorts of their twistedness, God's friends would not have been sent out to verify the realities, teach the sciences, and seek demonstrations so as to clarify *tawḥīd* and the cause of the occurrence of the cosmos, through unveiling, certainty, and so on.

(53) So also is the case with character traits and deeds, for example. Were it not for the backbiting of the backbiters and the prying of those who pry into people's faults, no one would totally shun the hidden faults that his loved ones do not see. These faults' fixity is made manifest to him only by the inspection of his enemies, their prying into his faults, and their making them manifest. How many an enemy there is, foul in essence, from whose enmity man benefits more than from the love of his sincere friend! For love is something that yields ignorance of the beloved's defects and blindness and deafness toward [seeing] his defective traits and hearing about his blemishes. Thus it has been said,

(٥٠) واسم الملك والعقل كاسم شجرة طيبة أصلُها ثابتٌ وفرعها فى السماء تُؤتى أُكُلَها كلَّ حين بإذن ربّها، كما أشير اليه فى القرآن. وثمارها الحاصلة منها هى العلوم الكلية والمعارف الالهية. وهى أيضاً شجرة طوبى التى غرسها يد الرحمن. وهى أيضاً شجرة مباركة زيتونة لا شرقية ولا غربية لتجرّدها عن شرل العالم وغربه وعدم اختصاصها بمكان او زمان. فلا يوجد فى جانب دون جانب كما لا يوجد فى وقت دون وقت.

## الفصل التاسع

### فى وجه الحكمة فى خلق الشياطين

(٥١) إنّ الانسان كما ينتفع من إلهام الملك ينتفع من وسوسة الشيطان بوجه، فإنّ وجودها من الله لا محالة لحكمة ومصلحة، والا لم يوجد لاستحالة العبث والتعطيل عليه تعالى.

(٥٢) فإنّ أتباع الشياطين كلّهم تبعة الوهم والخيال. ولو لم يكن أوهام المعطّلين وخيالات المتفلسفين والدهريين وسائر أولياء الطاغوت ومراتب جربزتهم وفنون اعوجاجاتهم، لما انبعث أولياء الله فى تحقيق الحقائق وتعليم العلوم وطلب البراهين لبيان التوحيد وعلّة الحدوث للعالم بالكشف واليقين وغير ذلك.

(٥٣) وكذا فى الأخلال والأعمال مثلاً. لو لم يكن اغتياب المغتابين وتجسّس المتجسّسين لعيوب الناس لم يجتنب كل الاجتناب من العيوب الخفية التى لا يراها أحبّاؤه. وإنّما يظهر له ثبوتها من تدقيقات أعدائه وتجسّسهم عيوبه وإظهارهم إيّاها. فكم من عدو خبيث الذات انتفع الانسان من عداوته أكثر ممّا انتفع من محبّة صديقه، فإنّ المحبّة ممّا يورث الجهل بعيوب المحبوب والعمى والصمم من معايبه وسماع مثالبه، كما قيل:

*The eye of satisfaction is dull to every defect,*
*the eye of enmity brings out every ugliness.*

(54) So it has become manifest that the existence of satanic deeds has great benefits for people. Among the profits of the pains and trials that reach the servant from the folk of wrongdoing and ungodliness is that these necessitate his speedy return to God, his abandonment of lingering in the earth, his avoidance of the folk of this world, and his seeking out the folk of the afterworld. All this is because of what he sees from the children of time and what reaches him because of them—the trials and intense pains that drive him away from the creatures and make him weary of this world and its happiness. So his nature flees from them; he returns to God, clings fast to the Causer of the causes and the Easer of affairs, and acquiesces to His words—*So flee unto God* [51:50]. So also, in the Persian *Mathnawī:*

*The creatures' cruelty to you in the world—*
*did you but know—is a secret stash of gold.*
*The creatures show their bad natures to you*
*so that you can only turn in* that *direction.*[41]

## Chapter Ten

### *Mentioning what was gained from these chapters*

(55) In the words that have preceded were mentioned the states of the origins of acts, the clarification of the human soul, the manner in which she becomes perfect, and her insight through witnessing solitary things and roots, as was mentioned in the chapters. Now that you have probed and searched after the origin of man's configuration and the levels of his advances and steps toward perfection, you should probe and search after the final goal of his coming to be and his being made and the levels of his final goal. Although the origin is one and the final goal is one, each of the two has levels and degrees. Just as the origin has levels and degrees, each of which is counted as origin, so also the final goal has levels and degrees, each of which is counted as final goal.

وعين الرضا عن كل عيب كليلة
وعين العداوة قد تبدّى المساويا

(٥٤) فظهر أنّ لوجود الاعمال الشيطانية منافع عظيمة للناس. ومن فوائد الآلام والمحن التى تصل الى العبد من أهل الظلم والفسق أنّه يوجب له سرعة الرجوع الى الله تعالى وترك الإخلاد الى الأرض والاجتناب عن أهل الدنيا وطلب أهل الآخرة لما يرى من أبناء الزمان ويصل اليه بسببهم من المحن والآلام الشديدة ما يزعجه عن الخلق ويملّه عن الدنيا ونعيمها. فيفرّ طبعه عنهم راجعاً الى الله وتشبّثاً منهم الى مسبّب الأسباب ومسهّل الأمور امتثالاً لقوله تعالى: ففرّوا الى الله، كما فى المثنوى الفارسى:

اين جفاى خلق با تو در جهان
گربدانى گنج زرآمد نهان
خلق را با تو چنين بد خو كند
تا تو را ناچار رو آنسو كند

## الفصل العاشر
### فى الذكر المحصول من هذه الفصول

(٥٥) قد ذكر فيما سبق من الأقوال أحوال مبادئ الأفعال وبيان النفس الانسانية وكيفية استكمالها واستبصارها بمشاهدة المفردات والأصول حسبما مضى ذكره فى الفصول. فالآن ينبغى لك اذا تفحّصت والتمست عن مبدأ نشو الانسان ومراتب ترقياته واستكمالاته أن تتفحّص وتلتمس عن غاية كونه وصنعه ومراتبها، فإنّ المبدأ وإن كان واحداً والغاية وإن كانت واحدة لكن لكلّ منهما مراتب ودرجات. كما أنّ للمبدأ مراتب ودرجات يكون كلّها فى عداد المبدأ فللغاية أيضاً مراتب ودرجات يكون كلّها فى عداد الغاية.

(56) It came to be known in the second and third parts that man has two faces and two configurations. One is a bodily, changing face, receptive to corruption, and the other a soulish face—illuminating, fixed, perpetual through the perpetuity of its effusing Cause, and living through the life of its subsistent Lord. Thus are His words, *Everyone upon [the earth] is undergoing annihilation, and there subsists the face of thy Lord, possessor of majesty and generous giving* [55:26–27]. The bodily face has life and subsistence only through the soulish face, from which aid and effusion reach it. Were the effusion to be severed from it for an instant, it would quickly go to ruin, its building would be destroyed, its organs would become ineffectual, and its form would disintegrate. So, when you seek the origin of man and scrutinize it, you should seek and scrutinize the origin of all his substantiality, both the bodily and the spiritual.

(57) The origins of his bodily substance are [first] the level of unqualified body and first hyle, which has no description in its essence, no ornament, and no form, save extension and deployment in the dimensions; upon it depend potency, ignorance, failure to find, absence from coming together and from presence, and distance from oneness and linkage in existence. This is because of the absence of every part from other than itself and the distance of some of its extremities and segments from others. So, the totality fails to find the totality, because it is identical with the parts.

(58) Then there is the natural body. It has a natural form that is the origin of the active and passive qualities, like mineral substances. Then there is the vegetal body, which has the form from which is configured the movement of growth and seeking food; like the sperm drop, within which comes to be the potency of attraction and growth so that it may become a flesh lump. Then there is the animal body, whose form is the origin of sensation and volitional movement, like the infant. Then there is the human body, which has the potency of distinguishing between harmful and beneficial, good and evil. These are five bodily origins of man with respect to his bodily ipseity and configuration.

(٥٦) وقد علم فى الباب الثانى والثالث أنّ الانسان ذو وجهين وذو نشأتين، أحدهما وجه جسمانى متغيّر قابل للفساد، والآخر وجه نفسانى منير ثابت دائم بدوام علّته الفيّاضة حىّ بحياة ربّه الباقى كما فى قوله تعالى: كلّ من عليها فانٍ ويبقى وجهُ ربّك ذو الجلال والإكرام. والوجه الجسمانى إنّما حياته وبقاؤه بالوجه النفسانى ومنه يصل المدد والفيض الى هذا. ولو انقطع فيضه منه لحظة لخرب سريعاً وانهدم بناؤه وتعطّلت آلاته وتفسّخت صورته. فانت اذا طلبت مبدأ الانسان وتفتّش عنه فعليك أن تطلب وتفتّش عن مبدأ جوهريته جميعاً الجسمانى والروحانى.

(٥٧) فمبادئ الجوهر الجسمانى منه مرتبة الجسم المطلق والهيولى الأولى التى لا نعت لها فى ذاتها ولا حلية ولا صورة سوى الامتداد والانبساط فى الأبعاد. وهو مناط القوّة والجهل والفقد والغيبة عن الاجتماع والحضور والبعد عن الوحدة والاقتران فى الوجود. وذلك لغيبة كلّ جزء عن غيره وتباعد الأطراف والأبعاد بعضها عن بعض. فيفقد المجموع عن المجموع لأنّه عين الأجزاء.

(٥٨) ثم الجسم الطبيعى وله صورة طبيعية هى مبدأ الكيفيات الفعلية والانفعالية كالجواهر المعدنية. ثم الجسم النباتى الذى له صورة ينشأ منها الحركة فى النماء وطلب الغذاء كالنطفة التى حصلت فيها قوّة الجذب والنشوء لصيرورتها كالمضغة. ثم الجسد الحيوانى الذى صورته مبدأ الحسّ والحركة الاختيارية كالطفل. ثم البدن الانسانى الذى له قوّة التمييز بين الضارّ والنافع والخير والشرّ. فهذه خمسة مبادئ جسمانية للانسان بحسب هويته ونشأته الجسمانية.

(59) As for the levels that he has with respect to his spiritual ipseity, they are gauged similarly in the view of the folk of insight. The first of his soulish origins is like the state of the soul at the moment of her conjunction with the solitary body, within which she has no description save the attribute of bodiment. Here her name is "nature." Next is like her state in her coming to be in the compound body, at which her name is "the constitutional potency." Next is like her falling into the degree of vegetal bodies, and here her name is "the growing soul." Next is like her becoming an animal soul, as in man's years of infancy and childhood; and then a human soul, as in the level of his adulthood.

(60) When acts and deeds emerge from her on the basis of deliberation and advantage, she is named "the practical intellect" and "the writing soul."[42] When she considers the knowledge of things and cogitates the intellective guideposts, she is named "the theoretical intellect" and "the reflective soul." When she obtains the potency of memory and recall, she is named "the remembering soul." When she obtains the potency of deducing the roots and uncovering the realities, she is named "the rational soul." When she conjoins with God's encounter and the witnessing of the realities, she is called "the spirit of holiness."

(61) Next you should know that the joining together of these two things—I mean the body and the spirit—is only for the sake of their unified compoundedness, because they are one in essence, but plural through the plurality of attributes and respects. Thus the two are unified in substantiality, but opposed through potency and act, deficiency and perfection, and darkness and light.

(62) In the first of the levels, man is an unqualified matter in one regard and an unqualified body in another regard. In the second of the levels, he is a species of body in one regard and a species-specific form in another regard. In the third of the levels, inasmuch as he is a receptacle for growth, he is named "a vegetal body," and inasmuch as he is the actor of vegetal activities such as growth, replication, and reproduction,

(٥٩) واما المراتب التى له بحسب هويته الروحانية فعلى هذا القياس عند أهل البصيرة، فإنّ أوّل مبادئه النفسانية هو كحال النفس وقت اتّصالها بالجسم المفرد الذى لا نعت لها فيه سوى صفة الجسمية ويكون اسمها حينئذ الطبيعة، ثم كحالها عند كونها فى الجسم المركّب واسمها القوّة المزاجية عند ذلك، ثم كوقوعها فى درجة الأجسام النباتية واسمها حينئذ النفس النامية، ثم كصيرورتها نفساً حيوانيةً كما فى سنّ الطفولية والصبى للانسان، ثم نفساً انسانيةً كما فى مرتبة البلوغ له.

(٦٠) فاذا صدرت عنها الأفعال والأعمال على وجه الرويّة والمصلحة تسمّى بالعقل العملى والنفس الكاتبة. واذا نظرت فى معرفة الأشياء وتأمّلت فى المعالم العقلية تسمّى بالعقل النظرى والنفس الفاكرة. واذا حصلت لها قوّة الحفظ والاسترجاع تسمّى بالنفس الحافظة. واذا حصلت لها قوّة استنباط الأصول واستكشاف الحقائق تسمّى بالنفس الناطقة. واذا اتّصلت بلقاء الله ومشاهدة الحقائق تسمّى بروح القدس.

(٦١) ثم اعلم أنّ الوصلة بين هذين الأمرين، أعنى الجسم والروح، إنّما هى لأجل التركيب الاتّحادى بينهما لأنّهما واحد بالذات متعدّد بتعدّد الصفات والحيثيات. فهما متّحدان فى الجوهرية متخالفان بالقوّة والفعل والنقص والكمال والظلمة والنور.

(٦٢) فالانسان فى أولى المراتب يكون مادّة مطلقة باعتبار وجسماً مطلقاً باعتبار، وفى ثانية المراتب يكون نوعاً من الجسم باعتبار وصورة نوعية باعتبار، وفى ثالثة المراتب يسمّى من حيث كونه قابلاً للنشوء جسماً نباتياً، ومن حيث كونه فاعلاً للأفاعيل النباتية من النشوء وايراد

"a vegetal soul." In the fourth level, inasmuch as he is acted upon by sense objects and undergoes transitions in diverse locations with respect to desire, [he is named] "an animal body," and with respect to employing the tools of sensation and movement through desire, "an animal soul." In the fifth level, he is named "a human body" in one respect and "a human soul" in another.

(63) In the same way should be gauged the other levels and way stations, until the removal of this duality that had come to his reality with respect to its descent and coming forth from the world of the divine oneness and the gatheredness of the [divine] names, because deficiency and inadequacy are the fountainhead of multiplicity and slackening. Do you not see how the movement of the pulse, when its potency is strengthened, becomes continuous and regular, but when weakened, becomes discontinuous and intermittent? Or how, when the matter of a flame's wick becomes little, its cone becomes plural because its active potency is inadequate to give shape, since the oil gives little aid?

(64) So also is the state of the human soul, her coming forth from the Presence of Gatheredness and her falling into the world of dispersion. As long as she does not return to her original home for the sake of the perfection and completion that come to be in the afterworld for the felicitous and perfect, unity in the Entity of Gathering does not come to be for her.[43] It is then that all the soul becomes hearing, eyesight, potencies, and bodily parts, so that she is identical with the body because of her utmost potency and luminosity, while the body is identical with the soul because of its utmost limpidness and subtlety. To this alluded the one who said,

*The glass is clear, the wine is clear,*
*the two are alike, the affair confused—*
*As if there is wine without cup,*
*or cup without wine.*[44]

البدل والتوليد للمثل نفساً نباتيةً، وفى المرتبة الرابعة من حيث كونه منفعلاً عن المحسوسات منتقلاً فى الأماكن المختلفة من جهة الإرادة بدناً حيوانياً وباعتبار كونه مستعملاً لآلات الإحساس والتحريك بالإرادة نفساً حيوانيةً، وفى المرتبة الخامسة يسمّى بدناً انسانياً من جهة ونفساً انسانيةً من جهة.

(٦٣) وهكذا القياس فى سائر المراتب والمنازل الى أن ترتفع هذه الإثنينية الحاصلة لحقيقته من جهة نزولها وخروجها من عالم الوحدة الالهية والجمعية الأسمائية، فإنّ النقص والقصور منبع الكثرة والفتور. أَوَلا ترى حركة النبض اذا قويت القوّة اتّصلت وانتظمت واذا ضعفت انفصلت وتواترت، والى الشعلة التى قلّت مادّة فتيلتها كيف تعدّدت صنوبرتها لقصور قوّتها الفاعلة للتشكيل لقلّة المدد من الدهن.

(٦٤) فهكذا حال النفس الانسانية وخروجها عن الحضرة الجمعية ووقوعها فى عالم التفرقة. فما لم ترجع الى مأواها الأصلى لأجل الكمال والتمام الذى يحصل فى الآخرة للسعداء الكاملين لم يحصل لها أحدية فى عين الجمع. وعند ذلك تصير النفس كلّها السمع والبصر والقوى والجوارح، فتكون عين البدن لغاية قوّتها ونورانيتها والبدن عين النفس لغاية صفائه ولطافته. واليه أشار من قال:

رلّ الزجاج ورقّت الخمر
فتشابها وتشاكل الأمر
فكأنّه خمر ولا قدح
وكأنّها قدح ولاخمر

(65) Thus it is known that the state of man at the beginning is the same as his state at the end, as He says, *As He began you, so you will return—a group that He has guided,* which is to say that they have reached oneness, *and a group against whom the misguidance is realized* [7:29–30],[45] so they have remained in dispersion and chastisement.

(66) Those who consider with the eye of insight and verification will see that in each thing, oneness has an actualized reality that is original and initial, and within it, multiplicity is among the subsequent accidents. Once the realities have been verified and the accidents have disappeared, multiplicity disappears and the derivative, accidental dispersion disintegrates. So also when man returns to his true reality, comes back to the clime of the oneness that he possessed with respect to the original innate disposition, and is delivered from the abode of opposites and the dwelling place of numbers—all this through acquiring potency, perfection, and conjunction with the Fully Active Intellect—then his bodily defects and husks disappear from him and the hylic bonds are clipped away from him, by the leave of Him *in whose hand is the Sovereignty of each thing* [36:83], from whom is the origination at the beginning and to whom is the going back at the end. It has been said, "The end is the return to the beginning."[46]

(67) *The Rising of a Gathering Light from the Horizon of a Sapiential Secret.*[47] Know that the form of the natural, elemental body is potentially inanimate, and the form of mineral things is actually inanimate and potentially plant. The plant's form—that is, the vegetal soul—is actually a growing, self-nourishing, and reproducing substance and potentially an animal. The animal's form—that is, its soul—is actually a sensate substance and potentially a human. Children's souls are actually sensate and potentially intellecting. Adults' souls are actually intellecting and potentially philosophers. Philosophers are actually sages and potentially angels, so when they depart from their bodies, they actually become angels.

(68) Thus minerals are transmuted into the bodies of plants, the bodies of plants are transmuted into the bodies of animals, and the most eminent of animals is man. These transmutations and steps toward perfection are manifest in the matter that is the human sperm drop and embryo.

(٦٥) فعلم أنّ حال الانسان فى البداية هى بعينها حاله فى النهاية، كما قال سبحانه: كما بدأ كم تعودون فريقاً هدى – أى وصل الى الوحدة – وفريقاً حقَّ عليهم الضلالة، فبقوا فى التفرقة والعذاب.

(٦٦) ومن نظر بعين البصيرة والتحقيق رأى أنّ الوحدة فى كلّ شئ لها حقيقة متحصّلة هى أصلية ابتدائية، والكثرة فيه من العوارض اللاحقة. فاذا حقّقت الحقائق وزالت العوارض زالت الكثرة وانفسخت التفرقة الفرعية العارضة. فكذا الانسان اذا رجع الى حالّ حقيقته وعاد الى إقليم وحدته التى كانت له بحسب الفطرة الأصلية، وخلص عن دار الأضداد ومنزل الأعداد، وذلك باكتساب القوّة والكمال والاتّصال بالعقل الفعّال، زالت عنه العيوب والقشور الجسمانية وحذفت عنه القيود الهيولانية بإذن من بيده ملكوت كلّ شئ ومنه البدؤ فى الابتداء واليه العود فى الانتهاء. وقد قيل النهاية هى الرجوع الى البداية.

(٦٧) طلوع نور جمعى من أفق سرّ حكمى. اعلم أنّ صورة الجسم الطبيعى العنصرى جماد بالقوّة وصورة المعدنيات جماد بالفعل نبات بالقوّة، وصورة النبات أى النفس النباتية جوهر نام متغذٍّ مولّد للمثل بالفعل حيوان بالقوّة، وصورة الحيوان أى نفسه جوهرٌ حسّاس بالفعل انسان بالقوّة، ونفوس الصبيان حسّاسة بالفعل عاقلة بالقوّة، ونفوس البالغين عاقلة بالفعل فلاسفة بالقوّة، والفلاسفة حكماء بالفعل ملائكة بالقوّة، فاذا فارقت أجسادها صارت ملائكة بالفعل.

(٦٨) فإذاً المعادن يستحيل الى أجسام النبات وأجسام النبات يستحيل الى أجسام الحيوان وأشرف الحيوانات هو الانسان. وهذه الاستحالات والاستكمالات ظاهرة فى المادّة النطفية والجنينية للإنسان.

(69) It is as if the human soul has fallen to the last of the gates of Gehenna, because she is midway between the two worlds and intermediary between the two way stations. Just as, in this station, she passes through all the levels of the existent things that are below her in way station, so also when she becomes perfect in knowledge and deed, comes to be disengaged, and reaches the level of the illuminating, acquired intellect in the world of the Return, she becomes all existents, for she has become an Actual Intellect. For the Actual Intellect is all existent things below it in level. Thus the soul that rises up to her Lord through these steps is as it were *on a straight path* [6:39]. Or rather, she is *a straight path* through her essence, while other souls are twisted or inverted paths.

(70) Do you not see the form of plants and the fact that it is a path inverted towards depth? The animal soul has passed beyond this form and has been saved from it, and the form of the animal is a lengthened path. The human soul has passed beyond it, and the form of man is a standing path, raised up between the lowest and the highest with respect to its innate disposition. However, when the form deviates toward twistedness through corrupt views, or toward bending through ugly deeds, it is *pushed back to the lowest of the low* [95:5]. When it goes straight, travels God's road, and betakes itself to the world of the afterworld through knowledge and deed, it is saved from the chastisement of Gehenna and reaches the gate of mercy and good-pleasure, the locus of the noble angels.

(71) So strive, O soul, and cogitate, for you have nearly reached the gate of the Garden. If you make haste before separation from the body and if you gain the preparedness for and provision of godwariness,[48] worthy deeds,[49] sound views, beautiful character traits, and true sciences, then you will have been saved from the fires of the Pit and the painful chastisement. You may hope that you will be in the row[50] of the high ones, those who lodge in the seats of the highest holiness in the Garden of Bliss among *the prophets, the truthful, the witnesses, and the worthy—good companions they!* [4:69].

(٦٩) والنفس الانسانية كأنّها واقعة فى آخر باب من أبواب جهنّم لأنّها متوسّطة بين العالمين وواسطة بين المنزلتين. فكما أنّها فى هذا المقام جازت جميع رتب الموجودات التى دونها فى المنزلة، فكذلك اذا استكملت بالعلم والعمل وتجرّدت وبلغت مرتبة العقل المستفاد المنير فى عالم المعاد صارت كلّ الموجودات لأجل صيرورتها عقلاً بالفعل، إذ العقل بالفعل جميع الموجودات التى دونه فى الرتبة. فالنفس الصاعدة الى ربّها بهذه الخطوات كأنّها على صراط مستقيم، بل هى صراط مستقيم بذاتها، وسائر النفوس على صرط معوجّة أو منكوسة.

(٧٠) أوَلا ترى الى صورة النبات وكونها صراطاً منكوساً الى العمق. وقد جاوزتها النفس الحيوانية ونجت منها، وصورة الحيوان صراط ممدود. وقد جاوزتها النفس الانسانية، وصورة الانسان صراط قائم ينتصب بين الأسفل والأعلى بحسب فطرتها، لكن اذا انحرفت الى الاعوجاج بالآراء الفاسدة او الانتكاس بالأعمال القبيحة ردّت الى أسفل السافلين، واذا استقامت وسلكت سبيل الله وتوجّهت الى عالم الآخرة بالعلم والعمل نجت من عذاب جهنّم وبلغت الى باب الرحمة والرضوان محلّ الملائكة الكرام.

(٧١) فاجتهدى يا نفس وتأمّلى، فإنّكِ قد بلغتِ قريباً من باب الجنّة، فإن بادرت قبل مفارقة الجسد واستعددت وتزوّدت بالتقوى والأعمال الصالحة والآراء الصحيحة والأخلال الجميلة والعلوم الحقيقية فقد نجوت من نيران الهاوية والعذاب الأليم ورجوت أن تكون من صفّ الأعالى المقيمين فى مقاعد القدس الأعلى من جنّة النعيم مع النبيين والصديقين والشهداء والصالحين وحسن أولئك رفيقاً.

*PART FOUR*

*On the Knowledge of the Ends*

*In it are ten chapters.*

## Chapter One

*On the highest knowledge*

(1) Know that knowledge of the final goal is linked to knowledge of the origin. Allusion has already been made that in reality each thing's origin is the same as its final goal. We also pointed out that the more the origin and final goal are elevated and high beyond falling under the sway of being, the more they are near to and inclined toward the direction of oneness and gatheredness. The lower and more descended they are, the quicker they go to plurality and separation and the more deeply they drop into the Pit.

(2) Know now that creatures must pass over these way stations and states during the descent from the world of oneness and gatheredness and the rising up to it. Hence they must know the final goals and the origins, because, in reality, these are the most excellent parts of the universal, sapiential sciences and the knowledges of certainty.

(3) It has also been confirmed in the investigations of the technique of demonstration pertaining to the Wisdom of the Scale [that is, logic] that whether knowledge is particular or universal in the case of a priori[1] demonstrations depends upon investigation of the origins of the object. If the investigation concerns the near origins of its object, then the knowledge is particular, but if it concerns the far origins, then the knowledge is universal.[2]

# الباب الرابع

## فى معرفة النهايات
## وفيه عشرة فصول

### الفصل الأوّل

(١) اعلم أنّ معرفة الغاية ترتبط بمعرفة المبدأ. وقد وقعت الاشارة الى أنّ المبدأ لكل شـئ هو عين الغاية له فى الحقيقة. وأومأنا أيضاً الى أنّ المبدأ والغاية كلّما كانا أرفع وأعلى من الوقوع تحت الكون كانا الى جهة الوحدة والجمعية أقرب وأميل، وكلّما كانا أدنى وأنزل كانا الى التعدّد والافتراق أسرع وفى الهُوىّ الى الهاوية أوغل.

(٢) ثمّ اعلم أنّه لا بدّ للخلق من المرور على هذه المنازل والأحوال عند النزول عن عالم الوحدة والجمعية والصعود اليها. فلا بدّ من معرفة الغايات والمبادئ لأنّها بالحقيقة أفضل أجزاء العلوم الكلية الحكمية والمعارف اليقينية.

(٣) وقد ثبت أيضاً فى مباحث فنّ البرهان من حكمة الميزان أنّ مناط كون العلم جزئياً أو كونه كلياً إنّما يكون بحسب البحث عن المبادئ لموضوعه فى البراهين اللمّيات. فإن كان البحث عن المبادئ القريبة لموضوعه كان العلم جزئياً وإن كان البحث عن المبادئ البعيدة كان العلم كلياً.

(4) It may be that one question, like the circularity of the celestial sphere's movement, is investigated in two diverse sciences—the particular, natural; and the universal, divine. Then, at one time, it is possible for it to be confirmed in the natural sciences that the sphere has a mutual similarity of movement with respect to its matter and form, which are the two near causes. The natural investigator will say, "Here the nature is one and the matter is one and simple, so the guise and the attribute are not diverse." Thus the knowledge is particular, coming to be from the direction of the near origins, because the middle term is taken from "nature," which has no opposite; and there is no diversity within simple matter. Hence it is impossible for corruption or change to occur for it.

(5) At another time this can be confirmed in the divine things. The gnostic philosopher says, "The actor [that is, the efficient cause][3] is an intellective, separate thing, and it is sheer good; the final cause is the furthest occasion, which is Unqualified Existence, more complete than that which is nothing."

(6) The natural investigator offers an a priori demonstration [that is valid] as long as matter and nature abide as existents. But the gnostic philosopher offers an a priori demonstration that abides in an unqualified sense. He offers the cause of the abidance of matter and of the nature that has no opposite, so what it demands abides.

(7) In short, if the demonstration offers some of the proximate causes, it pertains to the low and particular knowledge, but if it offers some of the separate causes, it pertains to the high and universal knowledge. The proximate causes are the matter and the form that are situated in the world of movements. The separate causes are the actor and the final goal that are situated above the world of movements, that is, [in] the world of holiness. All this belongs to what has been mentioned in the books of the sages, like [Ibn Sīnā's] *al-Shifāʾ* and others.

(8) It follows that the highest of sciences is that which considers and inquires after the state of the Highest Origin and the Furthest End of the cognitive topics. This is the "Lordly Science,"[4] which is the most eminent of sciences and the most excellent of arts. Through it man obtains the degree of the high angels, because the level of the thing's knower qua knower is the same as the level of the known thing, if he is firmly rooted in his knowledge of it, as has been verified in its place.

(٤) وقد يكون مسألة واحدة كاستدارة حركة الفلك يبحث عنها فى علمين مختلفين طبيعى جزئى وإلهى كلى، حيث يمكن أن يثبت تشابه الحركة للفلك مرّةً فى الطبيعيات من جهة مادّته وصورته وهما علّتان قريبتان، فيقول الباحث الطبيعى الطبيعة هناك واحدة والمادّة واحدة بسيطة، فيكون الهيئة والصفة غير مختلفة. فيكون العلم جزئياً حاصلاً من جهة المبادئ القريبة لأنّه يأخذ الأوسط من الطبيعة التى لا ضدّ لها والمادّة البسيطة لا اختلاف فيها. فيمتنع أن يعرض لها فساد أوتغيّر.

(٥) ويثبت مرّةً فى الالهيات، فيقول الفيلسوف العارف الفاعل أمر عقلى مفارل وهو خير محض والعلّة الغائية هى السبب الأقصى الذى هو الوجود المطلق الذى لا أتمّ منه.

(٦) فالباحث الطبيعى يعطى برهاناً لّمياً ما دامت المادّة والطبيعة موجودتين، والفيلسوف العارف يعطى البرهان اللمّى الدائم مطلقاً. ويعطى علّة دوام المادّة والطبيعة التى لا ضدّ لها فيدوم مقتضاها.

(٧) وبالجملة فإذا أعطى البرهان من العلل المقارنة كان من العلم السافل والجزئى، وإن أعطى من العلل المفارقة كان من العلم الأعلى والكلى، والعلل المقارنة هى المادّة والصورة الواقعتان فى عالم الحركات، والعلل المفارقة هى الفاعل والغاية الواقعتان فول عالم الحركات وهو عالم القدس. هذا ممّا ذكر فى كتب الحكماء كالشفاء وغيره.

(٨) فعلى هذا أعلى العلوم ما ينظر فيه ويسأل عن حال المبدأ الأعلى والغاية القصوى للموضوعات العلمية، وهو العلم الربوبى الذى هو أشرف العلوم وأفضل الصنائع، وبه يحصل للانسان درجة الملائكة العلويين لأنّ مرتبة العالم بشئ من حيث أنّه عالم به مرتبة المعلوم بعينها اذا كان راسخاً فى العلم به كما حقّق فى مقامه.

(9) This meaning[5]—that is, the unification of the intellecter and the intelligible—was unveiled to the foremost of the Peripatetics, Porphyry, who was the most excellent student of the most ancient teacher and the greatest philosopher, Aristotle. And we have recognized (to God be the praise) that a large number of followers of Islam *who preceded us in faith* [59:10] and were possessors of the spiritual sciences that come through unveiling and demonstration have maintained what was maintained by Porphyry and those who agree with him.

(10) So also, the Chief Shaykh [Ibn Sīnā] (may his secret heart be made holy) turned away from his denial of the unification of the intellecter and the intelligible in one of his books. As for our own time, we have found no one who has obtained this question through verification except one individual whom God specified for this magnificent bounty.

(11) In short, knowledge of the Origin and Return and knowledge of that to which the souls of the servants go back are among the most important goals and the most elevated aims. This is the beneficial remedy, the greatest antidote, and the red elixir. But ignorance of it, especially when paired with denial and obstinacy, is the foul poison and fatal illness through which souls ill with the malady of ignorance will have the bitter extraction at death and terror at the Uprising.

(12) In the preceding part, we clarified the knowledge of the reality of the origins prior to the existence of man. Knowledge of the final goal depends only on knowledge of the origin. Those who recognize from whence they have come recognize where they are going. Those who cogitate on each one of the activities that have volitional or natural final goals and who ponder what is the essential origin of their emergence and what is the essential final goal of their entrance will know for certain that the final goal in these is the origin itself in a more perfect manner.

(13) For example, in the emergence of eating, the actor, for example, is the essence of man—on condition that he be hungry and conceive of satiety or pleasure in himself. The final goal is the existence of his satiety or pleasure. Hence, the quiddity of satiety, for example, with respect to its imaginal existence, is the active cause of the eating; and, with respect

(٩) وقد انكشف هذا المعنى أى اتّحاد العاقل والمعقول لمقدّم المشّائين فرفوريوس وهو أفضل تلامذة المعلّم الأقدم والفيلسوف الأعظم أرسطاطاليس. ونحن قد عرفنا بحمد الله عدداً كثيراً فى الاسلاميين الذين سبقونا بالايمان من أصحاب العلوم الروحانية الحاصلة بالكشف والبرهان قد ذهبوا الى ما ذهب اليه فرفوريوس ووافقوه.

(١٠) والشيخ الرئيس قدّس سرّه أيضاً قد رجع عن إنكاره لاتّحاد العاقل والمعقول فى بعض كتبه. واما فى هذا الزمان فلم نجد أحداً حصّل هذه المسألة تحقيقاً الّا شخصاً واحداً قد خصّه الله بهذه النعمة العظيمة.

(١١) وبالجملة معرفة المبدأ والمعاد والعلم بما يؤول اليه نفوس العباد من أهمّ المقاصد وأرفع المآرب. وهو الدواء النافع والترياق الأكبر والإكسير الأحمر. والجهل به خصوصاً اذا كان مشفوعاً بالإنكار والعناد هو السمّ الناقع والمرض المهلك وبه يكون مرارة النزع عند الموت والفزع عند البعث للنفوس المريضة بداء الجهالة.

(١٢) ونحن قد بيّنا العلم بحقيقة المبادئ المتقدّمة لوجود الانسان فى الباب السابق. والعلم بالغاية إنّما ينوط بالعلم بالمبدأ. فمن عرف أنّ مجيئه من أين، يعرف أنّ ذهابه الى أين. ومن تأمّل فى واحد واحد من الأفاعيل التى لها غايات اختيارية أو طبيعية وتدبّر فيما هو المبدأ بالذات لصدورها وفيما هو الغاية بالذات لورودها، يعلم يقيناً أنّ الغاية فيها هى بعينها كان هو المبدأ على وجه أكمل.

(١٣) مثلاً الفاعل لصدور الأكل هو ذات الانسان مثلاً بشرط كونه جائعاً متصوّراً للشبع أو اللذّة فى نفسه، والغاية هى وجود الشبع أو اللذّة له. فماهية الشبع مثلاً بحسب وجودها الخيالى علّة فاعلية للأكل وهى بعينها بحسب وجودها العينى غاية ذاتية له. والوجود العينى أقوى وأشدّ

to its entified existence,[6] it itself is its essential final goal. Here, the entified existence is stronger and more intense for man than the imaginal existence. Thus, in this example, existence has moved from deficiency toward perfection and from weakness toward potency. The actor itself is the final goal, though there is disparity in the mode of existence. So also is the state in all activities that happen in this cosmos. Gauge in the same terms the state of man's reality according to its vicissitudes in its existence!

(14) What is intended by this can be elucidated properly only through two premises. The first is for it to be known that from the moment of his occurrence as a sperm drop, man possesses a natural form. He never ceases undergoing vicissitudes and transitions in nature and matter, in soul and body—from stage to stage, from form to form, and from state to state—up to this moment in which he has come to be according to these two. This will be manifest when anyone witnesses the states of his own soul and body.

(15) As for the states of his body, this is because he witnesses that he has been forever in transformation and transition in his essential stages from when he was a sperm drop, an embryo, and an infant until he came to be a youth, mature, and old.

(16) As for the states of his soul in her stages and vicissitudes, there was a moment when she had no task save preserving the body. Then there came to be for her the potency of growing and nourishing the body. Then there came to be for her the potency of reproducing her body. These are her levels with respect to inducing movement.

(17) As for her levels with respect to perception, there was a moment when she was in the station of being aware of and sensing only particulars. The first and most deficient degree of sensation is the sense of touch, of which no animal is empty, even worms in the soil. For when they are poked with a pin, they contract, and through this they are distinguished from plants. Next is the level of smell, then the remaining outward senses. Then she obtains the inward perceptions—the sensory and then the intellective according to their degrees.

مــن الوجود الخيالى للإنســان ههنا. فالوجود فى هــذا المثال قد تحرّك من النقص الى الكمال ومن ضعف الى قوّة. فالفاعل بعينه هو الغاية مع تفاوت فــى نحو الوجود، وهكذا الحال فى جميع الأفاعيل الواقعة فى هذا العالم. فقس عليها حال حقيقة الانسان بحسب انقلاباته فى وجوده.

(١٤) وهــذا المقصــود إنّما يتّضح حقّ الأتضــاح بمقدّمتين. الأولى أن يعلم أنّ الانسان من لدن حدوثه عند كونه نطفة ذات صورة طبيعية لا يزال فى الانقلاب والانتقال طبيعةً ومادّةً ونفساً وبدناً من طور الى طور وصورة الى صورة وحال الى حال الى هذا الوقت الذى يكون فيه بحسبهما. وهذا الأمريظهر من مشاهدة كلّ أحد أحوال نفسه وبدنه.

(١٥) أمّــا أحوال البدن فحيث شــاهد أنّه أبداً فى التحوّل والنقلة فى أطــواره الذاتية مــن لدن كونه نطفــةً وجنيناً وطفلاً الى كونه شــابّاً وكهلاً وشيخاً.

(١٦) وأمّا أحوال النفــس فى أطوارها وانقلاباتها فوقت لم يكن لها شــأن الا حفظ الجســم، ثمّ حصلت لها قــوّة الإنماء والتغذية للجســم، ثم حصلت لها قوّة التوليد للمثل لبدنها. هذه مراتبها بحسب التحريك.

(١٧) واما مراتبها بحســب الإدراك فوقت كانت فى مقام الشــعور والإحســاس للجزئيات فقط. وأوّل درجة الحسّ وأنقصها حاسّــة اللمس التــى لا يخلــوا عنها حيوان حتى الدود فى الطين، فإنّهــا اذا غرز فيها إبرة انقبضــت، وبهذا تمتاز عن النبات. وبعده مرتبة الشــمّ، ثــمّ باقى الحواسّ الظاهــرة، ثــم يحصــل لهــا الادراكات الباطنية الحسّــية ثــم العقلية على درجاتها.

(18) Thus it is known that both soul and body are in movement, transition, journey, and departure from state to state. Such is the situation in this abode until the this-worldly life is nullified, the form of the combination of the two is nullified, and they come to be separated and disjoined. Then, in this disjoining, they do not come to a halt. Rather, the body applies itself to dissolution until it reaches earthiness, or rather, sheer hylicity; and the soul applies herself to returning to the One, the All-Subjugating. So understand!

(19) The second of the two [premises] is that it be known that if something betakes itself and undergoes transformation from one level to another and from one way station to another according to nature [in general] or [individual] nature,[7] then, inasmuch as it departs and undergoes transition from one level to another, it inevitably has a natural, essential, final goal, which is the last thing at which it comes to rest, finds repose, and takes a homestead. The dwelling place of its settlement and the abode where it settles must be for it the most worthy of homesteads and the most appropriate of levels and degrees in its substance and essence. This can only be what was the origin of its essence and the establisher of its existence.

(20) Hence, the final goal toward which something journeys is necessarily the first thing from which it journeyed. It is this that is the natural homestead and the original mine, not any of the other way stations and boundaries in the middle realms. If any of them had been the original, natural settling place, there would have been no flight from it or betaking oneself to something else. For the custom of the divine mercy and solicitude is to hold the thing in the most eminent of states befitting it and the highest of stations conceivable for it, without transition from there to something that is not of the same sort, unless by a constraining accident. However, the "constraining" is not perpetual or frequent but rare and infrequent. This is because there is no prevention, niggardliness, or stinginess in His mercy, and no competition or rivalry in the world of His munificence and His solicitude. In such manner has come to pass *God's wont,* for which there is no *altering* and from which there is no *turning away* [35:43].

(١٨) فعلم أنّ كلاً من النفس والبدن فى الحركة والانتقال والسفر والارتحال من حال الى حال، وهكذا فى هذه الدار الى أن بطلت هذه الحياة الدنياوية وبطلت صورة التأليف وحصل الافتراال بينهما والانفصال. ثم لا يقفان فى هذا الانفصال، بل يمعن البدن فى الاضمحلال حتى ينتهى الى الأرضية بل الى الهيولية المحضة، وتمعن النفس فى الرجوع الى الواحد القهّار. فافهم.

(١٩) وثانيهما أن يعلم أنّ كلّ متوجّه ومتحوّل عن مرتبة الى مرتبة ومن منزلة الى منزلة بحسب الطبيعة او الطباع فله لا محالة حيث يرتحل وينتقل من مرتبة الى مرتبة أخرى يكون غاية طبيعية ذاتية هى آخر ما يطمئنّ به ويسكن لديه ويتوطّن فيه. ولا بدّ أن يكون منزل استقراره ودار قراره أصلح المواطن له وأنسب المراتب والدرجات اليه فى جوهره وذاته. وما ذلك الا ما كان مبدأ ذاته ومقوّم وجوده.

(٢٠) فغاية ما يسافر اليه الشئ يجب أن يكون أوّل ما سافر منه، وهو الموطن الطبيعى والمعدن الأصلى دون غيره من المنازل والحدود التى فى الأواسط، لأنّ كلاً منها لو كان مقرّاً أصلياً طبيعياً لم يقع الهرب منه والتوجّه الى غيره، فإنّ دأب الرحمة والعناية الالهية أن يمسك الشئ على أشرف الحالات اللائقة به وأعلى المقامات المتصوّرة فى حقّه من غير انتقال منه الى ما ليس كذلك الا لعارض قاسر. والقاسر ليس دائماً ولا أكثرياً بل نادراً أقلّياً. وذلك لأنّه لا منع فى رحمته تعالى ولا بخل ولا تقتير ولا تزاحم ولا تشاحّ فى عالم جوده وعنايته. وبذلك جرت سنّة الله التى لا تبديل لها ولا تحويل عنها.

(21) So, the effusion is freely given, the mercy is all-embracing, and everything receives the most elevated of what is conceivable for it, appropriate for its configuration, sustainable by its essence, and embraced by its existence. Hence the cosmos in its wholeness and its parts is upon the most beautiful manner and the most excellent arrangement.[8]

(22) As for the impairments and blights that adhere to the things that are betaking themselves, these happen only in this cosmos, in individual beings, and in a few constitutions by way of anomaly and on occasion. Within the blights there is often an advantage going back to their essences or something else, whether in this world or the afterworld. Our discussion concerns the original natures and their essential[9] activities and passivities, not their constrained activities and passivities.

(23) Everything betaking itself in a direction with respect to its own nature inevitably has an essential final goal that is the most eminent state for it. It will assuredly go back to it if not prevented by an external impediment or a thief on the road. The impediments to the natural aims of things are rare affairs, not perpetual, as was pointed out. It was also clarified in its place that when the constraints are removed, whether quickly or slowly, the return and homecoming of everything will be to the Furthest Good. *Surely unto God all things come home* [42:53].

(24) *An Instruction and Remark.* No one should let himself imagine that time and moment are taken into account in what is meant by "origin" and "final goal." Then it would be understood that the "priority" of childhood over old age is simply that one of them is in the past time and the other in the coming time. Rather, what is meant accords with nature and essence.

(25) Every occurring effect has affairs preceding it, in the sense that they are essential occasions for its existence and things that prepare for it and bring it near—that is, [they are] its cause and the summoners of its realization. It also has perfections subsequent to it, through which it may achieve perfection and toward which it travels. Why not? Even the quiddity of time itself, with respect to its individual ipseity that is quantitative and continuous, is one of the things that has an origin and a final goal in the just-mentioned meaning—not in the meaning of the precedence and subsequence that are temporal. Otherwise, it would be required that time would have a time precedent to it or subsequent to it, and that is absurd.

(٢١) فالفيض مبذول والرحمة واسعة وكلّ شئ قابل لأرفع ما يتصوّر فى حقّه ويناسب نشأته ويحتمله ذاته ويسعه وجوده. فالعالم بكليته وأجزائه على أحسن الوجوه وأفضل النظامات.

(٢٢) واما الآفات والعاهات اللاحقة للأشياء المتوجّهة فهى إنّما تقع فى هذا العالم وفى الأشخاص الكائنة وفى قليل من الأمزجة على سبيل الشذوذ أحياناً. وربّما كانت فيها مصلحة تعود الى ذوات العاهات وغيرها إمّا فى الدنيا وإمّا فى الآخرة. والكلام فى الطبائع الأصلية وأفاعيلها وانفعالاتها الذاتية لا أفاعيلها وانفعالاتها القسرية.

(٢٣) فكلّ متوجّه بحسب طبعه الى جهة فلا محالة له غاية ذاتية هى أشرف الحالات له وسيؤول اليها البتّة إن لم يمنعه عائق خارجى قاطع لطريقه. والعوائق عن المآرب الطبيعية للأشياء أمور نادرة غير دائمة كما وقعت الاشارة اليه. وقد بينّ فى مقامه أنّ عند ارتفاع القواسر سريعاً او بطيئاً يكون مرجع الكلّ الى الخير الأقصى والمصير اليه، ألا الى الله تصير الامور.

(٢٤) إعلام وتنبيه. ولا يذهب على أحد أن يتوهّم أنّ المراد من المبدأ والغاية ما يعتبر فيه الزمان والوقت حتى يفهم من تقدّم الصبى على الشيخوخية مجرّد كون أحدهما فى الزمان الماضى والآخر فى الآتى، بل المراد ما يكون بحسب الطبع والذات.

(٢٥) فلكلّ معلول حادث أمور سابقة عليه بمعنى كونها أسباباً ذاتيةً لوجوده ومعدّات ومقرّبات له من علّته ودواع لتحقّقه. وله أيضاً كمالات لاحقة به يستكمل بها ويسلك اليها. كيفَ ونفس ماهية الزمان بحسب هويته الشخصية الكمية الاتّصالية ممّا له مبدأ وغاية بهذا المعنى الذى ذكرناه لا بمعنى السبق واللحوق الزمانيين، والا يلزم أن يكون للزمان زمان سابق عليه او لاحق به وهذا محال.

# Chapter Two

*Clarifying and explaining the quiddity of the final goal toward which man betakes himself*

(26) It was pointed out that a thing comes to be complete at the end of its traveling and that this is nothing but the original state that conforms with its nature and is agreeable to its essence. As long as there are states other than this last state, they are alien to its essence and loaned to it. States alien to a thing will inevitably disappear from it, so the thing will return finally to the attribute that it had at the first, as was pointed out. It will obtain the original state only in its natural home. The natural home of the soul is in the world of the afterworld, which is the inwardness of this cosmos and the Absent of this Witnessed. It is the world of human souls, their homestead, and their true place of return. As long as the soul has not reached it, she will not find repose or come to rest from her troubledness and uneasiness.

(27) In her original home, the soul was alive, freely choosing, subtle, powerful, knowing through the potency of her Innovator, roaming in her world, joyful, at rest with her Author, *in a seat of truthfulness with an All-Powerful King* [54:55]. This is the "Garden" within which were her intellective father and her soulish mother, Adam and Eve. *O Adam, repose, you and your spouse, in the Garden, and eat of it carefree, you two, wherever you will* [2:35].

(28) When the soul fell from her world, her home, and the Garden of her Lord because of an offense that happened from her father and mother, and when she sank to lowness and was turned over to this cosmos, her life turned into death and her light into darkness. Her power was altered to incapacity, her free choosing to coercion, her settledness to agitation, her subtlety to density. Her nobility, eminence, and perfection disappeared into abasement, meanness, and deficiency. Her gatheredness and oneness were drawn into dispersion and multiplicity.

## الفصل الثانى

### فى الابانة عن ماهية الغاية الأخيرة التى يتوجّه اليها الانسان وشرحها

(٢٦) قد مرّت الاشارة الى أنّ تمامية الشئ يحصل عند نهاية سلوكه، وإنّما هى الحالة الأصلية التى توافق طبعه وتلائم ذاته. وكلّما يكون غير تلك الحالة الأخيرة من سائر الحالات فهى غريبة عن ذاته عارية عليه. والحالات الغريبة عن الشئ يزول عنه لامحالة، فيرجع الشئ آخر الأمر الى الصفة التى كانت له أوّلاً كما مرّت اليه الاشارة. والحالة الأصلية إنّما تحصل له فى مأواه الطبيعى، والمأوى الطبيعى للنفس فى عالم الآخرة التى هى باطن هذا العالم وغيب هذه الشهادة، وهو عالم النفوس الانسانية وموطنها ومعادها الحقيقى. وما لم تصل النفس اليها لم تسكن و لم تطمئنّ من انزعاجها واستقرارها.

(٢٧) والنفس كانت فى مأواها الأصلى حيّة مختارة لطيفة قادرة عالمة بقوّة مبدعها سائحة فى عالمها فرحانة مطمئنّة عند بارئها فى مقعد صدل عند مليك مقتدر، وهى الجنّة التى كان فيها ابوها العقلى وأمّها النفسية آدم وحواء. يا آدُم اسكن انت وزوجك الجنّة وكُلا منها رَغَداً حيث شئتما.

(٢٨) فاذا هبطت النفس عن عالمها ومأواها وجنّة ربّها لخطيئة وقعت من أبيها وأمّها وانحطّت الى السفل وحوّلت الى هذا العالم، انقلبت حياتها موتاً ونورها ظلمةً وتبدّلت قدرتها عجزاً واختيارها اضطراراً واستقرارها اضطراباً ولطافتها كثافةً، وزالت كرامتها وشرفها وكمالها الى المذلّة والخسّة والنقص، وانجرّت جمعيتها ووحدتها الى التفرقة والكثرة.

(29) [The soul is] like someone who is stricken by an intense illness and becomes feverish. From him many alien traces become manifest, like intense heat, which is the mark of fire, and great heaviness, which is the attribute of earthiness. His extremities become swollen and irritated, and this is from air. Perspiration flows from his pores and vessels, like drops of rain. Thus it goes until he returns to his precedent, original state. So, these generated things[10] cease to exist little by little, until they disappear entirely as if they had never been. Thus he finally becomes as he was at first.

(30) So also is the state of the soul in her falling away from her original level and configuration, inasmuch as diverse affairs—like the potencies, the pillars,[11] and the organs—come into being from her when deficiency and weakness adhere to her. In the same way, the spheres, elements, and compound things are configured from the Universal Soul when she descends from the station of the Intellect to the station of nature, since distance from the original homestead stirs up weakness, impairment, multiplicity, and division. So, when she returns to her original place of return, multiplicity and dispersion disappear from her entirely, as if they had never been.

(31) Such is the state in everything that departs from its original location for an alien location. It will be impaired and dispersed until it goes back to its location. Do you not see that water in its original home is gathered, settled, at rest, and limpid, such that forms and imprints are seen within it? When it goes to the confines of fire, gatheredness alters to dispersion, heaviness to lightness, rest to agitation, limpidness to opacity, and straightness to twistedness. Then, when it goes back to its home, the alien states disappear and the original state returns. So also should the other pillars be gauged in all plants and animals—like the fish in the location of the salamander and the salamander in the location of the fish.[12]

(٢٩) كمن عرض له مرض شـديد وحمّ، فظهر منه آثار كثيرة غريبة كالحرارة الشـديدة وهى علامة النار، والثقـل العظيم وهو صفة الأرضية. وتورّمت أطرافه وتهيّجت وهو من الهواء، وسال العرل من مسامّه وعروقه كقطرات المطر. هكذا الى أن يعود الى الحالة السابقة الأصلية. فينعدم منه هذه التولّدات شيئاً فشـيئاً الى أن تزول بالكلية كأنّها لم تكن أصلاً، فصار أخيراً كما كان أولاً.

(٣٠) فهكذا حال النفس فى سـقوطها عن مرتبتها ونشأتها الأصلية حيث تكوّنت منها أمور مختلفة كالقوى والأركان والأعضاء عند نقصانها وضعفها الذى يلحقها، كما نشـأت من النفس الكليـة الأفلاك والعناصر والمركّبات عند نزولها من مقام العقل الى مقام الطبيعة، اذ البعد عن الموطن الأصلـى مثار الضعف والآفة والكثرة والانقسـام. فاذا عادت الى معادها الأصلى زالت الكثرة والتفرقة عنها بالكلية كأنّها لم تكن.

(٣١) وهكـذا الحال فى كلّ شـئ زال عن مكانـه الأصلى الى مكان غريـب. يكون مع آفة وتفرقة الى أن يعود الى مكانه. أَوَلا ترى الماء كيف يكون مجموعاً فى مأواه الأصلى ذا قرار واطمينان وصفاء يتراءى فيه الصور والنقوش. واذا انتقل الى حيّـز النار تبدّلت الجمعية بالتفرقة والثقل بالخفّة والاطمينان بالاضطراب والصفاء بالكدورة والاسـتقامة بالاعوجاج. ثم اذا رجـع الى مأواه زالت الأحوال الغريبة وعـادت الحالة الأصلية. وكذا القيـاس فى غيره مـن الأركان فى كلّ نبات وحيوان كالسـمك فى مكان السمندر والسمندر فى مكان السمك.

# Chapter Three

## *That the source of the soul's imprisonment in this world and the lowest level and of her being deprived from climbing to the highest world is the elemental body*

(32) Know that the soul in this body is like a sheep with three legs bound, and one free.[13]

(33) The clarification of this is that the soul, when she first descends to this cosmos, is in the level of sheer hylicity, imprisoned [1] by the gate of natural bodiment against moving from location to location except with a potency external to her essence that moves her in one direction; [2] by the gate of growth and nourishment against moving in measure except with an external potency that attracts another body to her and moves her correspondingly in her sides and extremities; [3] by the gate of animality against diverse volitional movements in locational directions except with a sensate potency, a yearning, and a desire; and [4] by the gate of humanness and angelness against moving within the imaginal and intellective meanings and roaming in the world of the Absent except with a potency external to the potencies of this cosmos.

(34) When she undergoes transition to the degree of nature, one of her four legs is released, so that by the demand of nature she moves from one location to another location according to a single pathway. When she passes beyond the degree of nature to the degree of plants, her second leg is also released, so that she moves from one measure to another measure through her growth potency. When she undergoes transition to the degree of animals, her third leg is also released, so she can move toward that which is agreeable to her animal constitution, seek it through appetite, and, through wrath, move away from and flee from what is incompatible with her constitution.

(35) She still remains prevented by her fourth leg from arriving at the absent forms that she conceptualizes and imagines—those for *which the souls have appetite and which the* inward *eyes enjoy* [43:71] (namely, what "no eye has seen and no ear has heard"[14] in this cosmos)—until *God decrees an affair that was done* [8:42, 44]. Then she comes to possess a

## الفصل الثالث

### فى أنّ منشأ احتباس النفس فى الدنيا والمرتبة السفلى وحرمانها عن الارتقاء الى العالم الأعلى هو البدن العنصرى

(٣٢) اعلم أنّ مثل النفس فى هذا البدن كمثل شاة قيّدت بثلاثة أرجل وأطلقت بواحدة.

(٣٣) وبيان ذلك أنّ النفس فى أوّل نزولها الى هذا العالم كانت فى مرتبة الهيولية المحضة محبوسة فى باب الجسمية الطبيعية عن الحركة من مكان الى مكان الا بقوّة خارجة عن ذاتها يحرّكها فى جهة واحدة، وفى باب النموّ والتغذية عن الحركة المقدارية الا بقوّة خارجة يجذب جسماً آخر اليها ويحرّكها فى جوانبها وأطرافها على التناسب، وفى باب الحيوانية عن الحركات الإرادية المختلفة فى الجهات المكانية الا بقوّة حسّاسة وشول وإرادة، وفى باب الانسانية والملكية عن الحركة فى المعانى المثالية والعقلية والسياحة فى عالم الغيب الا بقوّة خارجة عن قوى هذا العالم.

(٣٤) فاذا انتقلت الى درجة الطبيعة أطلقت إحدى قوائمها الأربع فتحرّكت من مكان الى مكان آخر بمقتضى الطبيعة على سمت واحد. ثم اذا تجاوزت من درجة الطبيعة الى درجة النبات أطلقت رجلها الثانية أيضاً فتحرّكت من مقدار الى مقدار بقوّتها النامية. واذا انتقلت الى درجة الحيوان أطلقت رجلها الثالثة أيضاً فلها أن تتحرّك الى ما يلائم مزاجها الحيوانى ويطلبه بالشهوة وتتحرّك عن ما ينافى مزاجها ويهرب عنه بالغضب.

(٣٥) وبقيت برجلها الرابعة ممنوعة عن الوصول الى ما تتصوّرها وتتخيّلها من الصور الغيبية التى تشتهيها الأنفس وتلذّ الأعين الباطنة مما لا عين رأت ولا أذن سمعت فى هذا العالم الى ان يقضى الله أمراً كان

Sovereigntarial potency through which she roams in the space of the Sovereignty, *making* her *dwelling place wherever* she *wills in the Garden* [39:74].

(36) Thus it becomes manifest that in this cosmos, the soul is released by three of her legs and imprisoned by one. When she arrived at the level of nature, she was released by one. When she went beyond to the growth potency, she was released by two. When she passed on to the animal potency, she was let go, so she walked wherever she desired in this earth. In the same way, when she arrives at the potency of the Sovereignty, she obtains total release and unmixed freedom because of the potency of her perfection, her independence in roaming and flying in the space of the Kingdom and the Sovereignty, [her] vision of the signs of the Lord in the horizons and the souls, and [her] arrival at the stations and degrees of the Kingdom and Sovereignty that come to be for the types of angels in the world of inwardness and the absent—[types] that are like the varieties of animals in the world of outwardness and the witnessed.

(37) In the divine scripture, allusion is made to the first levels in His words, *who appointed the angels to be messengers having wings two, three, and four; He increases in creation what He wills* [35:1]. [He alludes] to the second levels with His words, *God has created every beast from water, and some of them walk upon their bellies, some walk upon two feet, and some walk upon four feet; God creates what He wills* [24:45].

(38) *A Fine Point and Allusion.* Know that the soul is let loose in this bodily world with respect to one level and one potency—that is, her reflective and imaginal potency, which is what belongs to her in her essence. She is imprisoned with respect to three levels, which are the levels of her animal, vegetal, and inanimate potencies, which belong to her with respect to the body. This is the reverse of what we just mentioned about her release from the three legs and her imprisonment by one leg, because the standpoint in the two is different. Here the discussion is according to the substance of the soul in the descent from the world of holiness to

مفعولاً، فتكون ذات قوّة ملكوتية تسيح بها فى فضاء الملكوت وتتبوّء من الجنّة حيث تشاء.

(٣٦) فظهر أنّ النفس فى هذا العالم مطلقة بثلاثة أرجل محبوسة بواحدة. فكما أنّها اذا وصلت الى مرتبة الطبيعة أطلقت بواحدة، واذا تعدّت الى القوّة النامية أطلقت بإثنتين، واذا جاوزت الى القوّة الحيوانية أرسلت، فمشت حيث أرادت فى هذه الأرض، فاذا بلغت الى القوّة الملكوتية يحصل لها الانطلال الكلى والحرّية الصرفة بسبب قوّة كمالها واستقلالها فى السياحة والطيران فى فضاء الملك والملكوت ورؤية آيات الربّ تعالى فى الآفال وفى الأنفس والوصول الى المقامات والدرجات المُلْكية والملكوتية الحاصلة لقبائل من الملائكة فى عالم الباطن والغيب على مثال أصناف الحيوان فى عالم الظاهر والشهادة.

(٣٧) وأشير فى الصحيفة الالهية الى المراتب الأولى بقوله: جاعل الملائكة رسلاً أُولِى أجنحة مَثْنى وثلاث ورباع يزيد فى الخلق ما يشاء، والى المراتب الثانية بقوله تعالى: والله خلق كلَّ دابّة من ماء فمنهم من يمشى على بطنه ومنهم من يمشى على رجليه ومنهم من يمشى على أربع يخلق الله ما يشاء.

(٣٨) نكتة وإشارة. اعلم أنّ انحلال النفس فى هذا العالم الجسمانى بحسب مرتبة واحدة وقوّة واحدة وهى قوّتها الفكرية والخيالية وهى ما لها فى ذاتها. وانحباسها بحسب ثلاث مراتب هى مراتب قواها الحيوانية والنباتية والجمادية، وهى مالها بحسب البدن على عكس ما ذكرنا آنفاً من انطلاقها بثلاثة أرجل وانحباسها برجل واحدة، لأنّ الاعتبار فيهما مختلف لأنّ الكلام ههنا بحسب جوهر النفس فى النزول عن عالم القدس الى هذا

this cosmos. In the preceding, it was according to the root of her matter in the climb and ascent from this cosmos to the world of holiness. From one of the two standpoints, she is approaching, and from the other, turning away.

(39) The Real (glorious and high exalted is He) alludes to these levels and legs belonging to the human soul in this cosmos from the standpoint mentioned here in that He created four varieties of elemental beings. Each is overcome by certain bonds and veils pertaining to the levels of imprisonment and the stumbling places of the legs. These are inanimate things, plants, animals, and man. Thereby it is known and unveiled that the substance of man's essence is released with respect to the root of the innate disposition—if he is not defiled by unbelief and acts of disobedience—because he is nearer than the others to deliverance from imprisonment in the world of natural defilements, vegetal filths, and animal disquiets.

(40) Moreover, He confirmed the allusion by creating among the animals alone—aside from the beings in an unqualified sense—four varieties belonging to four levels that are fixed in man. Thus, when the possessors of illuminated insights ponder them, they will come to know the manner in which the folk of hellfire are veiled and imprisoned in dark veils and, with respect to their reliance upon this cosmos and its three beings, have fallen into three *darknesses, one above another* [24:40], [which prevent them] from witnessing the encounter with God and the world of holiness. [And they will come to know] the manner in which the faces of the folk of mercy are unveiled, how they are released to the highest world and are not veiled from God.

(41) This is because the mark of being opened up and released is realized only in one of these four varieties, which is man, not in the other three varieties—I mean the dumb beasts, the wild animals, and the birds. In [man] is the mark of the folk of the Garden and forgiveness, those who are "hairless, beardless, [eyes] daubed with kohl."[15] The others have the mark of the imprisoned and the jailed, which is to be veiled by coverings and darknesses and to be obstructed by fetters on the necks and ties on the hands and the legs. *Surely We have put on their necks fetters up to the chins,*

العالم وفى السابق بحسب سِنْخ مادّتها فى الترقّى والعروج عن هذا العالم الى عالم القدس. فهى فى أحد الاعتبارين مقبلة وفى الآخر مدبرة.

(٣٩) فالحقّ سبحانه وتعالى أشار الى هذه المراتب والأقدام للنفس الانسانية فى هذا العالم بالاعتبار المذكور ههنا بأن خلق فى الأكوان العنصرية أصنافاً أربعة غلب فى كل منها بعض القيود والحجب من مراتب الاحتباس ومزلات الأقدام هى الجماد والنبات والحيوان والانسان، ليعلم وينكشف انطلال جوهر ذات الانسان بحسب أصل الفطرة اذا لم يتدنّس بالكفر والمعاصى لأنّه أقرب منها الى الخلاص من الاحتباس فى عالم الأدناس الطبيعية والأرجاس النباتية والوساوس الحيوانية.

(٤٠) بل آكد فى الاشارة بأن خلق فى الحيوان فقط فضلاً عن الأكوان مطلقاً أصنافاً أربعة لمراتب أربع ثابتة فى الانسان، ليعلم أولو البصائر المستنيرة اذا تدبّر فيها كيفية احتجاب أهل الجحيم واحتباسهم فى حجب ظلمانية ووقوعهم فى ظلمات ثلاث بعضها فول بعض حسب ركونهم الى هذا العالم وأكوانه الثلاثة عن مشاهدة لقاء الله وعالم القدس وكيفية انكشاف وجوه أهل الرحمة وانطلاقهم الى العالم الأعلى وعدم احتجابهم عن الله.

(٤١) حيث لم يتحقّق علامة الانفتاح والطلاقة الا فى واحد من هذه الأصناف الأربعة وهو الانسان دون الأصناف الثلاثة، أعنى البهائم والوحوش والطيور. ففيه علامة أهل الجنّة والمغفرة الذين هم جُرْدٌ مُرْدٌ مكحّلون. ولغيره علامة المحبوسين والمسجونين وهى الاحتجاب بالأغشية والظلمات والانسداد بالأغلال فى الأعنال والعقد فى الأيدى والأرجل. إنّا جعلنا فى أعناقهم أغلالاً فهى الى الأذقان فهم مقمحون

*so they bear their heads high, and We have put before them an obstruction, and behind them an obstruction; and We have covered them, so they do not see* [36:8–9]. *Fettered are their hands, and cursed are they for what they have said* [5:64].

(42) *Another Fine Point,* alluding to what was mentioned concerning the soul's becoming bound in this cosmos by the three bonds of her three feet. It is this: Within each of the three animals other than man are found three of the marks of the folk of hellfire and chastisement, but within man are found three marks counter to these—that is, marks of the folk of the Garden and forgiveness.

(43) For, in each [animal] are found three ties: One is the tie of blindness in the eyes, lest they witness God's signs and read the book of the horizons and the souls. Another is the tie of deafness in the ears, lest they hear the clarification and demonstration and accept the admonitions and counselings. Third is the tie of ignorance and forgetfulness in the hearts. *They have hearts with which they do not understand, they have eyes with which they do not see, they have ears with which they do not hear* [7:179].

(44) These three ties have three other ties giving witness to them. One is the tie of the tongue, which gives witness to the deafness of the ears, for the tongue is like the vicegerent of the ear. Second is the tie of the two hands, giving witness to the blindness of the eyes—*Fettered are their hands, and cursed are they for what they have said* [5:64]—for the writing hand is like the eye's vicegerent. Third is the tie of being inverted and turned over in the body, for the body is the soul's vicegerent, so its being inverted is the proof of her being inverted, just as the curve of the sheath is proof of the sword's curve.

(45) *Another Fine Point.* These three animals are in the form of the book of the depraved: *Surely the book of the depraved is in Sijjīn* [83:7]. This is because some of them are in the form of *him who is given his book in his left hand* [69:25], and this is the form of the beasts, the possessors of "twisted" legs—that is, distorted and prevented from writing, so they are incapable of gaining perfection through the activities of the folk of perfection.

(46) Some of them are in the form of *him who is given his book behind his back* [84:10]. This is like the form of the birds.

وجعلنا من بين أيديهم سدّاً ومن خلفهم سدّاً فأغشيناهم فهم لا يبصرون. غلّت أيديهم ولعنوا بما قالوا.

(٤٢) نكتة اخرى. للاشارة الى ما ذكر من تقيّد النفس فى هذا العالم بقيود ثلاثة لأقدامها الثلاث. هى أن فى كل واحد من الحيوانات الثلاثة سوى الإنسان يوجد ثلاث علامات من علامات أهل الجحيم والعذاب، وفى الانسان ثلاث علامات مقابلة لها من علامات أهل الجنّة والمغفرة.

(٤٣) فإنّ لكل واحد منها يوجد ثلاث عقد. إحداها عقدة العمى فى الأعين من مشاهدة آيات الله وقراءة كتاب الآفال والأنفس. والأخرى عقدة الصمم فى الأذن من استماع البيان والبرهان وقبول المواعظ والنصائح. والثالثة عقدة الجهل والنسيان على القلوب. لهم قلوب لا يفقهون بها ولهم أعين لا يبصرون بها ولهم آذان لا يسمعون بها.

(٤٤) ولهذه العقد الثلاث ثلاث عقد أخرى شاهدة عليها. إحداها عقدة اللسان شاهدة على صمم الأذن، فإنّ اللسان كخليفة الأذن. والثانية عقدة اليدين شاهدة على عمى العين. غلّت أيديهم ولعنوا بما قالوا، فإنّ اليد الكاتبة كخليفة العين. والثالثة عقدة الانتكاس والانقلاب فى البدن، فإنّ البدن خليفة النفس، فانتكاسه دليل انتكاسها كما أنّ انحناء الغلاف دليل لانحناء السيف.

(٤٥) نكتة أخرى. هذه الحيوانات الثلاثة على صورة كتاب الفجّار. إنّ كتاب الفجّار لفى سجّين. وذلك لأنّ بعضاً منها على صورة من أوتى كتابه بشماله، وهى صورة الدوابّ ذوات القوائم المعوّجة، يعنى المنحرفة الممنوعة عن الكتابة، فهى عاجزة عن الاستكمال بأفاعيل أهل الكمال.

(٤٦) ومنها على صورة من أوتى كتابه وراء ظهره، وهى كصورة الطيور.

(47) Some are in the form of the book of the folk of Sijjīn, like the snakes that are in the guise of the folk of chastisement, because they are imprisoned in the depths of the earth, their hands and legs severed.

(48) As for the fourth animal, which is man, his form is the form of *him who is given his book in his right hand* [17:71], so these are the pious, the Illiyyūn. For the human form is elevated toward the high direction, ennobled, and purified of the filths of the elemental things and the dung and impurities of the beasts. Within it are plain signifiers of the nobility of its writer's soul, while those brought nigh witness to its way station with the King, the Real, the Clear, and with the world of the Highest Sovereignty, with respect to this innate disposition. He has alluded to this with His words, *Surely the book of the pious is in Illiyyūn; and what shall teach you what Illiyyūn is? A book engraved, witnessed by those brought nigh* [83:18–21]. This signifies that, in his original substance, man has the preparedness to climb up to the highest world and the presence of those brought nigh and to sit in *a seat of truthfulness* [54:55] with the angels, *the prophets, [. . .] the witnesses, and the worthy* [4:69].

(49) This happens when he travels God's road, walks straight on the straight path, flies with the wings of the cherubim, and does not sink down from the degree of the human form to the degree of the animals whose heads are inverted, whose bodies are turned over, and whose hands and legs are fettered. Otherwise, the mere outward form is not sufficient to arrive at the level of afterworldly felicity and to attain sempiternal nobility, for blameworthy animals are not those that are dumb beasts with respect to form and guise. On the contrary, the blameworthy are only those who are dumb beasts in the form of man. *They are but as the cattle; nay, they are further astray from the road* [25:44]. So, although with respect to body, ignorant and depraved man may have the most beautiful aspect in form, with respect to the soul's ignorance he has the ugliest aspect in meaning.

(٤٧) ومنهـا ما علـى صورة كتاب أهل السـجّين كالهوامّ التى على هيئة أهل العذاب لانحباسها فى قعر الأرض مقطّعة الأيدى والأرجل.

(٤٨) وأمّا الحيوان الرابع الذى هو الانسان فصورته صورة من أوتى كتابه بيمينه، فهم الأبرار العلّيّون، فإنّ الصورة الانسـانية مرفوعة الى جهة العلوّ مكرّمة مطهّرة عن أرجاس العنصريات وأرواث الدوابّ ونجاسـاتها. فيها دلائل واضحة على كرامة نفس كاتبها وشـهادة المقرّبين على منزلتها عند الملك الحقّ المبين وعالم ملكوته الأعلى بحسـب هذه الفطرة كما أشير اليـه بقوله تعـالى: انّ كتاب الأبرار لفى علّيّين ومـا أدراك ما علّيّون كتاب مرقوم يشـهده المقرّبون. فهذه دالّة على أنّ للانسـان فى جوهره الأصلى اسـتعداد الارتقـاء الى العالم الأعلـى وحضور المقرّبين والقعـود فى مقعد صدل مع الملائكة والنبيين والشهداء والصالحين.

(٤٩) وذلك اذا سـلك سبيل الله واستقام على الصراط المستقيم وطار بأجنحـة الكروبيين ولم ينحطّ عن درجتها الى درجة الحيوانات المنتكسـة الـرؤوس، المقلوبـة الأبـدان، المغلولـة الأيـدى والأرجـل. والا فمجرّد الصـورة الظاهرة غير كافية فى الوصول الى رتبة السـعادة الأخروية ونيل الكرامـة السرمدية، فإنّ المذموم من الحيوانات ليس ما هو بهيمة بحسـب الصورة والهيئة بل إنّما المذموم من هو بهيمة فى صورة الانسان. إن هم الا كالأنعام بل هم أضلّ سـبيلاً. فالجاهل والفاجر من الانسـان وإن كان من جهة البدن على أحسـن وجه فى الصورة فهـو من جهة جهل النفس على أقبح وجه فى المعنى.

## Chapter Four

*On the divine solicitude toward man and His firm cord and His most reliable handle; when the soul attaches herself to it and holds fast, she stands up from her natural, vegetal, and animal stumbling and slipping*

(50) This is because people stand up from the stumbling places of the legs and ascend to the world of the Sovereignty and the encounter with God only with the assistance of the heavenly books and the casting of the lordly words in one of three manners. One is to witness explicit revelation because of conjunction with the world of the highest, intellective Sovereignty. The middle is to behold revelation and witness the revealing angel from behind the veil of sensory imaginalization, because of conjunction with the world of the middlemost, soulish, heavenly Sovereignty. The nethermost is to hear the signs and warnings with respect to conjunction with the nethermost, mortal, earthly Sovereignty. These three levels are alluded to in His words, *It belongs to no mortal that God should speak to him save by revelation, or from behind a veil, or that He send a messenger* [42:51].

(51) The gates that are the means of being aware of and perceiving these words and signs are hearing, eyesight, and heart, specifically. This is why the causes of knowledge of God and the origins of gaining cognizance of His Sovereignty arrive at the human essence by these three paths, whose number corresponds to the levels of the heavenly books sent down upon three communities—the Torah for the Jews, the Gospel for the Christians, and the Furqān for the Muslims.

(52) From this allusion is known that the strongest of the causes for the soul's deliverance from the world of the darknesses, by which man ascends to the highest world, is God's sending forth the prophets and sending down to them revelation and angels, and their guiding the creatures so *that the possessors of minds may ponder His signs* in the horizons and the souls, *and remember* [38:29]. Thus He says, *We shall show them Our signs in the horizons and in their souls until it becomes clear to them that He is the Real* [41:53].

## الفصل الرابع

### فى العناية الالهية للانسان وحبله المتين وعروته الوثقى التى اذا تعلّقت النفس بها واستمسكت قامت عن عثراتها وزلّاتها الطبيعية والنباتية والحيوانية

(٥٠) وذلك لأنّ الناس إنّما يقومون من مزالّ الأقدام ويعرجون الى عالم الملكوت ولقاء الله تعالى بإمداد الكتب السماوية وإلقاء الكلمات الربّانية على أحد الوجوه الثلاثة التى أحدها مشاهدة الوحى الصريح بسبب الاتّصال بعالم الملكوت الأعلى العقلانى. وأوسطها ملاحظة الوحى ومشاهدة المَلَك الموحى من وراء حجاب التمثيل الحسّى بسبب الاتّصال بعالم الملكوت الأوسط النفسانى السماوى. وأدناها استماع الآيات والنذر من جهة الاتّصال بالملكوت الأدنى البشرى الأرضى. والى هذه المراتب الثلاث أشير فى قوله تعالى: وما كان لبشر أن يكلّمه الله الا وحياً أو من وراء حجاب أو يرسل رسولاً.

(٥١) والأبواب التى تكون مشاعر ومدارك لهذه الكلمات والآيات هى السمع والبصر والفؤاد خاصّة. ولهذا يكون أسباب معرفة الله ومبادئ الاطّلاع على ملكوته واردة على ذات الانسان على هذه الطرل الثلاث التى يكون عددها بإزاء مراتب الكتب السماوية المنزلة على ثلاث أمم، وهى التوراة لليهود والانجيل للنصارى والفرقان للمسلمين.

(٥٢) فعلم من هذه الاشارة أنّ أقوى الأسباب لخلاص النفس من عالم الظلمات التى يعرج بها الانسان الى العالم الأعلى هى بعثة الأنبياء من الله وإنزال الوحى والملائكة اليهم وهدايتهم للخلق ليدّبّروا آياته فى الآفال والأنفس وليتذكّر أُولو الألباب، كما فى قوله تعالى: سنريهم آياتنا

So, these signs are God's firm cord and His most reliable handle. When the human soul holds fast to them, she stands up from her slips and the three mentioned stumbles of her legs through God's solicitude and His beautiful success-giving.

# Chapter Five

*On the clarification of the signs of the horizons and the souls*

(53) Know that God created heaven and made it like a veil midway between this world and the other world and like a veil of shadow between light and darkness. Hence it has a portion of oneness and completeness and a portion of what is counter to both. With respect to the form of its essence, its measure, its qualities, and its settled accidents, it is actual. There is no potency within it save relations and positions, and these are among the weakest of accidents adhering to a thing and the most external to its essence and substance. So, celestial occurrences are merely relational affairs that change and turn into each other. Mutual opposition and corruption happen among them in their least purpose and most insignificant attribute, because God has divided them into four divisions in the likeness of the elements—like the quarters of spring, summer, autumn, and winter. The first quarter is like air, the second like fire, the third like earth, and the fourth like water.[16]

(54) Then He ordered the cosmos as an empire is ordered.[17] He appointed from among His servants an elect, who are the angels, the sitting companions of the Real in remembrance and glorification.[18] They *do not claim to be too great to serve Him, neither grow weary, glorifying Him by night and in the daytime and never failing* [21:19–20]. Then He took a veil-keeper from among the cherubim, and He gave it His knowledge concerning His creation, which is a differentiated knowledge within undifferentiation. So His knowledge disclosed itself to it from His name Knowing. He named it "Nūn" and a "greatest spirit."[19] It remains forever retired in the Presence of His knowledge, and it is the head of the divine registry.

(55) Then He took an angel-scribe, teaching it the knowledge of differentiation from the undifferentiated knowledge by means of Nūn. This angel is the scribe of His registry, and He disclosed Himself to it from His name Powerful. He set its gaze toward the world of Registering

فى الآفال وفى أنفسهم حتّى يتبيّن لهم أنّه الحقّ. فهذه الآيات هى حبل الله المتين وعروته الوثقى التى اذا استمسكت بها النفس الانسانية قامت من عثراتها وزلات أقدامها الثلاث المذكورة بعناية الله وحسن توفيقه.

## الفصل الخامس

### فى بيان آيات الآفال والأنفس

(٥٣) اعلم أنّ الله تعالى خلق السماء وجعلها بمنزلة حجاب متوسّط بين هذا العالم والعالم الآخر وبمنزلة حجاب الظلّ بين النور والظلمة. فلها نصيب من الوحدة والتمامية ونصيب من مقابل كلّ واحد منهما. فهى بحسب صورة ذاتها ومقدارها وكيفياتها وأعراضها القارّة بالفعل، وليس فيها قوّة الا النسب والأوضاع، وهى من أضعف الأعراض اللاحقة بالشئ وأخرجها عن ذاته وجوهره. فالحوادث الفلكية هى مجرّد أمور نسبية يتغيّر وينقلب بعضها الى بعض، ويقع فيها التضادّ والتفاسد فى أسهل غرض وأيسر صفة منها، اذ قد قسمها الله أقساماً أربعة على مثال العناصر كالأرباع الربيعية والصيفية والخريفية والشتوية. فالربع الاوّل كمثال الهواء والثانى مثال النار والثالث مثال الأرض والرابع مثال الماء.

(٥٤) ثم رتّب العالم ترتيب المملكة. فجعل خواصّ من عباده، وهم الملائكة جلساء الحقّ بالذكر والتسبيح، لا يستكبرون عن عبادته ولا يستحسرون يسبّحون الليل والنهار لا يفترون. ثمّ اتّخذ حاجباً من الكرّوبيين واحداً أعطاه علمه فى خلقه، وهو علم مفصّل فى إجمال. فعلمه كان تجلّى له من اسمه العليم. وسمّاه نوناً وروحاً أعظم. فلا يزال معتكفاً فى حضرة علمه تعالى وهو رأس الديوان الالهى.

(٥٥) ثمّ اتّخذ مَلَكاً كاتباً فيعلّمه علم التفصيل من العلم الاجمالى بواسطة النون. فهذا الملك كاتب ديوانه وتجلّى له من اسمه القادر فجعل

and Inscribing, and He named it the "Highest Pen" and the "World of His Decree."[20] Then He created for it an Emerald Tablet and He commanded it to write everything that He willed to bring to pass in His creation until the Day of Requital, making [the Tablet] the world of His Measuring Out. Thus *everything* is *in a measuring out* [54:49], and *everything small and large is inscribed* [54:53] in the Preserved Tablet. In relation to [the Pen] He gave it the status of a student in relation to a teacher.

(56) It [that is, the Pen][21] has self-disclosures from the Real both without and with intermediary, but Nūn has only one self-disclosure, in a more eminent station. God commanded Nūn to give ink to the Pen through 360 sciences from among the sciences of undifferentiation. Under each science are differentiations that no one encompasses but God or whichever of His servants that He wills. Because of this reality, God made the sphere with 360 degrees; each degree is an undifferentiated summation because of what it comprises—that is, the differentiations of the minutes, the seconds, the thirds, and so on as far as God wills in what becomes manifest in His creation until the day of resurrection.

(57) Then God commanded that [the Pen] appoint over the world of Creation twelve administrators whose seat should be in the Towers [that is, the constellations] of the furthest sphere, like the towers of the wall [of a city]. Each Tower is a residence for one of these twelve administrators. God lifted the veil between them and the Preserved Tablet, so they saw within it the forms of all the creatures and beings; within it were inscribed their names, their provisions, and what the Real willed to bring out by their hands in the world of Creation until the day of resurrection. All of this was imprinted and engraved in their souls, and they came to know it.

(58) Then God commanded these administrators to appoint deputies and lieutenants for themselves in the seven heavens—in each heaven a lieutenant—like veil-keepers for them. These look over what is advantageous for the elemental world through what the administrators cast to them and command them. These are God's words, *He revealed in each heaven its command* [41:12]. God made the bodies of these lieutenant planets luminous, circular bodies, and He blew into them soulish spirits. He sent them down into these seven heavens—one in each heaven. He also appointed for each lieutenant one of the swift-moving spheres in which to swim,

نظره الى عالم التدوين والتسطير وسمّاه القلم الأعلى وعالم قضائه. ثم خلق له لوحاً زمرّديّاً وأمره أن يكتب فيه جميع ما شاء أن يُجريه فى خلقه الى يوم الدين، وجعله عالم قدره. فكلّ شى بقدر، وكلّ صغير وكبير مستطر فى اللوح المحفوظ. وأنزله منه منزلة التلميذ من الأستاذ.

(٥٦) فله تجلّيات من الحقّ بلا واسطة وبواسطة، وليس للنون سوى تجلٍّ واحد فى مقام أشرف. فأمر الله النون أن يمُدّ القلم بثلاثمائة وستّين علماً من علوم الاجمال تحت كلّ علم تفاصيل لا يحيط بها الا الله أو من شاء من عباده. ولهذه الحقيقة جعل الله الفلك بثلاثمائة وستّين درجة، كلّ درجة مجملة لما يحتوى عليه من تفاصيل الدقائق والثوانى والثوالث الى ما شاء الله ممّا يظهر فى خلقه الى يوم القيامة.

(٥٧) ثم أمر الله سبحانه أن يولّى على عالم الخلق إثنى عشر والياً يكون مقرّهم فى بروج الفلك الأقصى مثل أبراج السور، كل برج مسكناً لأحد هذه الولاة الاثنى عشر، ورفع الله الحجاب بينهم وبين اللوح المحفوظ فرأوا فيه صور الخلائق كلّهم والكائنات مستطراً فيه أسماؤهم وأرزاقهم وما شاء الحقّ أن يخرج به على أيديهم فى عالم الخلق الى يوم القيامة. فانتقش وارتقم ذلك كلّه فى نفوسهم وعلموه.

(٥٨) ثم أمر الله لهؤلاء الولاة أن يجعلوا الهم نوّاباً ونقباء فى السموات السبع فى كل سماء نقيباً كالحاجب لهم أن ينظر فى مصالح العالم العنصرى بما يلقى اليهم هؤلاء الولاة ويأمرونهم به، وهو قوله تعالى: وأوحى فى كلّ سماء أمرها. وجعل الله أجسام هذه الكواكب النقباء أجساماً نيرّة مستديرة ونفخ فيها أرواحاً نفسانياً. وأنزلها فى هذه السموات السبع فى كلّ سماء واحد. وجعل أيضاً لكل نقيب فلكاً يسبح فيه من الأفلاك السريعة الحركة

like epicycles and eccentrics, which, for them, are like chargers for riders. For they dominate over the occurrences of the world and supervise it through God's light. They also have custodians and helpers who exceed one thousand. Each of them has a sphere that includes other spheres and takes them circling around the empire once every day and night, so nothing whatsoever of the empire eludes them in those heavens and the earth.

(59) So the administrators, the lieutenants, and the custodians circle in the service of those deputies and scribes who have retired to the gate of the mercy of God, the most magnificent King. In the same way, it is appropriate that the King supervise the folk of His empire every day. He says, *Each day He is upon some task* [55:29], because *Everyone in the heavens and the earth asks of Him* [55:29] with the tongue of its state or its speech.[22] He gives to each what establishes it, perfects it, and preserves it from what would corrupt it and make it disappear. *The preservation* of the cosmos *does not burden Him, and He is the high, the magnificent* [2:255]. He has no occupation except with [the empire]. Thus has the divine wont come to pass. *He governs the affair from the heaven to the earth, then it ascends to Him* [32:5]. *He governs the affair, He differentiates the signs, that perhaps you will be certain of the encounter with your Lord* [13:2].

(60) For we are what is intended from the cosmos, and all these administrators, lieutenants, custodians, and veil-keepers are subjected for our sake. God says, *And He subjected to you what is in the heavens and what is in the earth, all together* [45:13]. God sent down in the Torah, "O son of Adam, I created the things for you, and I created you for Me."

(61) Since God put the reins of the affairs of this cosmos in the hands of these, and since He made the helpers and custodians subjected to these administrators, He made their subjection accord with layers and levels.[23] Among them are the folk of ascent and descent by night and day, from us to the Real and from the Real to us, in every morning and evening. Among them are those who ask forgiveness for everyone in the earth. Among them are those entrusted with conveying the shariᶜas and the rulings. Among them are those entrusted with inspirations and suggestions and those

كالتداويـر والخوارج هى لهم كالجوادّ للراكـب، اذ كان لهم التصرّف فى حوادث العالم والاستشراف عليه بنور الله. ولهم سدنة وأعوان يزيدون علـى الألف، وللكلّ فلك يشتمل على أفلاك يدور بهم على المملكة فى كلّ يوم وليلة مرّة. فلا يفوتهم شئ من المملكة أصلاً من تلك السموات والأرض.

(٥٩) فتدور الولاة والنقباء والسدنة كلّهم فى خدمة هؤلاء النوّاب والكتّاب العاكفين على باب رحمة الله المَلك الأعظم. وهكذا ينبغى أن يكون المَلك يستشرف كلّ يوم علـى أهلَ مملكته. يقول كلَّ يوم هو فى شأن، لأنّه يسأله كلّ من فى السموات والأرض بلسان حاله او مقاله. فهو يعطيه ما يقوّمه ويكمله ويحفظه عمّا يفسده ويزيله. ولا يؤوده حفظ العالم وهو العلى العظيم، فماله شغل الا بها. هكذا جرت السنّة الالهية. يدبّر الأمر من السماء الى الأرض ثمّ يعرج اليه. يدّبر الأمر يفصّل الآيات لعلّكم بلقاء ربّكم توقنون.

(٦٠) اذ كنّا المقصود من العالم، وكلّ من هؤلاء الولاة والنقباء والسدنة والحجّاب مسخّرون فى حقّنا. قال الله سبحانه: وسخّر لكم ما فى السموات وما فى الأرض جميعاً. وأنزل الله فى التوراة يابنَ آدم خلقتُ الأشياء من أجلك وخلقتك من أجلى.

(٦١) ولمّا جعل الله زمام أمور هذا العالم تحت أيدى هؤلاء وجعل أعواناً وسدنة مسخّرة تحت هؤلاء الولاة فجعل تسخيرهم على طبقات ومراتب. فمنهم أهل العروج والنزول بالليل والنهار منّا الى الحقّ ومن الحقّ الينا فى كلّ صباح ومساء، ومنهم المستغفرون لمن فى الأرض، ومنهم الموكّلون بايصال الشرائع والأحكام، ومنهم الموكّلون بالإلهامات واللمّات

who convey sciences to the hearts. Among them are those entrusted with giving form to what is in the wombs. Among them are those who blow the spirits into the bodies. Among them are those entrusted with provisions. Among them are those who drive back the clouds, those who escort the snow and the hail, and those who fall down with the drops of the rains. Among them are those entrusted with the storehouses of the seas and the mountains so that these will not disappear. Among them are the *emissaries,* the *noble,* the *pious* [80:16] and the *preservers,* the *noble scribes* [82:10–11]. Among them are the angels of the graves and those who circumambulate the Inhabited House.[24] Among them are Ridwan and the custodians of the Gardens. Among them are *the Thrusters* [96:18] who—when it is said to them, *Take him, and fetter him, and then roast him in hellfire, then in a chain of seventy cubits' length, insert him* [69:30–32]—quickly rush to him and grant him no delay.

(62) There are other than these, such that the knowledge of mortals does not encompass their enumeration, for there is no occurrence in the cosmos with whose bringing to pass the angels have not been entrusted—however, by the command of those who are the angels brought nigh. This is why God says, quoting from them, *None of us there is but has a known station* [37:164]. Thus, among them are the Rangers, the Scarers, the Swimmers, the Casters, and the Governors. Nonetheless, they all remain under the authority of those [rulers, except the][25] enraptured spirits, for they are God's special elect.

(63) The common people witness nothing but the dwelling places of the high and low angels, but the elect witness the angels in their dwelling places.

(64) God placed in the elemental world from the human species the vicegerents of God, who are likenesses of the highest angels. Among them are the messengers, the Imams, the judges, the just kings, the administrators, and the sultans. He put the most excellent of the prophets (upon whom be peace) in the way station of the Greatest Spirit and the most excellent of the Imams in the way station of the Universal Soul, the Preserved Tablet, and the Mother of the Book. *Surely he is in the Mother of the Book with Us, "high" [ᶜAlī], wise* [43:4].[26]

(65) Between the spirits of these administrators in the earth and those administrators in the spheres God placed tenuities and correspondences that extend to them from the celestial administrators and are purified of contaminations and hallowed beyond defects.[27] So they receive them in the measure of their potency and preparedness.

والموصلـون للعلوم الى القلوب، ومنهـم الموكّلون بتصوير ما فى الأرحام، ومنهم النافخون للأرواح فى الأجساد، ومنهم الموكّلون بالأرزال، ومنهم زواجر السحاب ومشيّعو الثلج والبرد والهوابط مع أقطار الأمطار، ومنهم الموكّلـون علـى خزائن البحار والجبـال فلا تزول، ومنهم السـفرة الكرام الـبررة والحفظة الكرام الكاتبون، ومنهم ملائكة القبور والطائفون بالبيت المعمور، ومنهم رضوان وسـدنة الجنان، ومنهـم الزبانية الذين اذا قيل لهم خذوه فغلّوه ثمّ الجحيم صلوة ثمّ فى سلسلة ذرعها سبعون ذراعاً فاسلكوه ابتدروه سراعاً و لم يُنظروه.

(٦٢) وغير هـؤلاء ممّا لا يحيط علم البشر بإحصائه، اذ ما من حادث فى العالم الا وقد وكّل بإجرائه الملائكة ولكن بأمر أولئك الملائكة المقرّبين. ولذلـك قال الله تعالى حكايةً عنهـم: وما منّا الا وله مقام معلوم، كما كان منهم الصافات والزاجرات والسـابحات والملقيات والمدبّرات، ومع هذا فلا يزالون تحت سلطان أولئك الأرواح المهيّمة، فهم خصائص الله.

(٦٣) ثم العامّة ما يشاهدون الا منازل هذه الملائكة العلوية والسفلية، والخاصّة يشاهدونهم فى منازلهم.

(٦٤) وجعـل الله فى عـالم العنصرى من نوع البشر خلفاء الله أشـباه الملائكة الأعلون. فمنهم الرسـل ولأئمّـة والقضاة والملوك العدل والولاة والسـلاطين، وجعـل أفضل الأنبيـاء عليه السـلام بمنزلة الـروح الأعظم وأفضـل الأئمّة بمنزلة النفس الكلية واللوح المحفوظ وأمّ الكتاب. وإنّه فى أمّ الكتاب لدينا لعلى حكيم.

(٦٥) وجعل الله بين أرواح هؤلاء الولاة فى الأرض وبين هؤلاء الولاة فى الأفلاك رقائق ومناسبات تمتدّ اليهم من هؤلاء الولاة الفلكية مطهّرة من الشوائب مقدّسة عن العيوب، فيقبلها هؤلاء بقدر قوّتهم واستعدادهم.

(66) *Another Fine Point.* God made the earth, as the location of perfect man, like an imam at which all the creatures gather—the simple things, the compound things, the elemental beings, the heavenly traces, various types of angels, and ranked troops from the world of the Absent—so that his states may gain equilibrium from their gathering. He made the brightness of the sun and the light of the moon two prostrators at the earth's door. [He made] night and daytime its two habitués, circumambulating its courtyard and its extremities. In the same way, He made water and air two devotees of its surface, both circling around it. In the same way, He made the planets, with respect to the falling of their rays, like those who put their heads down for prostration. So also the plants, with respect to their natural, inverted position, are like those who place their heads on a carpet for prostration. *The stars and the trees prostrate themselves* [55:6]. Similar is the state of the animals in their bowing toward the earth and their meekness.

(67) All this is for the sake of the existence of God's vicegerent in this earth, as He says: *Surely I am setting in the earth a vicegerent* [2:30]. *When thy Lord said to the angels, surely I am creating a mortal from a clay of stinking mud, so when I have proportioned him and blown into him of My spirit, fall down before him as prostrators. So, all the angels prostrated themselves together, save Iblīs. He refused to be one of the prostrators* [15:28–31].

(68) For, [man] is the original final goal in the existence of the cosmos and the creation of the beings. He is the highest fruit and the most limpid core. That is why God made all these high and low created things subjected and obedient to him, as He says: *He subjected to you the night and the daytime, and the sun and the moon. And the stars are subjected by His command. Surely in that are signs for a people who use intelligence. And that of which He has multiplied for you in the earth, diverse in colors—surely in that is a sign for a people who remember. And He it is who subjected the sea, that you may eat of it fresh flesh, and bring forth from it ornaments that you wear* [16:12–14].

(٦٦) نكتة أخرى. إنّ الله جعل الأرض لمكان الانسان الكامل بمنزلة إمام يجتمع عنده الخلائق من البسائط والمركّبات والكائنات العنصرية والآثار السماوية وقبائل من الملائكة وجنود مجنّدة من عالم الغيب ليعتدل باجتماعها أحواله. وجعل ضوء الشمس ونور القمر ساجدين على بابها، والليل والنهار دائبين لها طائفين على ساحتها وأطرافها. وكذلك جعل الماء والهواء عاكفين على سطحها دائرين حولها. وكذلك جعل الكواكب من جهة وقوع أشعّتها بمنزلة من يهوى برأسه الى التحت للسجود. وكذلك النباتات بحسب وضعها الطبيعى الانتكاسى بمنزلة من يضع رأسه على البساط للسجدة، والنجم والشجر يسجدان. وكذلك حال الحيوانات فى انكبابها الى الأرض وخضوعها.

(٦٧) كلّ ذلك لأجل وجود خليفة الله فى هذه الأرض كما قال تعالى: إنّى جاعل فى الأرض خليفة. واذ قال ربّك للملائكة إنّى خالق بشراً من صلصال من حماء مسنون، فإذا سوّيته ونفخت فيه من روحى فقعوا له ساجدين، فسجد الملائكة كلّهم أجمعون، الا إبليس أبى أن يكون مع الساجدين.

(٦٨) فانّه الغاية الأصلية فى وجود العالم وخلقة الكائنات وهو الثمرة العليا واللباب الأصفى، ولهذا جعل الله هذه المخلوقات العالية والسافلة كلّها مسخّرة له مطيعة إيّاه كما قال تعالى: وسخّر لكم الليل والنهار والشمس والقمر والنجوم مسخّرات بأمره إنّ فى ذلك لآيات لقوم يعقلون، وما ذرأ لكم فى الأرض مختلفاً ألوانه إنّ فى ذلك لآية لقوم يذّكرون، وهو الذى سخّر لكم البحر لتأكلوا منه لحماً طرياً وتستخرجوا منه حلية تلبسونها.

Thus, in these verses, He alludes to the subjection to us of the stars, animals, plants, and inanimate things. Then He summarizes and says, *He subjected to you what is in the heavens and what is in the earth* [31:20]. So also are His words, *He subjected to you [. . .] what is in the earth all together* [45:13].

(69) *Another Fine Point.* God made the earth, because of its potency to receive traces, like a leaven through which was readied the creation of the beings. The original purpose in it was the creation of man, the vicegerent of the All-Merciful. From his leftover He created the other beings, for two reasons—because man needs them, and so that He might not neglect any element's right or hold back from any receptacle what it deserves.

(70) God stirred up a vicegerent from the leavened earth through three inblowings. Through the first inblowing it obtained the potency of growing and increasing in measure with respect to attracting nourishment and utilizing it in the sides and regions. This is like someone who blows into a skin to increase it in measure. Through the second inblowing is born the potency of sensation and movement, like someone who blows on charcoal with a bellows so that it glows after having been heated. Through the third inblowing is born within it the potency of reflective thought, knowledge, and the conception of the intelligibles with the intellective light, like someone who blows on charcoal so that it flames up and brightens its surroundings.

(71) Thus man, with respect to these three inblowings, is like a sleeper in intense sleep. Through the first he moves a little. Through the second he is aroused while perplexed and bewildered. Through the third he awakens, standing up straight from the slumber of nature and the sleep of heedlessness, knowing the gauges of affairs and the reckonings of things by reflective thought and deliberation. He recalls past deeds by memory and remembrance. He anticipates coming states by intuition and understanding. He recognizes things' specificities, roots, definitions, representations, causes, origins, and final goals by the potency of wisdom and demonstration. He also uncovers the measures of every deed, the manners of every quiddity's existence, and the reality of everything possessing a reality, along with its worlds and its configurations, through the complete, inward power.

فأشار فى هذه الآيات الى تسخيره لنا الكواكب والحيوانات والنباتات والجمادات. ثم أجمل وقال أيضاً: وسخّر لكم ما فى السموات وما فى الأرض، وكذا قوله: وسخّر لكم ما فى الأرض جميعاً.

(٦٩) نكتة أخرى. جعل الله الأرض لقوّة قبولها الآثار بمنزلة خميرة تهيّأ بها خلقة المكوّنات. والغرض الأصلى منها خلقة الانسان خليفة الرحمن، وخلق من فضالته سائر الأكوان لأمرين: لحاجة الآدمى اليها، ولئلا يهمل كلّ عنصر حقّه ولا يمنع من القابل ما يستحقّه.

(٧٠) فبعث الله خليفة من الأرض المخمّرة بثلاث نفخات. فبالنفخة الأولى حصل لها قوّة النموّ والزيادة فى المقدار من جهة جذب الغذاء وصرفها فى الجوانب والأقطار بمنزلة من ينفخ فى زلّ فيزداد فى مقداره. وبالنفخة الثانية يتولّد قوّة الحسّ والحركة كمن ينفخ فى الكير فى فحم ينجمر بعد أن يتسخّن. وبالنفخة الثالثة يتولّد فيه قوّة الفكر والمعرفة وتصوّر المعقولات بالنور العقلى كمن ينفخ فى جمر يشتعل ويضيئ جوانبه.

(٧١) فالإنسان بحسب هذه النفخات الثلاث بمنزلة نائم فى نوم شديد يتحرّك قليلاً بالأولى ويتنبّه بالثانية هائماً متحيّراً ويستيقظ بالثالثة قائماً مستوياً من رقدة الطبيعة ونوم الغفلة عارفاً مقاييس الأمور ومحاسبات الأشياء بالفكر والروية ويسترجع الأعمال الماضية بالحفظ والذكر ويستنظر الأحوال الآتية بالحدس والفهم ويعرف خواصّ الأشياء وأصولها وحدودها ورسومها وعللها ومبادئها وغاياتها بقوّة الحكمة والبرهان ويستكشف أيضاً مقادير كلّ عمل وأنحاء وجود كل ماهية وحقيقة كلّ ذى حقيقة وعوالمه ونشآته بالقدرة التامّة الباطنية.

(72) Such is the state until, through the radiant light and the flashing blaze, he arrives at the world of Lordship. Within it he sees wonders that tongues are too weak to describe and ears too deaf to hear. So, my beloved, it is necessary for you to know all this and to have faith that the cosmos is like a tree whose fruit is man; he is like a tree whose fruit is the rational soul and the acquired intellect, and the intellect is like a tree whose fruit is the encounter with God. This is the goal of all goals and the end point of all yearnings and longings.

# Chapter Six

*On the clarification of the root of true felicity and the root of true wretchedness*

(73) Know that it is possible for those who consider the states of the human body and the attributes of its constitution, its color, and the movements of its extremities to deduce from these, through the craft of bodily medicine, the body's immediate health and felicity or sickness and wretchedness. In the same way, it is possible for those who consider the states of the human soul and her soulish attributes, habitudes, and character traits to deduce from these, through the craft of spiritual medicine, her deferred health and felicity or sickness and wretchedness.

(74) Know then, that with respect to people's outward states and sensory forms, God created them in the most beautiful form and the most beauteous state, just as God says: *We indeed created man in the most beautiful stature* [95:4]. Hence, they have the receptivity to arrive at the most complete perfection because of the beauty of their preparedness. This is because the body is a receptive substance created for the soul's preparedness, for the perfection that befits her, and for her climb to the world of the afterworld at God. It is like a beast that someone rides so as to arrive at a longed-for home or an original homeland. Otherwise, the mere fact of riding on it or taking care of it is a weariness and a service, a point to which He alludes with His words, *Surely man is in loss, save those who have faith and do worthy deeds,* and so on [103:2–3].

(٧٢) وهكذا الحال الى أن يصل بالنور الشارل والوميض البارل الى عالم الربوبية، فيرى فيها من العجائب ما يكلّ عن وصفه الألسن ويصمّ عن سماعه الأذن. فيا حبيبى يجب عليك أن تعلم من هذه الجملة وتؤمن بأنّ العالم بمنزلة شجرة ثمرتها الانسان، وهو كشجرة ثمرتها النفس الناطقة والعقل المستفاد، والعقل كشجرة ثمرتها لقاء الله، وهو غاية الغايات ومنتهى الأشوال والرغبات.

## الفصل السادس

### فى بيان أصل السعادة وأصل الشقاوة الحقيقيتين

(٧٣) واعلم أنّ الناظر فى أحوال بدن الانسان وصفات مزاجه ولونه وحركات أطرافه يمكن له أن يستنبط منها بصناعة الطبّ الجسمانى صحّته وسعادته أوسقمه وشقاوته العاجلتين، كذلك الناظر فى أحوال نفسه وصفاتها وملكاتها وأخلاقها النفسانية يمكن له أن يستنبط منها بصناعة الطبّ الروحانى صحّتها وسعادتها أوسقمها وشقاوتها الآجلتين.

(٧٤) ثم اعلم أنّ الله خلق الناس بحسب أحوالهم الظاهرة وصورهم المحسوسة فى أحسن الصور وأجمل الأحوال كما قال الله تعالى: لقد خلقنا الانسان فى أحسن تقويم. فله قابلية الوصول الى الكمال الأتمّ لحسن استعداده لأنّ البدن جوهر قابلى خلق لأجل استعداد النفس وكمالها اللائق بها وارتقائها الى عالم الآخرة عند الله كالدابّة المركوبة عليها لأجل الوصول الى منزل مرغوب اليه أو وطن أصلى. والاّ فمجرّد الركوب عليها أو رعيها تعب وخدمة كما أشير اليه بقوله: إنّ الإنسان لفى خسر الاّ الذين آمنوا وعملوا الصالحات الآية.

(75) It is not the outward form upon which true felicity depends, because it disappears and changes. So, the truly felicitous is he whose soulish conduct—like his bodily form—has the most beautiful and perfect guise and the most beauteous and eminent dress. The truly wretched is he whose inward form is ugly because of ugly deeds and vile character traits. The soul that has neither felicity nor wretchedness is like an abandoned beast that deserves neither reward nor punishment.

(76) However, God's mercy embraces everything, so the mere fact of thingness and possibility sets in place the reception of a certain level of mercy, so long as this is not prevented by some preventer opposed to it and incompatible with it. So, when doing beautiful deeds adds deservingness to it, this necessitates[28] the winning of the degrees [of paradise], as He says: *My mercy embraces everything, so I shall write it for those who are godwary* [7:156]. However, the root of every true felicity is knowledge and certainty, and the matter of every wretchedness is doubt and ignorance. One sort of the latter, which is that opposed to knowledge and paired with denial and obstinacy, is a vice that necessitates endless chastisement and sempiternal wretchedness.

(77) Souls naked of imprints are like pages of paper empty of writing. When they are imprinted with intellective sciences and practical wisdom, they become worthy to be the storehouse for the king's secrets. But if they themselves are imprinted with inane embellishments and with idle, base, and false or lying words, then they are worthy only to be burned in the fire.

(78) So the roots of true reward and punishment grow from knowledge and ignorance. This is because the fruits of deeds and the results of acts will come to be either in this cosmos or in the afterabode. The first are like the wages paid to the masters of crafts, professions, and commercial transactions. These come under the heading of dirhams and dinars, or reception by and nearness to kings and sultans, in which there is the body's ease. The second sort is like the recompense for worthy deeds, such as acts of worship, invocations, standing [in *ṣalāt*], fasting, alms-tax, and circumambulation, for these are among the affairs of the afterworld within which are the refreshment and delight of the spirits and the Gardens of Bliss.

(٧٥) فليست الصورة الظاهرة مناط السعادة الحقيقية لزوالها وتغيّرها. فالسعيد الحقيقى من كان سيرته النفسانية كصورته الجسمانية على أحسن هيئة وأكملها وأجمل كسوة وأشرفها، والشقى الحقيقى من كانت صورته الباطنية قبيحة لأجل قبائح الأعمال ورذائل الأخلال. والنفس التى لا سعادة ولا شقاوة لها كبهيمة معطّلة لا يستحقّ الثواب والعقاب.

(٧٦) الّا أنّ رحمة الله واسعة لكلّ شئ. فمجرّد الشيئية والإمكان مصحّحة لقبول مرتبة من الرحمة إن لم يمنع منها مانع مضادّ مناف لها. فاذا ضمّ اليه الاستحقال بفعل الحسنات يوجب الفوز بالدرجات كما قال: ورحمتى وسعت كلَّ شئ فسأكتبها للّذين يتّقون، الّا أنّ أصل كلّ سعادة حقيقية هو العلم واليقين، ومادّة كل شقاوة هى الشكّ والجهل. وضرب منه وهو المضادّ للمعرفة المشفوع بالإنكار والعناد رذيلة يوجب العذاب الأبدى والشقاء السرمدى.

(٧٧) والنفوس الساذجة من النقوش بمنزلة صحيفة قرطاس خالية عن الكتابة بحيث اذا انتقشت بالعلوم العقلية والحكمة العملية صلحت لأن تكون خزينة أسرار الملك. واذا انتقشت هى بعينها بالمزخرفات الواهية والكلمات المعطّلة الدانية الباطلة والكاذبة لم يصلح الا للاحترال بالنار.

(٧٨) فأصل الثواب والعقاب الحقيقيين ينشآن من العلم والجهل. وذلك لأنّ ثمرات الأعمال ونتائج الأفعال إما أن يكون فى هذا العالم أو فى الدار الآخرة. فالأولى كأجور أرباب الصنائع والحرف والمكاسب، وهى من باب الدراهم والدنانير أو القبول والتقرّب للملوك والسلاطين التى فيها راحة الأبدان. والثانية كجزاء الأعمال الصالحة من العبادات والأذكار والقيام والصيام والزكاة والطواف، فإنّها يكون من الأمور الأخروية التى فيها رَوْح الأرواح وريحانها وجنّات النعيم.

(79) Just as the man with propertied wealth and current coinage can do without the weariness of commercial transactions and the hardship of crafts and professions, so also lordly knowers with the true wealth of knowledge can do without the hardship of supererogatory deeds and supposed good works, for knowledge is the goal of every deed and movement and the fruit of every act of obedience and worship—*and worship thy Lord until certainty comes to thee* [15:99]. This is because all the acts of worship and obedience bring about the limpidness of the heart's mirror from the wrappings of soulish turbidities so that it may be prepared to be imprinted with the form of what is sought. As for the final goal of the divine sciences and the noninstrumental knowledges of certainty, it comes to be from them themselves.[29]

(80) It has come in the traditions that when someone does a beautiful deed, then a wage is written for him, an ugly deed is effaced, and he is lifted up by a degree.[30] Thus, someone said, "When someone hears a word and understands its meaning, a knowledge comes to be for him, an ignorance disappears from him, and his way station is uplifted corresponding to this measure of knowledge."[31] This is because knowledge is by its essence an eminence and a perfection, and ignorance by its essence is an impairment and a disappearance. In the same way, whenever man increases in certainty, his way station in the Sovereignty increases.

## Chapter Seven

### *On the quiddity of death*

(81) Death is counter to life just as nonexistence is counter to possession. Now, since it has been clarified that life is of two sorts—bodily, which is the origin of sense-perception and volitional movement; and soulish, which is the source of wisdom and certainty—death will also be of two sorts. One is bodily, and it is the nonexistence of the origin of sensation and volitional movement, and the second is the perishment of the source of wisdom and certainty.

(82) Bodily life may be accidental and by subordination, not by essence, like the life of hair and nails, whose movements are subordinates to the sensate organs adjacent to them. In the same way, soulish life may be

(٧٩) وكما أنّ الإنسان يستغنى بالغنية المالية والنقود الرائجة من تعب المكاسب ومشقّة الصنائع والحِرَف، فكذلك بالغنية العلمية الحقيقية يستغنى العالم الربّانى عن مشقّة النوافل والخيرات المظنونة، فإنّ المعرفة غاية كلّ عمل وحركة وثمرة كلّ طاعة وعبادة؛ واعبد ربّك حتّى يأتيك اليقين، لأنّ حاصل سائر العبادات والطاعات تصفية مرآة القلب عن غشاوة الكدورات النفسانية ليستعدّ بذلك للانتقاش بصورة المطلوب. وأمّا غاية العلوم الالهية والمعارف اليقينية الغير الآلية فحصولها أنفسها.

(٨٠) وما وقع فى الآثار أنّ من فعل حسنةً فكتب له أجر ومحيت عنه سيّئة ورفعت له درجة، كما قال بعضهم من سمع كلمة وفهم معناها حصلت له معرفة وزالت عنه جهالة وارتفعت منزلته بإزاء هذا القدر من العلم، لأنّ العلم هو بذاته شرف وكمال، والجهل بذاته آفة وزوال. وهكذا كلّما ازداد الانسان يقيناً ازداد منزله فى الملكوت.

## الفصل السابع
### فى ماهية الموت

(٨١) الموت يقابل الحياة مقابلة العدم والملكة. ثم لمّا بينّ أنّ الحياة على وجهين جسمانية وهى مبدأ الإحساس والتحريك الإرادى ونفسانية وهى منشأ الحكمة واليقين، فكذا الموت يكون على وجهين، أحدهما الجسمانى وهو عدم مبدأ الحسّ والحركة بالارادة، والثانى هلاك منشأ الحكمة واليقين.

(٨٢) وكما أنّ الحياة الجسمانية قد يكون بالعرض وبحسب التبعية لا بالذات كحياة الشعر والظفر، فإنّ حركاتها بتبعية الأعضاء الحسّاسة المجاورة لها، فكذلك الحياة النفسانية قد يكون بالعرض وبحسب التبعية

accidental and by subordination, not by essence, as when someone subordinates himself to a knower by imitating true beliefs, or makes himself similar to him in worthy conduct, or hears from him true words without coming to understand their significance or clearly seeing their meaning. In this respect he does not possess an afterworldly life or a real faith that is established by itself with the Real, for imitative knowledge is not a true knowledge of certainty that comes to be from inward insight, which is why it is receptive to transformation. However, it is a kind of subordination and a making oneself similar to the Folk of Life. "And he who makes himself similar to a people is one of them,"[32] so he will be mustered along with them.

(83) You should not suppose that the prophets used to hear revelation from the angels by virtue of imitation. What an idea! For imitation is not knowledge, whether the one imitated be a mortal man or an angel. But the prophets are knowers of God, His signs, His Sovereignty, His books, and His messengers, and the Last Day. This is only a witnessing by the heart and an inward conversation with respect to insight and certainty, not mere imitation and surmise.[33]

(84) The sperm drop and the embryo's matter, because of their deficiency in bodily life, are transformed into the level of infancy. So also the level of infancy is transformed into another level above it, until it reaches the final goal in bodily life and corporeal growth. There it halts, and it is not transformed into another animality in this cosmos. However, it may take a route and travel a pathway other than this natural, bodily way.

(85) So also, when man begins to perceive the first and self-evident things, this is the first of his journey to the world of the Sovereignty. His soulish life with respect to this level corresponds to the bodily life that belongs to the *embryos in the bellies of* their *mothers* [53:32]. It is receptive to transformation because of the deficiency of its degree. In each transformation, there is a corruption and a disintegration of the preceding life.

(86) Such is the state in transformation from any imitation to another imitation, until his potency in receiving the soulish life reaches the degree of inward insight. Then he obtains the complete life of the

لا بالذات كما يتبع أحد عالماً بالتقليد فى العقائد الحقّة أو يتشبّه به فى سيرة صالحة أويسمع منه الكلمات الحقّة من غير أن يقف على مؤدّاها أويستبصر معناهــا. فهو من جهــة ذلك ليس ذا حياة أخرويــة وذا ايمان حقيقى يقوم بنفســه عند الحــقّ، لأنّ العلم التقليـدى ليس بعلم حقيقـى يقينى حاصل مــن البصيرة الباطنية، ولهذا يقبل التحوّل، الا أنّه نوع متابعة وتشـبّه بأهل الحياة. ومن تشبّه بقوم فهو منهم، فيكون محشوراً معهم.

(٨٣) ولا يذهبنّ عليك أنّ الأنبياء كان سـماعهم الوحى من الملائكة من جهة التقليد، هيهات، فإنّ التقليد ليس معرفة، سواء كان المقلّد له بشراً أو مَلَكاً، والأنبياء عرفاء بالله وآياته وملكوته وكتبه ورسـله واليوم الآخر. إنّما ذلك مشـاهدة قلبية ومكالمة باطنية بحسب الاستبصار واليقين لا مجرّد التقليد والتخمين.

(٨٤) وكمـا أنّ النطفـة والمـادّة الجنينية تحوّلت لنقصانهـا فى الحياة الجسمانية الى مرتبة الطفولية، وكذا مرتبة الطفولية تحوّلت الى مرتبة أخرى فوقهـا حتى بلغت الغايــة فى الحياة الجسـمانية والنشـوء البدنى، فوقفت عندهـا ولم يتحوّل الى حيوانيــة أخرى فى هذا العـالم، الا أنّ لها أن ينهج منهجاً ويسلك مسلكاً غير هذا المذهب الطبيعى الجسمانى.

(٨٥) فكذلـك الإنســان اذا شرع فى إدراك الأوّليـات والبديهيات، فيكون ذلك أوّل سـفره الى عالم الملكوت وحياته النفسـانية بحسب هذه المرتبة بإزاء الحياة الجسـمانية التى للأجنّة فى بطون أمّهاتهم، فتكون قابلة للتحوّل لنقص درجتها ويكون فى كلّ تحوّل فساد وفسخ للحياة السابقة.

(٨٦) وهكـذا الحـال فى التحوّل من كلّ تقليـد الى تقليد آخر الى أن بلغت قوّته فى قبول الحياة النفسـانية الى درجة البصيرة الباطنية. فحصلت

heart, which is the origin of clear-sighted knowledge and the complete, afterworldly power that makes present the form of the entities whenever he wills and desires in the world of the Gardens. Thus, God says, *They will have what they call for* [36:57]. He also says, *Therein shall be that for which the souls have appetite and which the eyes enjoy* [43:71], and *they will be therein everlastingly* [2:25].

(87) Thus they will be delivered from death, and their undergoing transformation from one world to another will be nullified. "Abrogation," which is the death of the imitators, will be lifted from them. A prophetic hadith says,

> When the folk of the Garden repair to the Garden and the folk of the Fire repair to the Fire while in the state of chastisement, death will be brought in the form of a salt-colored ram and placed between the Garden and the Fire. The Faithful Spirit will hold it down on its side, and John will come, a knife in his hand. He will slaughter it, and it will be said to the inhabitants of the Garden and the Fire, "Everlastingness without death!"[34]

(88) In this there is an allusion to the fact that the form of the bodily beast through which the soul dies will be brought in the soulish world, which is midway between bodily and sheer intellective life. With the severance of its matter, the termination of its impairments, and the slaughter of its potency by knowledge, the soul will have intellective life. The "Faithful Spirit" is that which brings forth the souls from potency to act by effusing cognitive life upon them. "John" is an allusion to the human intellective potency, which becomes an Actual Intellect through the confirmation of the holy angel that effuses the realities, by God's leave.[35]

(89) Once ignorance is lifted from the soul, then endless death is lifted, perpetual subsistence and everlasting life come to be, and the resurrection stands forth. This is why God's Messenger said, "I and the Hour are like these two."[36] And God's Messenger has been called "the messenger of the Last of Time," which is to say that his time is the last of the time of bodily life and the first of the manifestation of the soulish life for human spirits, without the alteration and disintegration that are found in other times, preceding centuries, and past nations.

لـه حينئذ الحياة التامّـة القلبية التى هى مبـدأ العلم العيانـى والقدرة التامّة الأخرويـة التى تحـضر صورة الأعيان متى شـاء وأراد فى عالم الجنان، كما قـال تعالى: ولهم فيها ما يدّعون، وقال أيضاً فيها ما تشـتهيه الأنفس وتلذّ الأعين، وهم فيها خالدون.

(٨٧) فخلـص من الموت وبطل منه التحوّل مـن دنيا الى دنيا وارتفع منه النسـخ الذى هو مـوت المقلّدين، كما ورد فـى الحديث النبوى صلى الله عليـه وآلـه اذا صـار أهل الجنّة الى الجنّـة وأهل النـار الى النار وهم فى حـال العذاب يُجاء بالموت على صورة كبش أملح فيوضع بين الجنّة والنار فيضجعـه الروح الأمين ويأتى يحيى عليه السـلام وبيده الشـفرة فيذبحه ويقال لساكن الجنّة والنار خلود بلا موت.

(٨٨) وفيه إشارة الى أنّ فى العالم النفسانى المتوسّط بين الحياة البدنية والعقليـة المحضة يُجـاء بصورة البهيمـة البدنية بها يكون مـوت النفس، وبقطـع مادّتها وحسـم آفاتها وذبـح قوّتها بالعرفان يكـون الحياة العقلية للنفس. والروح الأمين هو مُخرج النفوس من القوّة الى الفعل بإفاضة الحياة العلمية عليها، ويحيى كناية عن القوّة العقلية من الانسـان التى تصير عقلاً بالفعل بتأييد المَلَك المقدّس المفيض للحقائق بإذن الله.

(٨٩) فـاذا ارتفع الجهل مـن النفس ارتفع المـوت الأبدى وحصل البقاء الدائم والحياة الأبدية وقامت القيامة. ولهذا قال رسـول الله صلى الله عليه وآله: أنا والسـاعة كهاتين، ودعى رسـول الله بأنّه رسـول آخر الزمـان، يعنـى زمانـه آخر زمان الحيـاة الجسـمانية وأوّل ظهـور الحياة النفسـانية للأرواح الأنسـية من غير تبدّل وفسـخ كما فى سـائر الأزمنة والقرون السـابقة والأمم الماضية.

# Chapter Eight

## *On the meaning of forgiveness and its realization from God's bounty as He has promised and announced to His servants*

(90) This is known from the precedents of His mercy and beneficence toward man, His forgiveness of [man's] precedent, creaturely sins, and His purifying him of the defilement of his natural filths and hylic impurities. Do you not see how He has brought forth the embryo from the tightness of its mother's belly into the space of this world and how He has forgiven the sins that it committed and the ugly deeds that it performed when it was a sperm drop, a blood clot, a flesh lump, and an embryo? For it was stained with impurities and nourished with the forbidden blood of menstruation, and it lingered in the earth of the womb in the company of the darknesses. He purified it from the defilement of the impurities and foulnesses, and, in place of the *blood* of menstruation, He gave it *pure milk, sweet to* drink [16:66], so that it may nourish itself and its body become strong. Then it may roam in the expanse of the world however it desires and wills. Thus it comes forth from its precedent sins on the day its mother gives birth to it.

(91) In the same way, when man reaches the degree of knowledge and faith and comes forth from the sleep of ignorance and the slumber of nature, *God forgive*s him *the sin*s *that have gone before* [48:2]—the ignorance and darkness and the ugly deeds of blindness and deprivation. He purifies him from the defilement of the offenses of bodies,[37] and the appetites of soul, and caprice. In place of bodily nourishments and various foods, He gives soulish nourishments, which are the diverse sorts of knowledge and the varieties of the sciences.

(92) *An Unveiling and Verification.* That which grasps the earth's spirit is the vegetal soul, which is a fully active word[38] and a potency from among the potencies of the angels entrusted to the surface of the earth, a potency whose task is to transform the earth. It strips from it the earthly form so that it may replace it with a more beautiful form and a purer dress. Thus *He forgive*s it its *sin that has gone before* [48:2] and He brings it out of its lowliness and its distance from the world of mercy.

## الفصل الثامن
### فى معنى المغفرة وتحقّقها من فضل الله تعالى كما وعدها عباده وبشّرهم

(٩٠) وذلك معلوم من سوابق رحمته وإحسانه فى حق الانسان وغفرانه لذنوبه السابقة الخلقية وتطهيره إيّاه من دنس أرجاسه الطبيعية وأنجاسه الهيولوية. أَوَلا ترى كيف أخرج الجنين من مضيق بطن أمّه الى فضاء عالم الدنيا، وغفر ذنوبه التى اقترحها وسيئاته التى اجترحها عند كونه نطفة ومضغة وعلقة وجنيناً من تلطّخه بالأنجاس وتغذّيه بحرام دم الحيض وإخلاده فى أرض الرحم بصحبة الظلمات، وطهّره عن دنس الأنجاس والأخباث، وعوّض له عن دم الحيض بلبن خالص سائغ شرابه، لأن يتغذّى به ويتقوّى بدنه فيسرح فى سعة العالم كيف يريد ويشاء، فخرج من ذنوبه السابقة يوم ولدته أمّه.

(٩١) وكذا اذا بلغ درجة العلم والايمان وخرج من نوم الجهالة ورقدة الطبيعة، غفر الله له ما تقدّم من ذنوب الجهالة والظلمة وسيئات العمى والحرمان وطهّره عن دنس جرائم الأجرام وشهوات النفس والهوى وعوّض له عن الأغذية الجسمانية وألوان الطعوم بالأغذية النفسانية التى هى فنون المعارف وأقسام العلوم.

(٩٢) كشف وتحقيق. إنّ قابض روح الأرض هى النفس النباتية التى هى كلمة فعّالة وقوّة من قوى ملائكة موكّلين على أديم الأرض شأنها إحالة الأرض. فينسلخ عنها الصورة الأرضية ليعوّض عنها بأحسن صورة وأطهر كسوة، فيغفر لها ما تقدّم من ذنبها ويخرجها عن تسفّلها وبعدها عن عالم الرحمة.

(93) So also, that which grasps the plant's spirit, makes it die, and lifts it to the heaven of animality is the soul specific to animals. She is among the helpers of the angels entrusted, by God's leave, with this act by taking into service the sensory and motor potencies.

(94) In the same way, that which grasps the spirit of the animal, makes it die, and lifts it up to the heaven of the degree of humanness is the soul specific to man. She is God's word named "the holy spirit." Her task is to bring forth the souls from the hylic potency[39] to the acquired intellect, by God's command, and to convey the spirits to God's neighborhood and the world of the afterworldly Sovereignty.

(95) In these transformations, each subsequent level is more eminent than its preceding level. What undergoes transition from the precedent state to the subsequent state has no regret or remorse over the disappearance of the first configuration. Or rather, if there is any, it concerns something else.[40]

(96) In this way should one gauge the afterworldly configuration, which belongs to souls that climb up to it through science and knowledge.

(97) *A Qur'ānic Confirmation.* Know that the Wise Qur'ān sometimes ascribes making souls die to God, like His words, *God makes the souls die at the time of their death* [39:42]. This signifies that the one that makes to die is God. So also are His words, *Who created death and life* [67:2] and *My Lord is He who gives life and brings death* [2:258]. So also are His words, *How do you disbelieve in God, for you were dead things, so He gave you life, then He brings you death, then He gives you life?* [2:28].

(98) Sometimes making to die is ascribed to the angel of death, like His words, *Say: The angel of death, who has been entrusted with you, will make you die* [32:11]. And sometimes it is ascribed to God's messengers, as in His words, *Until, when death comes to one of you, Our messengers make him die* [6:61].

(٩٣) وكذلك قابض روح النبات ومتوفّيه ورافعه الى سماء الحيوانية هى النفس المختصّة بالحيوان، وهى من أعوان الملائكة الموكّلة بإذن الله تعالى بهذا الفعل باستخدام القوى الحسّاسة والمحرّكة.

(٩٤) وكذلك قابض روح الحيوان ومتوفّيه ورافعه الى سماء درجة الانسانية هى النفس المختصّة بالانسان، وهى كلمة الله المسمّى بالروح القدسى الذى شأنه إخراج النفوس من القوّة الهيولانية الى العقل المستفاد بأمر الله تعالى وايصال الأرواح الى جوار الله وعالم الملكوت الأخروى.

(٩٥) ففى هذه التحويلات كانت كلّ مرتبة لاحقة أشرف من سابقها، ولم يكن للمنتقل من الحالة السابقة الى الحالة اللاحقة حسرة وندامة على زوال النشأة الأولى، بل إن كانت ففى أمرآخر.

(٩٦) فهكذا ينبغى أن يقاس النشأة الأخروية للنفوس المرتقية اليها بالعلم والمعرفة.

(٩٧) تأييد فرقانى. اعلم أنّه قد وقع فى القرآن الحكيم نسبة التوفّى للنفوس تارةً الى الله، كقوله: الله يتوفّى الأنفس حين موتها، فيدلّ على أنّ المتوفّى هو الله، وكقوله: الذى خلق الموت والحياة، وربّى الذى يُحيى ويميت، وكقوله: كيف تكفرون بالله وكنتم أمواتاً فأحياكم ثمّ يُميتكم ثمّ يُحييكم.

(٩٨) وتارةً نسب التوفّى الى ملك الموت كقوله: قل يتوفّاكم مَلَك الموت الذى وُكّل بكم. وتارةً نسب الى رسل الله كما فى قوله: حتى اذا جاء أحدَكم الموتُ توفّته رسلُنا.

(99) Concerning the manner in which these verses agree, one of the commentators has mentioned that in reality the one who makes to die is God, but, in the world of the Witnessed, He delegates every sort of deed to one of the angels. So, He delegates grasping the spirits to the angel of death, who is a chieftain under whom are subordinates and servitors. Thus making to die is attributed in a verse to God, and this is the true attribution; in a verse to the angel of death, because he is a chieftain in this deed; and to the other angels, because they are the subordinates of the angel of death. And God knows best what is correct. Thus ends his discussion.[41]

(100) *A Holy Interpretation.*[42] Know that man is an all-gathering configuration. The existence of this all-gathering ["congregational"] mosque has been built from four roots, each of which has troops, servitors, and branches whose detailed differentiation none knows but God. The true goal in building this all-gathering, human mosque, within which the individuals of the species are gathered, is [1] the commencing of the *ṣalāt* by the address of the preacher-intellect on the pulpit that is man's brain by bearing witness that there is no god but God; [2] [the intellect's] signifying the unity of the Real through its gathered, unifying existence on the level of its simple, undifferentiated spirit; [3] the acquiescing of the "creatures," which are its perceptual and motor potencies, to its command; [4] their listening to its call when its voice penetrates their means of hearing; [5] their accompanying the spirit and following it in the *ṣalāt,* which is "the *miʿrāj* of the believer,"[43] to the encounter with God; and [6] their abandoning the use of the body in their bodily interactions and purposes, thereby acquiescing to God's command and responding to the Real's summons in His words, *O believers, when the* ṣalāt *is called on the Day of Gathering, hasten to God's remembrance,* and so on [62:9].

(101) Allusion has already been made that death is a natural affair and an innate hastening. To this God alluded in His words, *O man! You are laboring unto your Lord laboriously, and you shall encounter Him* [84:6]. We have clarified this in the proper place such that nothing can be added.[44]

(٩٩) وذكر بعض المفسّرين فى وجه الموافقة بين هذه الآيات أنّ المتوفّى فى الحقيقة هو الله الا أنّه فوّض فى عالم الشهادة كل نوع من أنواع الأعمال الى مَلَك من الملائكة، ففوّض قبض الأرواح الى ملك الموت وهو رئيس وتحته أتباع وخدم. فأضيف التوفّى فى آية الى الله وهو الاضافة الحقيقية، وفى آية الى ملك الموت لأنّه رئيس فى هذا العمل والى سائر الملائكة لأنّهم أتباع ملك الموت. والله أعلم بالصواب انتهى كلامه.

(١٠٠) تأويل قدسى. اعلم أنّ الانسان نشأة جامعة، قد بنى وجود هذا المسجد الجامع من أصول أربعة لكلّ منها جنود وخدم وفروع لا يعلم تفصيلها الا الله. والغاية الحقيقية فى بناء هذا المسجد الجامع الانسانى الذى اجتمعت فيه أفراد الأنواع إقامة الصلاة بخطابة خطيب العقل على منبر دماغه بشهادة أن لا اله الا الله؛ ودلالته بوجوده الجمعى المتوحّد فى مرتبة روحه البسيط الإجمالى على وحدانية الحقّ سبحانه وامتثال خلائق قواه الإدراكية والتحريكية أمره، واستماعها نداءه اذا نفذ فى مسامعها صداه، ومشايعتها للروح واقتداءها به فى الصلاة التى هى معراج المؤمن الى لقاء الله وتركها استعمال البدن فى معاملاتها وأغراضها البدنية امتثالاً لأمر الله وإجابة لداعى الحقّ فى قوله: يا أيّها الذين آمنوا إذا نودى للصلاة من يوم الجمعة فاسعوا الى ذكر الله الآية.

(١٠١) وقد مرّت اشارة الى أنّ الموت أمر طبيعى وسعى جبلّى كما أشير اليه فى قوله تعالى: يا أيّتها الإنسان إنّك كادح الى ربّك كدحاً فملاقيه. ونحن قد بيّنّا هذا فى مقام يناسبه بما لا مزيد عليه.

(102) Now, diverse accounts have come concerning the superintendent of the inhabitation of this sacred mosque and the one who takes up the clay of this Inhabited House. In some of them, what gathers the parts of Adam's body is the angels. In some, the one who takes up the dust of his frame is God's messengers, so that they may have messengerhood to His servants. In some, the angel of death takes up a handful of dust. In still others, God grasps with His hand a handful from the surface of the earth.

(103) What has become implanted in the perceptual means of intellects is that the grasper of the spirit of man and the one who makes him die is the grasper of his body's parts. So, all these accounts are truthful in purport and agree in meaning for those who have come to understand the reality of man's essence.

(104) For his essence was leavened from four clays and roots, so within it are the natural, vegetal, animal, and soulish clays. At root its vegetal clay is what was grasped by the angels who are entrusted with bringing about the inhabitation of this elemental world. So God gave it life through water: *And from water We made every living thing* [21:30].

(105) The matter of the clay of animality is what God's messengers brought, according to His words, *Say: The spirit is from the command of my Lord* [17:85]. In other words, it began to come from the world of the Command at the hands of angels intermediary between His Command and His Creation.

(106) The matter of his rational soul and his hylic intellect is that whose intellective life comes to be by His blowing His spirit into it, according to His words, *So when I have proportioned him and blown into him of My spirit* [15:29].

(107) As for the clay portion of him who is a servant, a knower of God, subsistent through His subsistence, and annihilated from his own essence, it is that to which He gives life through the spirit of holiness, as He says concerning Jesus: *We confirmed him with the spirit of holiness* [2:87].

(١٠٢) ثم إنّه قد وردت الروايات المختلفة في باب المتولّى لعمارة هذا المسجد الحرام والآخذ لطينة هذا البيت المعمور. ففي بعضها أنّ الجامع لأجزاء بدن آدم هم الملائكة، وفي بعضها أنّ الآخذ لتراب قالبه هم رسل الله ليكون لهم الرسالة الى عباده، وفي بعضها أنّ ملك الموت أخذ قبضة من التراب، وفي بعضها أنّ الله قبض بيده قبضة من أديم الأرض.

(١٠٣) وقد ارتكز في مدارك العقول أنّ القابض لروح الانسان المتوفّى له هو القابض لأجزاء بدنه، فهذه الروايات كلّها صادقة الفحوى متوافقة المعنى عند الواقف على حقيقة ذات الانسان.

(١٠٤) فإنّ تخمير ذاته من طينات وأصول أربعة ففيها الطينة الطبيعية والنباتية والحيوانية والنفسانية. فأما أصل طينتها النباتية فهي التي قبضتها الملائكة الموكّلة بعمارة هذا العالم العنصري. فأحياها الله تعالى بالماء وجعلنا من الماء كلّ شئ حيّ.

(١٠٥) وأما مادّة طينة الحيوانية فهي التي جاء بها رسل الله لقوله: قل الروح من أمر ربّي، أي ابتداء حصوله من عالم الأمر بيد ملائكة متوسّطة بين أمره وخلقه.

(١٠٦) وأما مادّة نفسه الناطقة وعقله الهيولاني فهي التي يكون حياتها العقلية بنفخه تعالى روحه فيها لقوله تعالى: فإذا سوّيتُه ونفختُ فيه من روحي.

(١٠٧) وأما حصّة طينة من كان عبداً عارفاً بالله باقياً ببقائه فانياً عن ذاته فهي التي أحياها بروح القدس كما قال في حق عيسى روح الله على نبينا وآله وعليه السلام وأيّدناه بروح القدس.

(108) Now, given that what grasps man's clay and gives him life is the same as what grasps his spirit and makes his precedent matter die, it is the vegetal clay whose dust is grasped by the earthly angels [and which God brought to life with water].[45] So, these same angels make the clay die and grasp its spirit to God, according to His words, *The angels make them die while they are wronging their souls* [16:28].

(109) As for the animal creation, it was grasped by the "messengers," and to it God gave life by His command. So, they grasp its spirit and make it die, according to His words, *Our messengers make him die and they neglect him not* [6:61].

(110) His rational soul, which was grasped by the angel of death and to which God gave life with a Seraphielian inblowing from Him, is made to die by the angel of death, according to His words, *Say: The angel of death, who has been entrusted with you, will make you die* [32:11].

(111) As for the intellective matter and holy, divine leaven which was grasped by God, to which He gave life through the spirit of holiness, and which was attracted by the attraction of the "return" in His words, *O soul at peace, return to your Lord, well-pleased, well-pleasing* [89:27–28], it is that which God makes to die and lifts up to Him, according to His words, *God makes the souls die at the time of their death* [39:42]; His words, *God will lift up in degrees those of you who have faith and those who have been given knowledge* [58:11]; His words, *He has lifted up some of you above others in degrees* [6:165]; and His words concerning Jesus, *Surely I will make thee die and lift thee up to Me and I will purify thee of those who disbelieve* [3:55].

## Chapter Nine

*On the clarification of the soul's establishment through herself, her independence in existence, and her subsistence after the ruination of the this-worldly body*

(112) It is necessary to know that everything that becomes nonexistent after having existed becomes nonexistent only by a cause. The cause of something's nonexistence is either the nonexistence of one of its four causes—actor,[46] final goal, matter, or form—or the fact that something that has existence opposed to it enters in upon its essence or its matter.

(١٠٨) ثم لمّا كان القابض لطينة الانسان المحيى له هو بعينه القابض لروحه المتوفّى لمادّته السابقة، فتلك الطينة النباتية التى قبضت الملائكة الأرضية ترابها، فتلك الملائكة بعينها تتوفّاها وتقبض روحها الى الله لقوله تعالى: تتوفّاهم الملائكة ظالمى أنفسهم.

(١٠٩) وأما الخلقة الحيوانية التى قبضتها الرسل وأحياها الله بأمره فهم يأخذون روحها ويتوفّونها لقوله تعالى: توفّته رسلنا وهم لا يفرّطون.

(١١٠) وأما نفسه الناطقة التى قبضها ملك الموت وأحياها الله بنفخة إسرافيلية منه فيتوفّاها ملك الموت لقوله: قل يتوفّاكم ملك الموت الذى وكّل بكم.

(١١١) وأما المادّة العقلية والخميرة المقدّسة الالهية التى قبضها الله وأحياها بروح القدس وجذبها بجذبة ارجعى فى قوله تعالى: يا أيّتها النفس المطمئنّة ارجعى الى ربّك راضية مرضية، فهو الذى يتوفّاها ويرفعها الله اليه لقوله تعالى: الله يتوفّى الأنفس حين موتها، وقوله تعالى: يرفع الله الذين آمنوا منكم والذين أوتو العلم درجات، وقوله: ورفع بعضكم فول بعض درجات، وقوله تعالى فى حقّ عيسىّ: إنّى متوفّيك ورافعك إلىّ ومطهّرك من الذين كفروا.

## الفصل التاسع

### فى الإبانة عن قيام النفس بذاتها واستقلالها فى الوجود وبقائها بعد بوار البدن الدنيوى

(١١٢) يجب أن يعلم أنّ كلّ ما يعدم بعد وجوده فإنّما يعدم بسبب، وسبب عدم الشئ إمّا عدم أحد أسبابه الأربعة الفاعل والغاية والمادّة والصورة أو بورود أمر وجودى مضادّ له على ذاته أو على مادّته.

(113) The actor and final goal of the soul is God when He puts to service one of the angels that subsists through His giving subsistence to it. The soul has no matter, because of her disengagement, nor does she have a form, because she is a formal substance, and her form is her essence, not another form. Since she has no matter, she has no opposite.

(114) Any existent thing realized in the soul can only be of the same kind as sciences, soulish concepts, and reflective cogitations. If the death of the body had the effect of nullifying the soul, this would happen when the soul conceived of it, and when it came to mind. But the soul often conceives of the body's death without harming itself in any way. So how could that be a cause of its perishing?

(115) Thus it is confirmed that the body's death in the external realm is not a cause that has the effect of annihilating the soul, as has been held. So, the fully knowing soul is secure from corruption at the occurrence of the death of the bodies. The root of the essence does not change at the loss of the tools. Indeed, the soul's ignorance is her death, and her knowledge is her life, since intellect is nothing other than conception and imaginalization. Whenever a soul lacks intellect, she fails to find her essence. Whoever fails to find his essence is dead. But this needs an explanation, which should be sought from our books on wisdom.[47]

(116) Someone may say: Just as the soul needs the body for her occurrence, so also she needs it for her subsistence, since the body is a precondition for [her] occurrence, though not its cause. This answer will be given: It is not necessary that the precondition for occurrence be the precondition for subsistence. Through its preparedness, the body is a net for catching the soul from the cause. After falling into existence by means of the net, she has no need for the subsistence of the net.[48]

(117) The explanation of this is that the body is prepared for a form that is its perfection. The soul, with respect to being a form for the body, has an interlinking existence, but with respect to being an intellective substance, she has an existence [that is] in itself, for itself.[49] When the body along with its preparedness is nullified, the soul's attachment and

(١١٣) والنفس فاعلها وغايتها هو الله تعالى باستخدام بعض الملائكة الباقيــة بإبقاء الله إيّاه. وليس لها مادّة لتجرّدها ولا لها صورة لأنّها جوهر صورى، وصورتها ذاتها لا صورة أخرى. وإذ لا مادّة لها فلا ضدّ لها.

(١١٤) وكلّ أمـر وجودى يتحقّق فى النفـس فلا يكون الا من قبيل العلـوم والتصوّرات النفسـية والتأمّلات الفكرية. فمـوت البدن لو كان مؤثّراً فى بطلان النفس لكان ذلك عند تصوّر النفس إيّاه وخطوره بالبال. ثــم إنّ كثيراً ما تتصوّر النفس مـوت البدن و لم تتضرّر أصلاً، فكيف يكون سبباً لهلاكها.

(١١٥) فقد ثبت أنّ موت البدن فى الخارج ليس سـبباً مؤثّراً فى فناء النفـس كما قيل ذلك. فالنفس العلّامة آمنة من الفســاد عند حادثة موت الأجســاد ولا يتغـيّر أصل الذات عند فقد الآلات. نعـم جهل النفس هو موتها وحياتها علمها لأنّ العقل ليس شئ غير التصوّر والتمثّل. وأىّ نفس عدمت العقل فقدت ذاتها، ومن فقد ذاته فهو ميت. فهذا يحتاج الى شرح يطلب من كتبنا الحكمية.

(١١٦) فـإن قيل كما افتقرت النفس الى البدن فى حدوثها، فكذلك تفتقـر اليــه فـى بقائها من حيـث أنّه شرط للحـدوث لا علّـة، يقال شرط الحـدوث لايجب أن يكـون شرط البقاء. فكان البدن باستعداده شـبكة اقتناص النفس من العلّة، فبعد الوقوع فى الوجود بواسطة الشبكة لا تحتاج الى بقاء الشبكة.

(١١٧) وشرح هذا أنّ البدن استعدّ لصورة هى كمال له، والنفس من حيـث كونها صورة للبـدن لها وجود رابطى، ومن حيـث كونها جوهراً عقليـاً لها وجود فى نفســه لنفســه، وعند بطلان البدن باسـتعداده انقطع

linkage with it is severed, but not her intellective existence. This is because one of the two existences is that which is called for by the body and for which it is prepared, but not the other existence, for, through God's configuring, [the intellective existence] is the effuser of the last configuration.[50] So understand, and take it as booty!

## Chapter Ten

*On the attachment of these three parts to each other*

(118) What was intended in everything that was detailed in the chapters of parts two and three was to make the road easy for the traveling seeker. Otherwise, what comes to be from what is mentioned in those two is knowledge of the origin and the final goal.

(119) It is also possible to deduce from part two, which was put together for the sake of the knowledge of the human soul, that the final goal of the soul's existence is the abode of holiness and the world of the afterworld. The final goal of her intention, toward which she turns by essence with respect to innate disposition, is gnosis and arrival at the encounter with God. Once the knowledge of *tawḥīd* becomes plain for someone and he understands the guideposts of the Lordship,[51] within which the first origins and the furthest final ends are investigated, he will know for certain that each thing's origin is the same as its final goal. So, the origin of the fully knowing soul is from God, and her end point is to God. *Their call therein is, "Glory to Thee, O God," and their greeting, "Peace," and the last of their call is, "Praise belongs to God, Lord of the worlds"* [10:10].

*Finished is the writing of this eminent treatise, named*
*"The Elixir of the Gnostics:*
*On the Knowledge*
*of the Real and*
*of Certainty."*

◆

علاقــة النفس وارتباطها بــه، لا وجودها العقلى لأنّ أحــد الوجودين هو الذى يستدعيه البدن ويستعدّ له دون الوجود الآخر، فإنّه فائض بإنشاء الله تعالى النشأة الآخرة. فافهم واغتنم.

## الفصل العاشر
### فى تعلّق هذه الأبواب الثلاثة بعضها ببعض

(١١٨) المقصود ممّا فصّل فى الباب الثانى والثالث سهولة السبيل على الطالب السالك. والا فحاصل ما ذكر فيهما هو معرفة المبدأ والغاية.

(١١٩) ويمكن أن يستنبط أيضاً من الباب الثانى المعقود لمعرفة النفس الانســانية أنّ غاية وجودها هى دار القدس وعــا لم الآخرة، وغاية قصدها الــذى يتوجّه اليها بالذات بحســب الفطرة هى المعرفــة والوصول الى لقاء الله. ومن اتّضح له علم التوحيد وتفطّن المعا لم الربوبية التى يبحث فيها عن المبادئ الأوّل والغايات القصوى علم يقيناً أنّ مبدأ كلّ شئ هو بعينه الغاية له. فالنفس العلاّمة من الله مبدأها والى الله منتهاها. دعواهم فيها سبحانك اللهمّ وتحيّتهم فيها سلام وآخر دعواهم أنِ الحمد لله ربّ العالمين.

قد وقع الفراغ من كتابة هذه الرسالة الشريفة
المسمّاة باكسير العارفين
فى معرفة الحقّ
واليقين.

# Notes to the English Text

*References to Sunni hadith collections follow the system employed by A. J. Wensinck in his* Concordance et indices de la tradition musulmane, *2d ed., 8 vols. (Leiden: E. J. Brill, 1992). To verify whether or not a given hadith is found in Shiʿite sources, I have consulted the encyclopedic collection of Majlisī,* Biḥār al-anwār. *Following are the bibliographical references for the consulted collections.*

## Abbreviations

| | |
|---|---|
| Aḥmad | Ibn Ḥanbal, Aḥmad ibn Muḥammad. *Al-Musnad.* 6 vols. Beirut: Dār Ṣādir, n.d. |
| *Biḥār* | Majlisī, Muḥammad Bāqir. *Biḥār al-anwār.* 110 vols. 1883–1887. Reprint, Beirut: Muʾassasat al-Wafāʾ, 1983. Also on the CD-ROM *Nūr.* Qom: Computer Research Center of Islamic Sciences, 1999. |
| Bukhārī | Al-Bukhārī, Muḥammad ibn Ismāʿīl. *Al-Ṣaḥīḥ.* 9 vols. N.p.: Maṭābiʿ al-Shuʿab, 1378/1958–59. |
| Dārimī | Al-Dārimī, ʿAbd Allāh ibn ʿAbd al-Raḥman. *Al-Sunan.* 2 vols. Beirut: Dār Iḥyāʾ al-Sunna al-Nabawiyya, n.d. |
| Ibn Māja | Ibn Māja, Muḥammad ibn Yazīd. *Al-Sunan.* 2 vols. Edited by M. F. ʿAbd al-Bāqī. Cairo: Dār Iḥyāʾ al-Kutub al-ʿArabiyya, 1952. |
| Muslim | Muslim ibn al-Ḥajjāj. *Al-Ṣaḥīḥ.* 8 vols. Cairo: Maṭbaʿa Muḥammad ʿAlī Ṣabīḥ, 1334/1915–16. |
| Tirmidhī | Al-Tirmidhī, Muḥammad ibn ʿĪsā. *Al-Jāmiʿ al-ṣaḥīḥ, wa huwa sunan al-Tirmidhī.* 5 vols. Edited by A. M. Shākir. Cairo: al-Maktaba al-Islāmiyya, 1938. |

## Notes to the Preface and Translator's Introduction

1. See especially Fazlur Rahman, *The Philosophy of Mullā Ṣadrā* (Albany: State University of New York Press, 1975); Seyyed Hossein Nasr, *Ṣadr al-Dīn Shīrāzī and his Transcendent Theosophy: Background, Life and Works,* 2d ed. (Tehran: Institute for Humanities and Cultural Studies, 1997).

2. The Persian title is *Kitābshināsī-i jāmi$^c$-i Mullā Ṣadrā;* compiled by Nāhīd Bāqerī Khurramdashtī with the assistance of Fāṭima $^c$Askarī (Tehran: Bunyād-i Ḥikmat-i Islāmī-i Ṣadrā, 1378/1999).

3. Ṣadr al-Dīn Shīrāzī, *Majmū$^c$ah-i rasāʾil-i falsafī-i Ṣadr al-Mutaʾallihīn,* ed. Ḥāmid Nājī Iṣfahānī (Tehran: Intishārāt-i Ḥikmat, 1378/1999).

4. References to the *Asfār* follow the nine-volume edition published in Qom in 1998 on the CD-ROM *Nūr al-ḥikma 2* by the Computer Research Center of Islamic Science; this is paginated according to the Ṭabātabā$^c$ī edition, which began appearing in Qom in 1378/1958–59. Wherever the slightest textual question has arisen, I have collated the CD-ROM with the Tehran lithograph (1282/1865–66), though the texts seem to be practically identical.

5. See Parviz Morewedge, *Essays in Islamic Philosophy, Theology, and Mysticism* (Oneonta, N.Y.: Department of Philosophy, State University of New York at Oneonta, 1995), introduction.

6. James Morris translated *Al-Hikma al-$^c$arshiyya* as *The Wisdom of the Throne: An Introduction to the Philosophy of Mullā Ṣadrā* (Princeton: Princeton University Press, 1981); Parviz Morewedge translated *Al-Mashā$^c$ir* as *The Metaphysics of Mullā Ṣadrā* (New York: SSIPS, 1992).

7. For a study of Bābā Afḍal and a translation of this and other treatises, see Chittick, *The Heart of Islamic Philosophy: The Quest for Self-Knowledge in the Teachings of Afḍal al-Dīn Kāshānī* (Oxford: Oxford University Press, 2001).

8. *Asfār,* 8:142–43. See *Asfār,* 7:9, where Ibn al-$^c$Arabī is mentioned specifically. Ṣadrā uses the term "folk of God" in the same way that Ibn al-$^c$Arabī does. For Ibn al-$^c$Arabī, see Chittick, *The Sufi Path of Knowledge: Ibn al-$^c$Arabī's Metaphysics of Imagination* (Albany: State University of New York Press, 1989), index under *Allah;* and Chittick, *The Self-Disclosure of God: Principles of Ibn al-$^c$Arabī's Cosmology* (Albany: State University of New York Press, 1998), index s.v. "God."

9. See the last chapter of his *Madārij al-kamāl* (The rungs of perfection), where he uses this expression in explaining the highest level of human existence. Bābā Afḍal, *Muṣannafāt,* ed. M. Mīnuwī and Y. Mahdawī (Tehran: Dānishgāh-i Tihrān, 1331–37/1952–58), 51; translated in Chittick, *Heart of Islamic Philosophy,* 269–71.

10. Ṣadrā calls Porphyry this in Elixir 4.9. In *Asfār,* he is a bit more circumspect, using phrases such as "among the greatest companions of the First Teacher" (5:242), and "the foremost of the Peripatetics, one of the greatest students of the First Teacher" (6:181).

11. Ṣadr al-Dīn Shīrāzī, *Tafsīr al-Qurʾān al-karīm,* 7 vols. (Qom: Intishārāt-i Bīdār, 1366–69/1987–90), 1:107–11.

12. These passages are the following (the first numbers are those of the part and paragraph of the present edition of *Iksīr,* the second those of the *Tafsīr*

*sūrat yāsīn,* which was published as vol. 5 of Ṣadrā's *Tafsīr al-Qurʾān al-karīm*). Italics indicate that the passages are translated from or inspired by *Jāwidān-nāma:* 1.50–53:34–35; *3.43–45:229–32; 3.51–54:245; 3.57–59:164–65;* 4.1–2:163; 4.11–12:163–64; *4.14–15:168–69; 4.19–20:169; 4.26–31:170–72; 4.40–41:263; 4.42–44:264; 4.72:155;* 4.83:301; *4.90–91:156–57.*

13. See 1.40–45 of the present edition, corresponding to *Tafsīr,* 7:152–54.

14. *Shawāhid al-rubūbiyya,* in *Majmūʿah-i rasāʾil,* 296. This newly published work should not be confused with Ṣadrā's better known book whose complete title is *Al-Shawāhid al-rubūbiyya fī al-manāhij al-sulūkiyya,* ed. Jalāl al-Dīn Āshtiyānī (Mashhad: Dānishgāh-i Mashhad, 1346/1967).

15. "Principial," according to Webster's, means "initial" or "primary." The Arabic *aṣāla* is a *maṣdar* designating the fact of being an *aṣl,* that is, a root, principle, or foundation. Briefly, the doctrine of the "principiality of *wujūd*" means that *wujūd* is the root, and everything else—every quiddity—is a branch of *wujūd.*

16. Elsewhere Ṣadrā writes, "Knowledge *[maʿrifa]* of the soul and her states is the mother of wisdom and the root of felicity." See *Al-Mabdaʾ wa al-maʿād,* ed. Sayyid Jalāl al-Dīn Āshtiyānī (Tehran: Imperial Iranian Academy of Philosophy, 1976), 6. Toward the beginning of *Sharḥ al-hidāya,* he writes, "The science *[ʿilm]* of the soul is the mother of wisdom and the root of the virtues *[faḍāʾil].*" Tehran lithograph edition, 1313/1895, 7.

17. In *Asfār,* 2:350, Ṣadrā employs "gnostics" and "folk of God" together in a way that shows he considered them synonyms.

18. *Asfār,* 6:9. On *tashabbuh*'s importance in philosophy in general, see Chittick, *Heart of Islamic Philosophy.* On the significance of *takhalluq,* used by the Sufis as a virtual synonym for *tashabbuh* (as Ibn al-ʿArabī points out explicitly), see Chittick, *Sufi Path of Knowledge,* 383ff.

19. *Asfār,* 7:72–73.

20. *Asfār,* 9:16.

21. *Asfār,* 1:265–66.

22. On various translations that have been offered for this term, see Chittick, *Heart of Islamic Philosophy,* 16–17.

23. *Uthūlūjiyā,* in *Aflūṭīn ʿind al-ʿArab,* ed. ʿAbd al-Raḥmān Badawī (Cairo: Dār al-Nahḍa al-ʿArabiyya, 1966), 22. Ṣadrā may be referring to this passage when he writes that it has been related from Aristotle that he said, "I saw during disengagement luminous celestial spheres" (*Asfār,* 2:50).

24. *Asfār,* 8:135–36.

25. *Asfār,* 3:461. The word *faʿʿāl,* an intensive form of the active participle *fāʿil,* is normally translated as "agent" or "active," but neither of these terms seems adequate; "Fully Active" suggests the meaning more clearly. Ṣadrā explains (*Asfār,* 8:398) that the word is used to modify Intellect for three reasons: "First, the Fully Active Intellect gives existence to our souls and brings them out of the bounds of the potential intellect into the bounds of the Actual Intellect. Second, it is actual in every respect—there is nothing of potentiality *[quwwa]* within it. Through its intellective existence it is all of the intelligibles, or rather, all of the existences. Hence [the intensive form] *faʿʿāl* was ascribed

to it by way of stressing its actuality *[fiʿl]*. Third, it gives existence to the cosmos and is the origin of its forms, which are effused from it upon their matters." As for the word *ʿaql* itself, Ṣadrā explains in the same passage that it signifies "a disengaged form, intelligible to its essence by its essence. For, everything disengaged from matter—as was mentioned in the discussions of the intellect and the intelligible—is necessarily intellecter of its own essence. Its intellection of its essence is the very existence of its essence; this is not because of the presence of another form [other than itself]. So its essence is intellect, intellecter, and intelligible." Compare *Al-Mabdaʾ wa al-maʿād,* 269–70.

26. *Asfār,* 9:278.

27. These are of course the three basic types of souls in the afterlife, mentioned in surah 56 of the Qurʾān and frequently discussed in the literature—the companions of the right hand, the companions of the left hand, and the foremost.

28. *Shawāhid al-rubūbiyya,* 290–91. Compare *Iksīr,* pt. 3, chap. 10; *Shawāhid al-rubūbiyya,* 228–29.

29. For a fine discussion of Aristotle's saying that humans have three souls—the vegetal, animal, and rational—see *Asfār,* 8:135. For a more elementary account of the meaning of this teaching, see Chittick, *Heart of Islamic Philosophy,* 29ff.

30. On the term "soulish," see the end of the introduction.

31. *Asfār,* 8:136–37.

32. *Asfār,* 5:195.

33. The "two faces" are frequently discussed by Ibn al-ʿArabī (see Chittick, *Self-Disclosure,* 124, 135–36, passim).

34. These two expressions are more or less synonymous. "The divine wisdom" is also called simply *al-ilāhiyyāt,* "the divine things," a word that is commonly translated as "metaphysics." "The lordly sciences" are the knowledges that pertain to God as the Lord *(rabb),* the one who nurtures, protects, and has authority over created things. *Rubūbiyya* or "Lordship" is commonly taken as the topic of philosophical theology. Thus, for example, the Greek loanword *uthūlūjiyā,* "theology," is glossed in the very title of the Arabic Plotinus by the words *qawl ʿalā al-rubūbiyya,* "a talk about Lordship." Historians of philosophy have translated *rubūbiyya* in various ways, such as "divinity" and "sovereignty."

35. The Greek loanword *hayūlā* typically refers to the universal matter *(mādda)* that acts as the receptacle for all "forms" *(ṣūra)* in the hylomorphism that is standard in Islamic philosophy. The word *mādda* is more likely to be used to refer to matter in the relative sense, that is, matter that is itself a form, and hence it is commonly used in the plural *(mawādd)* to refer to the various sorts of matter. For example, "shirt" is a form in the matter that is cloth, but "cloth" is a form in the matter that is cotton. When all forms are eliminated, we are left with hyle, which is simply matter without form. For a good summary of Ṣadrā's understanding of matter, see his *Al-Mabdaʾ wa al-maʿād,* 264ff.

36. In the *Asfār,* 6:294, and elsewhere, Ṣadrā identifies this with the world of the First Intellect, which stands below God but beyond the spiritual world or Sovereignty *(malakūt).* In *Al-Mabdaʾ wa al-maʿād,* 125, he explains that the name derives from the divine name *al-jabbār,* which traditionally has been

understood in two ways according to its root meaning—Compeller and Mender. Ṣadrā tells us that this world deserves the name with respect to both meanings. The Real effuses the forms and realities of things by means of this world. Then he effuses their attributes and secondary perfections, which "mend" their deficiencies; and he "compels" the creatures to have perfections, to pay attention to these perfections when they lack them, and to preserve then when they acquire them.

37. *Asfār,* 1:2–3.

38. See n. 7, above.

39. Shigeru Kamada, *Morrā Sadorā no reikonron: Shinchi o motsu monotachi no reiyaku* (Tokyo: Isurāmu Shisô Kenkyukai, Faculty of Literature, Tokyo University, 1984).

40. Yathribī often corrects Kamada's readings of Qur'ānic verses, readings that coincide with the Majlis manuscript, without noting in his apparatus that his sources do not agree. For the most part, I follow Yathribī on Qur'ān quotations, but where he disagrees with both the Majlis manuscript and the Kamada edition without noting variants, and where there is a significant change in the nuance of the meaning, I follow the latter two.

## Notes to Part One

1. Ṣadrā is clearly identifying the science of "states" *(aḥwāl)* with the science of "thoughts" *(afkār)* discussed in chapter four. The rationale for this is not clear, and it may be this fact that led the copyist of one of Yathribī's manuscripts to substitute *afkār* for *aḥwāl* in this passage. What Ṣadrā has in mind can perhaps be explained in terms of a detailed discussion of the "Ramparts" *(aʿrāf)* that he offers in the *Asfār.* There he throws some light on the connection he sees between the "states" of things and the middle position, which is that of knowing the real situation of things, and thus presumably of mastery over thought. He stresses the linguistic connection between "ramparts" and "to know" *(ʿarafa).* The Men of the Ramparts have been given knowledge of the states of all things, and, one can surmise, they have thereby mastered the science of thoughts. Ṣadrā writes: "Thus it is established that He means by His words *who know each by their mark* that in this world they know both the folk of good and faith, and the folk of evil and rebellion. Hence He sets them upon the Ramparts, which are high, elevated places, in keeping with their station and their level, so that they may gain cognizance of all and witness what befits each of the two groups. They know that the folk of reward have arrived at the [ascending] degrees [of paradise], and the folk of punishment at the [descending] reaches [of hell]." *Asfār,* 9:317.

2. Al-Ghazālī explains at the beginning of *Iḥyāʾ ʿulūm al-dīn,* 5 vols. (Beirut: Dār al-Hādī, 1992) that there are two types of religious knowledge—that of unveiling *(mukāshafa)* and that of interaction *(muʿāmala).* The first deals precisely with what Ṣadrā lists here, which are the basic articles of Islamic faith. The second pertains to all the practices that should be followed on the path to God, and those are the topics of al-Ghazālī's *Iḥyāʾ.*

3. By using *ᶜāmmī* (common) and *khāṣṣī* (elect) instead of Bābā Afḍal's *ᶜāmm* (general) and *khāṣṣ* (specific), Ṣadrā shows that Bābā Afḍal does not mean this pair of terms in the usual philosophical sense but rather as adjectives derived from *ᶜāmma* (the common people) and *khāṣṣa* (the elect).

4. Contrasted with each other in this way, *khabar* (or *ikhbār*) means a statement of fact, and *inshāʾ* means the uttering of a command or wish. See C. P. Caspari, *A Grammar of the Arabic Language,* trans. W. Wright (London: Cambridge University Press, 1967), ii.73c.

5. These three together are usually taken as the science of eloquence *(balāgha)*—that is, rhetoric. Specialists have suggested that what is meant by *maᶜānī* is "semantics of syntax" and by *bayān,* the "science of figurative expression." *Badīᶜ* then pertains to various figures of speech. For the technical uses of the terms, see the articles on "al-Maᶜānī wa'l-bayān" and "Badīᶜ" in H. A. R. Gibb et al., *The Encyclopaedia of Islam* (Leiden: E. J. Brill, 1986–).

6. On the meaning of the word *ṣalāḥ* ("well-being" or "worthiness"), see 2 n. 9, below.

7. "The path" *(al-ṭarīqa)* is of course a common designation for what is usually called "Sufism" in English. The idea that the goal of Sufism and the goal of the religion of Islam are identical was a commonplace in the premodern texts. Notice, however, that both *ṭarīqa* and *dīn* are taken as practical and ethical ways. In philosophical terms, the path and the religion are oriented toward developing the "practical intellect" *(ᶜaql ᶜamalī),* in contradistinction to philosophy and theoretical Sufism or "gnosis," which are oriented toward developing the "theoretical intellect" *(ᶜaql naẓarī).* The goal of the path and the religion is to live in the world correctly and worthily, whereas the goal of philosophy and gnosis is to see things as they actually are in the divine scheme of things. On the two sorts of intellect, see Chittick, *Heart of Islamic Philosophy,* 29ff.

8. In its technical sense, *ḥuṣūl* means for something to come into existence after nonexistence. By "things and their realities" Ṣadrā means the existent things as known (that is, the quiddities), or the intellective forms of things.

9. Here Ṣadrā speaks of "presence" (as opposed to "absence," *[ghayba]*) because, in his view, "Knowledge is the presence of something at *(ᶜind)* something" (*Asfār,* 2:237). When someone knows something, we are speaking of the presence in that person's mind either of the thing's "whatness" *(māhiyya)* (that is, its "quiddity," which is its intellective form) or its "whetherness" *(haliyya)* (that is, the recognition of whether or not it exists). In Western philosophy, this contrast between whatness and whetherness has often been discussed as the issue of "essence and existence." Note that Ṣadrā ties this into the two basic sorts of knowledge discussed in logic—concept *(taṣawwur)* and assent *(taṣdīq).* The first is the form *(ṣūra)* or quiddity of a thing perceived by the mind, and the second is the recognition of a connection between two or more concepts. For example, both "ice" and "melting" are concepts, but the sentence, "Ice melts," is an assent. Definitions provide concepts, and demonstrations assents. As for the translation of *māhiyya* as "quiddity" rather than "essence," I do this not only because quiddity is a well-established word that was coined

by the Latins as a translation of *māhiyya,* but also because "essence" is needed for the word *dhāt,* which has quite a different usage.

10. In other words, intellects are the higher form of spiritual reality, ruling over things without being connected to bodies. The lower form, souls, are connected to bodies through governing and controlling them. The term "subjugating" is borrowed from Suhrawardī, a point that is more obvious in a parallel passage in *Al-Mabdaʾ wa'l-maᶜād,* 125: "Those holy intellects are subjugating lights that exercise their effects *[taʾthīr]* in the souls and orbs below them through God's exercising effects. Their subjugatingness, which is their exercising effects in others, is the shadow of His subjugatingness and one of the effects of His majesty and power."

11. *Taᶜayyun* is used as a synonym for *tajallī* (self-disclosure) and *ẓuhūr* (manifestation) in theoretical Sufism. I use "entification" to preserve the connection with *ᶜayn* (entity), a connection that is lost in the alternative translations, such as "determination." As an important technical term, *taᶜayyun* seems to be the coinage of Ṣadr al-Dīn Qūnawī, though it was often used by Ibn al-ᶜArabī. It means to appear in the form of "entities," which are things. The entities may be "nonexistent" *(maᶜdūm)* in the cosmos though "fixed" *(thābit)* in the divine knowledge, or they may be "existent" *(mawjūd)* in the world and hence "external" *(khārijī).* In the discussion of the "Five Divine Presences," it is commonly said that the Presences are "entifications," in contrast to the Divine Essence, which can only be discussed in negative terms—that is, as "nonentification" *(lā taᶜayyun).* Thus, in Ṣadrā's formulation here, "the entifications required by His names and His attributes" are the various levels of manifestation that make up the created realm.

12. Much of this section along with the material that follows in § 3 seems to consist of briefer versions of passages found in a section of Ṣadrā's *Al-Mabdaʾ wa al-maᶜād,* 124–28, on the manner in which the divine knowledge gives rise to the universe. There he depicts three levels of descent from God—the First Intellect, the Universal Soul, and the Soul as imprinted in the Universal Body—as three great "books," in each of which all existence is inscribed. Then a fourth book, Perfect Man *(al-insān al-kāmil),* brings together and comprehends *(jāmiᶜ)* the other three.

13. In the Qurʾān (19:52, 20:80), the "right side of the mountain" is the direction from which God called to Moses at Mount Sinai. Hence the "right side" is the direction of the luminous, spiritual world, and the "left side" the direction of the dark, corporeal world. Notice here the distinction that is drawn between the "intellective" nature of the First Pen and the "soulish" nature of the First Tablet. "Soul" invariably denotes an intermediary realm, between spirit and body, or between intellect and sense perception, or between light and darkness. When the human soul realizes the fullness of its potential, it is no longer a soul but rather "an Actual Intellect" *(ᶜaql bi'l-fiᶜl).*

14. By using the term "fixity" here, Ṣadrā is alluding to the "fixed entities" *(al-aᶜyān al-thābita)* made famous by Ibn al-ᶜArabī. In *Al-Mabdaʾ wa al-maᶜād,* he defines *qaḍāʾ* as "the existence of the intellective forms of all existents

through the Author's innovating them in the intellective world in the universal mode without time." In *Asfār,* 6:291–92, he says that it is "the forms of knowledge required by His Essence . . . , eternal *[qadīm]* in essence and subsistent through God's subsistence."

15. Ṣadrā provides an expanded form of this definition of *qadar* in *Asfār,* 6:292–93: "The Measuring Out consists of the existence of the forms of the existents in the soulish, heavenly world in the particular mode. [These forms] coincide with what is in their external, individual sorts of matter; they are ascribed to their occasions and their causes, are necessary through them, and are requisite for their designated times and their specific locations. The Decree envelops them just as the [divine] solicitude envelops the Decree."

16. Judging by the parallel passage in *Al-Mabdaʾ wa al-maʿād,* 124, by "folk of the Real" Ṣadrā means the Stoics and Suhrawardī. He contrasts them with the Peripatetics, specifically al-Fārābī, Ibn Sīnā, and Bahmanyār. He explains that for the latter group, solicitude means "an impression *[naqsh]* extraneous *[zāʾid]* to His Essence and having a locus that is His Essence." It consists of God's knowing the actual situation of everything that exists in the universal order, and this demands the most excellent universe possible in keeping with God's good pleasure. In contrast, the Stoics and Suhrawardī do not allow that there can be forms in the Essence extraneous to it. In their view, solicitude is

> His Essence with respect to the fact that from it are effused the forms of the things that are intelligible to Him, witnessed within Him, and pleasing to Him. Hence, solicitude has no locus. Rather, it is a simple knowledge established through His Essence, hallowed beyond the stain of multiplicity and differentiation, encompassing all things, and ever creating the differentiated objects of knowledge that come after it, which are the essences of the things that emerge from Him along with their essences and their individualities inasmuch as they are "from" him, not inasmuch as they are "in" Him.

For more on God's knowledge as "solicitude," see *Asfār,* 6:290–91.

17. In a similar but more straightforward sentence in *Al-Mabdaʾ wa al-maʿād,* 126, Ṣadrā writes: "Just as the intellective world called 'the Pen' is the locus of the Decree, so the heavenly, soulish world is the locus of His Measuring Out and the tablet of His Decree."

18. Ṣadrā's explanations in *Al-Mabdaʾ wa al-maʿād,* 126–27, make clear that just as the Decree is a pen that writes in the world of the Measuring Out, so also the Measuring Out is a pen that writes in its own tablet, which is the world of universal imagination *(al-khayāl al-kullī)* or images *(mithāl).* This third world is the Sovereignty *(malakūt)*; it acts by God's permission, subjects *(taskhīr)* by his command, and governs *(tadbīr)* the universe by preparing the various sorts of matter and the causes.

19. "Absent" here designates "that which is absent (from our senses)," the invisible realm of being, the spiritual world. In Qurʾānic terms, God is "Knower of the absent and the witnessed" *(ʿālim al-ghayb wa al-shahāda),* and this is typically understood to mean that he has knowledge of all creation, the unseen as well as the visible parts. Moreover, everything in the earth (the witnessed or visible realm) comes down from heaven (the absent or invisible

realm). God has "storehouses," as the Qur'ānic verse tells us, and a verse quoted in 1.39 shows that the Absent has "keys." These can be the keys to God's storehouses.

20. Most of this fourth section, including the "Branching Out," is found in a less detailed and probably earlier version in Ṣadrā's *Tafsīr sūrat al-jumuʿa* (in vol. 7 of his *Tafsīr al-Qur'ān al-karīm*), 152–54. As noted in the introduction, Ṣadrā considers this passage among his specific contributions to philosophy.

21. "Angelic" translates *subbūḥī*, a word that is derived from the divine name *subbūḥ*, the Glorified. The adjective refers to the specific activity of the angels, because *subbūḥ quddūs* is said to be their constant invocatory refrain. In the Qur'ān they say, "We glorify *[nusabbiḥ]* You in praise and call You holy *[nuqaddis]*" (2:30). As for "casting" *(ilqā')*, it is a Qur'ānic term often used to mean throwing in general. More relevantly, the Qur'ān uses it to designate God's "casting the spirit of His command" to His servants (40:15) and to designate a type of angel (77:5). Like Ibn al-ʿArabī, Ṣadrā uses it generically for any sort of divine infusion of knowledge. For other examples here, see 3.28 and 4.50.

22. The term *wahm* (sense-intuition) is often used loosely to mean "imagination" or "illusion," and this may be what is meant here. In Ṣadrā's technical language, however, it is the third of four basic sorts of perception. These are *ḥiss* (sense-perception), *khayāl* (imagination), *wahm*, and *ʿaql* (intellect). Briefly, the senses perceive particulars in the outside world, imagination perceives particulars internally, sense-intuition perceives universals in the form of particulars, and intellect perceives universals within itself. For a summary of Ṣadrā's theory, see Chittick, "On the Teleology of Perception," *Transcendent Philosophy* 1 (2000): 1–18.

23. The word *shabaḥ* (apparition) is often used as a synonym for *jism* or *badan* (body), but it is more likely to be employed when there is discussion of imaginal bodies, as here. Later, Ṣadrā will use it to mean physical body, as in 2.59–60, and 3.32.

24. According to Ibn al-ʿArabi, prophets both see and hear the angel, but the saints, who follow in their footsteps, may either see or hear the angel, but not both at once. See Chittick, *Sufi Path of Knowledge,* 260.

25. *Biḥār,* 18:136; Muslim, Fitan 19; Tirmidhī, Fitan 14; Ibn Māja, Fitan 9.

26. The hadith begins with words that Ṣadrā may be assuming his reader knows, since they strongly support his argument: "Surely I see what you do not see and hear what you do not hear." *Biḥār,* 59:212; Tirmidhī, Zuhd 9; Ibn Māja, Zuhd 19; Aḥmad, 5:127, 128.

27. In the standard Sunni sources, this hadith is found in the version "I find the breath of your Lord coming from the direction of Yemen" (Aḥmad, 2:541). Ibn al-ʿArabī frequently quotes it in the form given here, and, like Ṣadrā, he takes the verb "find" *(wujūd)* to mean "smell."

28. *Biḥār,* 6:208; Bukhārī, Ṣawm 20, 48, 49; Muslim, Ṣiyām 57, 58.

29. *Biḥār,* 18:373; Dārimī, Ru'yā 12; Aḥmad, 1:378, 4:66, 5:243, 378. Ṣadrā cites all five of the hadiths in this paragraph in a similar context in *Asfār,* 9:73.

30. The Qur'ān uses both the plural form *shayāṭīn* and the indefinite form *shayṭān* as distinct from *al-shayṭān,* "the Satan," that is, Iblīs. Like many authors,

Ṣadrā discusses satans generically, often contrasting them with angels (as in 3.39 ff.).

31. *Nash'a* (configuration) means literally an instance of growing up, rising up, coming to be. In the Qur'ān, God "configures" *(inshā')* two things that are called *nash'a*: "the first *nash'a*" (56:62) and the "last" or "other" *nash'a* (29:20, 53:47), meaning this world and the next. The word was used at least from the time of Ibn al-ʿArabī as a synonym for "world" *(ʿālam)* in the narrower sense, that is, as a designation for each of the various cosmic realms, especially those that human beings pass through in the stages of the Origin and Return.

32. The reference is to Qur'ān 50:22, cited in the next paragraph.

33. The first two of these contrasting pairs of terms are Qur'ānic. The third is associated with the Qur'ānic expressions "knowledge of certainty" *(ʿilm al-yaqīn)* and "eye of certainty" *(ʿayn al-yaqīn)*, or indirect, rational knowledge as contrasted with direct, intellective knowledge (compare Ibn al-ʿArabī's use of these expressions as cited in Chittick, *Self-Disclosure,* 355). Given that *ʿiyān* is grammatically identical in meaning with *muʿāyana,* the fourth pair of terms can be said to be an allusion to the well-known hadith, *laysa al-khabar ka'l-muʿāyana,* "Reports are not like clear-sightedness." Aḥmad, 1:215, 271.

34. The exact meaning of *ʿilliyyūn* is much discussed by the commentators, but it certainly designates something "high," as indicated by its root and the obvious connection with paradise. The root meaning of the contrasting term *sijjīn,* also usually taken as a proper name, is to imprison.

35. Tirmidhī, Qiyāma 26. *Biḥār* gives the phrase as a part of numerous hadiths from both the Prophet and some of the Imams (for example, 6:205, 214, 218).

36. There are several versions of this hadith in *Biḥār,* usually ascribed to ʿAlī. This version is most likely taken from al-Ghazālī, *Iḥyā',* 4:724, especially because much of the next sentence, beginning with "One should not wonder," is taken from al-Ghazālī's explanation. For his sources in the Sunni hadith literature, see *The Remembrance of Death and the Afterlife: Book 40 of The Revival of the Religious Sciences,* trans. T. J. Winter (Cambridge: Islamic Texts Society, 1989), 138 and note.

37. *Biḥār,* 3:90. Al-Ghazālī quotes this as a hadith in *Al-Arbaʿīn fī uṣūl al-dīn,* ed. Muḥammad Mustaf'a Abū al-ʿAlā' (Cairo: Maktabat al-Jundī, 1970), 283.

38. Ṣadrā discusses these in many works; for some details, see James Morris's *Wisdom of the Throne* (Princeton: Princeton University Press, 1981).

39. *Biḥār,* 61:7. Al-Ghazālī cites this as a hadith in *Iḥyā'*, 4:94, and *Arbaʿīn,* 280.

40. The rest of this paragraph seems to be the reworking of a discussion by al-Ghazālī in *Iḥyā',* 4:95, given that the order of the verses and the correspondences between macrocosm and microcosm are basically the same.

41. *Taʿṭīl* is a label for theological positions that divest God of his attributes.

42. The *barzakh* or "isthmus" is also called the "grave" *(qabr)*. It is an imaginal world in which souls dwell between death and resurrection. The word is also used in a wider sense (as it is later on in the text) to designate the world of imagination in general.

## Notes to Part Two

1. Apparently all the manuscripts have a singular noun here, even though the grammar of the rest of the sentence demands a plural subject.

2. None of these four groups—*mujassima, mu*ᶜ*aṭṭila, malāḥida,* and *dahriyya*—can be clearly identified. Rather, the terms are labels that were applied to theological enemies. The third was often used for the Ismāᶜīlīs when they were a political force to be reckoned with.

3. *Ghulāt* refers to sects of Islam that were thought to have "exaggerated" *(ghuluww)* their beliefs concerning the Prophet, the Imams, or anyone else—for example, by ascribing divinity to them. *Nawāṣib* is used to designate early Muslims who were enemies of ᶜAlī.

4. A *fatwā* is a legal opinion given by an expert in the law, a mufti. In the Shiᶜite context, giving *fatwā*s is the prerogative of the "mujtahids," those who exercise independent legal judgment *(ijtihād)*. In the Sunni world, the "gate of *ijtihād*" is typically said to have been closed by the efforts of the great mujtahids of the past, though the ulama continue to give *fatwā*s. "Transmission" refers to the chains of authority that must be established if a hadith is to be considered authentic. The four topics together designate the three principles upon which jurisprudence is built. Ṣadrā does not mention the fourth Shiᶜite principle, *ᶜaql.*

5. *Farḍ ᶜayn* is a juridical term that is contrasted with *farḍ kifāya.* The first designates something that is incumbent upon each individual Muslim; the second, something that is incumbent upon the community. For example, the daily *ṣalāt* is *farḍ ᶜayn,* and knowledge of inheritance laws is *farḍ kifāya.*

6. That is, this world and the next world (see above, 1 n. 31).

7. As noted in the introduction, "Command and Creation" (derived especially from Qurᵓān 7:54) refer to the two worlds—the Absent and the Witnessed, or the spiritual and the corporeal, or the Sovereignty and the Kingdom. In the expression "horizons and souls" (derived from Qurᵓān 41:53), "horizons" refers to the macrocosm and "souls" to the microcosm. Both macrocosm and microcosm are divided into spiritual and bodily worlds, or Command and Creation, or Sovereignty and Kingdom.

8. Caprice *(hawā)* is an important Qurᵓānic term. It designates the worst sort of false god—that is, one's own desires and fancies. In Sufi texts it is much discussed, sometimes as a synonym for appetite *(shahwa)*. Its opposite is *ᶜaql,* the intelligence and moral integrity that is able to hold it back and act as its "fetter" *(ᶜiqāl)*. In philosophical texts, appetite and wrath (the medieval "concupiscence and irascibility") designate the two basic tendencies of the animal soul that *ᶜaql* needs to tame and redirect.

9. This is an important Qurᵓānic term. The verbal noun, *ṣalāḥ,* means well-being, goodness, soundness, and worthiness. Its opposite is *fasād,* which means corruption, rottenness, and decay. The philosophers also use *fasād* as the opposite of a second word, *kawn,* "being" or "generation" (as in the expression *al-kawn wa al-fasād*). Thus *ṣalāḥ* can be understood to designate the proper and worthy mode of being that people need to achieve. When Qurᵓān translators render *ṣāliḥ*—an

adjective that is applied both to people and to deeds—as "righteous," this obscures the ontological issues and draws the discussion into the biblical context, suggesting that the primary focus is on morality and deliverance from sin. (The Hebrew *ṣedheq* has its Arabic cognate in *ṣidq,* "truthfulness," an important Qurʾānic term, often discussed in Sufism and much closer to "righteousness" than *ṣalāḥ.*) Philosophers and Sufis read a verse like "Corruption has appeared in the land and the sea because of what people's hands have earned" (Qurʾān 30:41) not as a metaphor, but as an actual statement of the intimate, ontological nexus between microcosm and macrocosm. If human beings do not achieve worthiness to be the divine vicegerent, which is the purpose for which they were created, the universe as a whole will suffer (not just the physical environment, which is only the surface of a much deeper reality). In order to avoid stressing the moral implications of the word *ṣāliḥ,* I have often translated it as "wholesome," but the connotations of this English word are not especially appropriate. "Worthy" is perhaps better, as long as we understand this primarily as an ontological worthiness that then gives rise to moral and ethical worthiness.

10. "Adamic" *(ādamī)* is of course synonymous with "human" *(insānī),* so the discussion pertains to the human soul in general. The feminine pronoun is generated by the feminine noun "soul" *(nafs).*

11. Ṣadrā has apparently conflated two verses. The continuation of 14:32 reads "to run upon the sea of His commandment."

12. There is an allusion here to sound hadiths that state that the heart is "between two fingers of the All-Merciful, and He turns it about as He wills." In *Al-Mabdaʾ wa al-maᶜād,* 201, Ṣadrā cites a version of the hadith and explains that "finger" here designates the means to put something into motion and the power to change and separate.

13. Webster's gives the meaning of "satanity" as "satanism," but the connotations of the Arabic *shayṭana* are not especially negative. The issue here is not moral judgment but microcosmic function. What is it in man that corresponds to Satan? That the answer is *wahm* had long been discussed, among others by ᶜAbd al-Razzāq Kāshānī. (For relevant texts in al-Ghazālī and Kāshānī, see Sachiko Murata, *The Tao of Islam* [Albany: State University of New York Press, 1992], 258–59, 273–74). In *Al-Mabdaʾ wa al-maᶜād,* 308, Ṣadrā explains, "The potencies [of the soul] are given commands and prohibitions, and none of them is able to oppose and disobey except the one that is named 'sense-intuition.' It has a share of satanity, and through this it rebels against obeying the intellect, just as Iblīs rebelled against obeying the Real." In *al-Shawāhid al-rubūbiyya,* 225, he tells us that intellect, imagination, and sense-perception each has a world pertaining to it, but not *wahm,* the fourth sort of perception. "Sense-intuition perceives the meanings as ascribed to the sorts of matter, so no configuration pertains to it. Rather, its existence is that of a false *[kādhib]* intellect, just as Satan is an angel accidentally *[bi al-ᶜaraḍ].*"

14. *Taʾyīd* has a literal sense closer to "strengthening" and means giving strength to the heart through understanding and knowledge. The usage derives from the Qurʾān, as in the verse, "As for those, He has written faith upon their hearts and confirmed them with a spirit from Him" (58:22). Ibn al-ᶜArabī calls

the spirit that provides confirmation "the command spirit" *(al-rūḥ al-amrī)* on the basis of verses like 40:15: "He casts the spirit of His command upon whomsoever He will of His servants." See Chittick, *Self-Disclosure*, 276–77.

15. The word *maʿnā* here is used in a sense that was taken over from Sufi writings. It designates not abstract, mental notions, or ideas in the modern sense, but rather concrete, spiritual realities that exist independently of the mental faculties in the realm of the First Intellect. The term is used more or less synonymously with reality *(ḥaqīqa)*, quiddity *(māhiyya)*, and fixed entity *(ʿayn thābita)*. It is thus a synonym for form *(ṣūra)* in the philosophical sense, but not in the Sufi sense. In philosophical usage, as is suggested by the use of the word later on in this same sentence, form is contrasted with matter *(mādda)*. The forms are the *maʿqūlāt*, the "intelligibles" or eternal realities that come to be known when the intellect is actualized. In the Sufi usage, meaning is a thing's reality with God or in the First Intellect, whereas form is the thing's outward appearance. Thus "meanings" in the Sufi sense are the same as "forms" in the philosophical sense.

16. In a philosophical context, the verb *intizāʿ* is usually translated as "to abstract." I use a nontechnical, concrete term to underline the cosmic function of the perfect man that Ṣadrā is depicting here. By employing a parallelism between "extracting" and "grasping," he reminds us that *intizāʿ* is the eighth form of the verb *nazʿ*, which, along with *qabḍ*, is commonly used to designate the taking of the soul at death. Ṣadrā is pointing out that he sees an exact correspondence between the proper operation of the intellect, which is achieved by the perfect man and the true sage, and the angel of death, which grasps and extracts the soul. The sage pulls the spiritual reality out from the bodily shell, or the intellective substance out from the sensory accident, or the form out from the matter. The "universals" that he extracts are not "abstractions" in any modern sense, but rather the actual, concrete, permanent realities of the things. For further indications of the correspondence between the intellect and the angel of death, see the discussion of Azrael in 3.26–28.

17. It is important to note that much of this argument has to do with the nature of the "potency" *(quwwa)* that belongs to man. This term is difficult to translate consistently into English because it covers at least three concepts that we normally differentiate. First, it refers to a divine attribute and is usually translated as "strength" or "power." Second, it designates every strength and power latent in the soul, and here it is usually translated as "faculty." The vegetal soul has certain potencies, the animal soul possesses these plus others, and the human soul possesses the greatest number of potencies. The overall capacity (again *quwwa*) of the human soul, or the strength and power that it has to be human, is also its "potency." In this sense, however, the word is typically translated as "potentiality," and it is contrasted with *fiʿl*, "act" or "actuality." What is potential in the soul is actual in the intellect.

18. These are good examples of Ṣadrā's manner of using Qurʾānic phrases outside their own context to stress his point. In the Qurʾān, the two phrases refer to God and need to be translated in the present tense—"He does what He wills"; "He rules as He desires."

19. Encompassing all beings and having mastery over them is what Ibn al-ʿArabī calls the "all-comprehensiveness" *(jamʿiyya)* of the human configuration, an attribute that derives from the creation of Adam in God's form. The degree to which an individual actualizes the divine form in this world determines the manner of his being in the next. The fact that man embraces everything "within his own world" helps explain Ṣadrā's well-known teaching that each human soul becomes a total world in the afterlife. He writes, "Every human being, whether blessed or damned, has a world complete on its own, more immense than this world, and not strung on the same thread with any other world." *ʿArshiyya,* ed. Ghulām Ḥusayn Āhanī (Isfahan: Kitabfurushi-i Shahriyār, 1341/1962), 252. See also James Morris's translation of this passage, *Wisdom of the Throne,* 165.

20. My reading follows the Majlis manuscript. Yathribī's text has *fī baldat*$^{in}$ *ghālibat*$^{in}$ *wa ʿālimat*$^{in}$, "into the conquering and knowing city."

21. Given the mention of *muslim* in the previous sentence, Ṣadrā probably has in mind the verse, "To God is submitted *[islām]* everything in the heavens and the earth, willingly or unwillingly" (3:83). Compare 13:15: "To God prostrates itself everything in the heavens and the earth." To the objection that the pronoun *man* should be translated "everyone" and not "everything," one can reply that the Qurʾān does not clearly distinguish between animate and inanimate, and when it ascribes attributes of living beings to things that are apparently dead, it commonly personifies them. Since everything prostrates itself and submits itself, everything has animate qualities and deserves the pronoun *man.* Compare the verse, "God said to it [the heaven] and to the earth, 'Come willingly or unwillingly.' They said, 'We come willingly'" (41:11).

22. For more on the significance of this sort of "ransom" and its meaning in the context of good and evil, see *Asfār,* 7:91–94, a chapter called "That the divine desire may be connected to the occurrence of things in the cosmos considered evil by the majority for the sake of the worthiness of the state of the beings."

23. The Qurʾānic verse refers to angels. It is an appropriate proof text in this context because the potencies in the microcosm play the same role as the angels in the macrocosm. Both are invisible forces that animate the visible realm.

24. These are often called the "seven subtleties" *(laṭāʾif)* or the "seven subtle centers" and have been discussed in the context of Kubrawī teachings by Henry Corbin and others. They become a standard topic in Sufi texts from about the eighth/fourteenth century. See Chittick, "On Sufi Psychology: A Debate Between the Soul and the Spirit," in *Consciousness and Reality: Studies in Memory of Toshihiko Izutsu,* ed. S. J. Ashtiyani et al. (Tokyo: Iwanami Shoten, 1998), 341–66.

25. There are several ancient interpretations for the meaning of the Qurʾānic phrase "seven of the doubled and the magnificent Qurʾān." Most commonly, the doubled seven are said to be the seven verses of the Fātiḥa, "doubled" because they are recited so often or because they were revealed on two different occasions to the Prophet. In Bābā Afḍal's original text, the doubled seven are seven signs of the macrocosm (heaven, fire, air, water, earth, plants, animals) plus seven corresponding microcosmic signs (hearing, eyesight, smell,

taste, touch, rational speech, writing). It is not clear how Ṣadrā considers the seven subtleties to be "doubled," or if in fact he does.

26. In *Al-Taʿlīqāt*, ed. ʿAbd al-Raḥmān Badawī (Cairo: al-Hayʾa al-Miṣriyya al-ʿĀmma li'l-Kitāb, 1973), 90, Ibn Sīnā writes that from counting *(ʿadd)* and measurement *(misāḥa)* are derived "what is in the soul, and that is the numberer and the measurer, and what is in the thing, and that is the numbered and the measured." In *Kitāb al-muqāwamāt*, in *Majmūʿa fi al-ḥikma al-ilāhiyya*, ed. Henry Corbin (Istanbul: Maṭbaʿat al-Maʿārif, 1945), 137, Suhrawardī writes, " 'Numbering' *[ʿadad]* is to determine *[taqdīr]* the discontinuous, just as 'measurement' is to determine the continuous. Numberingness *[ʿāddiyya]* and measuringness *[māsiḥiyya]* are specificities of the perceiver."

27. The solitary numbers are 1 through 9, then 10, 20, 30, . . . 90; then 100, 200, 300, . . . 1000. They are "solitary" because in each case, only a single numeral is mentioned (zero not being considered a numeral). The *abjad* order of the alphabet (contrasted with the usual, *alif-bāʾ* order) gives each letter a numerical value, beginning with *alif* (1), *bāʾ* (2), *jīm* (3), *dāl* (4), and ending with *ghayn* (1000).

28. "All-Merciful Breath" is of course Ibn al-ʿArabī's term (see Chittick, *Sufi Path of Knowledge*, chap. 8). For a much longer version of this discussion, also in terms of the All-Merciful Breath, see *Asfār*, 7:10–13, a chapter called "On the difference between speech, book, speaking *[takallum]*, and writing *[kitāba]*."

29. *Maʿnawī* or "supraformal" is the adjective derived from *maʿnā* or "meaning." As already noted, meaning is contrasted with "form" *(ṣūra)*, which is the appearance of things to our senses. The "supraformal" realm lies beyond outward forms. However, it is not "formless" in the philosophical sense because the intelligibility of all things is indebted precisely to their "forms."

30. Grammatically, the two feminine pronouns ("its") go back to "state" *(ḥāl)*, though the meaning is basically the same if we understand them as referring to "cosmos."

31. Ṣadrā is saying that in the macrocosm, everything that appears in the earth (the bodily world) depends upon heaven (the spiritual world). So also in the microcosm: everything that appears in the analogous earth, which is the realm of writing and documents, depends upon the soul.

32. Usually "well-established" here would be translated as "straight," but that rendering would lose the wordplay that ties the passage together.

33. The two editions and the Majlis manuscript have *samāʿ* (hearing) instead of *samāʾ* (heaven), but this is a mistake, as shown both by the context here and by the passage in Bābā Afḍal's *Jāwidān-nāma* (*Muṣannafāt*, 280–81) upon which this discussion is based.

34. Notice that this whole section is comparing the soul as governor of the body to God as governor of the heavens and earth. In this paragraph, Ṣadrā seems to be alluding to a hadith that tells us, "Our Lord descends to the heaven of this world every night and says, 'Is there any repenter? Is there any supplicator? Is there anyone asking forgiveness?' " (Muslim, Musāfirīn 172).

35. "Absent of absents" *(ghayb al-ghuyūb)* is a term commonly used in Sufi texts to distinguish between what is absolutely absent and what is relatively

absent. The first is the Essence of God, which can never be known to any but God Himself, and the second is the world of the Absent that is contrasted with the world of the Witnessed; these are the two basic worlds, as already noted. For an explanation of the two sorts of absent domain by Ibn al-ᶜArabī, see Chittick, *Self-Disclosure*, 243–44. For a discussion of *ghayb al-ghuyūb* by Ṣadrā, see *Asfār*, 2:345–47 (compare *Asfār*, 5:232, 6:284, and 7:11).

36. The term "carriers" is derived from a reference in Qurᵓān 69:17 to eight angels who will carry God's Throne on the day of resurrection.

37. The use of the word "task" *(shaᵓn)* in this sort of context goes back to Ibn al-ᶜArabī, who takes a Qurᵓānic mention of the term—"Each day He is upon some task" (55:29)—as a reference to God's renewal of creation at each instant. The "day" of the "He-ness" or Ipseity (the divine Essence), he often remarks, is the present moment (see Chittick, *Sufi Path of Knowledge*, 98–99). In the writings of Ibn al-ᶜArabī's followers, the term comes to designate the divine properties and traces found in everything in the universe. For more explanation and examples in Jāmī's writings, see Sachiko Murata, *Chinese Gleams of Sufi Light* (Albany: State University of New York Press, 2000), 120, and index s.v. "task."

38. The full text of the verse cited here is this: "Were all the trees in the earth pens, and the sea—seven seas after it to aid it—yet the words of God would not run out." The word translated "aid" *(imdād)* also means to provide something with "ink" *(midād)*, and the ink is mentioned explicitly in a second verse that makes the same point (18:109). Thus the text tells us that the ink is the matter of all the "divine words," which are simply the creatures. On hyle, see 4 n. 39.

39. There is an allusion here to a well-known hadith: "Faith has seventy or sixty and some branches, the best of which is the words, 'There is no god but God,' and the least of which is the removal of harm from the road" (Muslim, Īmān 58 ff.). In a similar passage in *Al-Mabdaᵓ wa al-maᶜād*, 268, Ṣadrā goes on to quote the famous saying, usually attributed to Junayd, *wujūduka dhanb lā yuqās bihi dhanb*, "Your existence is a sin to which no sin can be compared."

40. An associator is someone who associates others with God. Hence, he has two faces, one turned toward God and the second toward others. The "face" of a thing, as Ibn al-ᶜArabī frequently remarks, is its reality. In the first chapter of his *Lawāᵓiḥ*, Jāmī warns the seeker of the dangers of dividing the face: "*God has not assigned to any man two hearts in his breast* [Qurᵓān 33:4]. The Howless Presence, who has given you the blessing of being, has placed within you only one heart, that you may be one-faced and one-hearted in love . . . not that you should make one heart into a hundred pieces." Murata, *Chinese Gleams*, 136.

41. The word *submitted* (that is, *muslim*) is found in both Kamada's edition and the Majlis manuscript, but Yathribī has dropped it and does not tell us of its existence in his apparatus. Ṣadrā may have purposefully interpolated the word with a view toward Qurᵓān 3:67, which says about Abraham that he was "unswerving, submitted, and not one of the associators."

42. Ṣadrā has taken some of the phrasing here from Naṣīr al-Dīn Ṭūsī's commentary on Ibn Sīnā's *Al-Ishārāt wa'l-tanbīhāt* (Tehran: Maṭbaᶜat al-Ḥaydarī,

1377–79/1957–60), 3:389. He quotes Ṭūsī's exact words with ascription to him in *Sharḥ al-hidāya,* 209.

43. There is an allusion here to the verse, "Say: 'If you love God, follow me; God will love you'" (3:31).

44. This *ḥadīth qudsī* is found in *Biḥār,* Bukhārī, Muslim, and other standard sources. The concept of two nearnesses, those of obligatory and supererogatory works, is derived from the full text of the hadith and is frequently discussed in Sufi texts from Ibn al-ᶜArabī onward. Ṣadrā does not mention the two in the *Asfār,* however. See Chittick, *Sufi Path of Knowledge,* 325–31.

## Notes to Part Three

1. "Undergoing renewal" is to change and be transformed moment by moment. Ṣadrā uses the word synonymously with *istiḥāla, taghayyur,* and *ḥaraka.* It does not have the same technical sense as *ḥudūth,* "occurrence," which is the opposite of *qidam* ("eternity") and denotes coming into being after not having been. By using the word *tajaddud,* Ṣadrā is recalling Ibn al-ᶜArabī's famous doctrine, *tajdīd al-khalq fi al-ānāt,* "the renewal of creation at each instant."

2. The term "withness" *(maᶜiyya)* is derived from the Qurʾānic verse, "He is with you wherever you are" (57:4), and is much employed by Ibn al-ᶜArabī. See, for example, Chittick, *Sufi Path of Knowledge,* 88, and index s.v. "withness."

3. It may seem strange that Ṣadrā here equates hell's castigation with going astray *(ḍalāl),* which is typically understood as the soul's activity in this world that leads to chastisement in the next. However, in Ṣadrā, the next world is nothing but the world of the soul, so "going astray" here is identical with "castigation" there. In *Asfār,* 9:346, he explains that hell's very existence derives from human sin: "Gehenna has no real existence with respect to being an abode of chastisement. Rather, its source is the existence of going astray and disobedience in the souls. So much is this so that, were there no disobedience in Adam's children, God would not have created the Fire."

4. Ṣadrā specifies the Measuring Out here because of a purported hadith, "Measuring Out is God's secret, so do not make it manifest!" Ibn Sīnā cites this hadith and then takes a stab at making the secret manifest in his three-page treatise, *Fī sirr al-qadar,* in *Majmūᶜ rasāʾil al-shaykh al-raʾīs* (Hyderabad: Dāʾirat al-Maᶜārif al-ᶜUthmāniyya, 1953). For some of Ṣadrā's remarks on the secret, see *Asfār,* 2:297, 351.

5. It seems that the verb has now become feminine, because Ṣadrā has reverted to *huwiyya* (ipseity) as the subject of the sentence. For a while he had been taking an implied *insān* as the subject (as is indicated not so much by the masculine form of the verbs as by the masculine pronoun in *fahmihi,* "his understanding").

6. Ṣadrā quotes this saying in a similar context in *Asfār,* 8:327, and *Al-Mabdaʾ wa al-maᶜād,* 361.

7. The title of this chapter can be more fluently translated into English as "On the nature of place" or "What is place?" I use the heavier English words

to highlight the technical terms and to avoid loose usage. "Quiddity," as noted earlier, is contrasted with *wujūd.* By asking about a thing's quiddity, we are asking for a definition of the thing, not an explanation of its existence. Ṣadrā turns to the question of existence in temporal matters in chapter four of this part. As for "location" as a translation for *makān,* this makes it possible to use "place" without any technical sense for the many other words that demand it, such as "nouns of place" *(ism makān),* for example, "falling place" *(mahbat),* "hiding place" *(makman),* and "stumbling place" *(mazilla).* Also, in contrast to place, "location" allows for a derived adjective, "locational" (for *makānī).* As for "nature," it is the standard translation for *ṭabīʿa,* and this is far too important a technical term to be applied where it does not belong. In the philosophical vocabulary, one would not say *ṭabīʿat al-makān,* "the nature of location," because location has no nature, in contrast to things that can be located, such as minerals, plants, and animals.

8. This definition of *makān* is given almost word for word in Ibn Sīnā's *Ḥudūd* and Jurjānī's *Taʿrīfāt* and can be traced back to Aristotle's *Physics,* 4.4. Clearly, by "sages" is meant "philosophers." Ṣadrā, like many others, often uses *ḥakīm* and *faylasūf* interchangeably, but on occasion he also differentiates between the two, and then he makes the *ḥakīm* stand at a higher level. It was never lost on the tradition that the *faylasūf* is the "lover of *ḥikma,*" not necessarily the true possessor of *ḥikma.*

9. In *Shawāhid,* 396, Ṣadrā cites this point as one of the particularities of his own philosophy: "The abode of the afterworld is another configuration, not strung with this configuration on one pathway. Hence its location is not of the genus of the locations of this world, nor is it within one of its directions. So also, its time is not of the genus of these times, nor does it fall in its future. On the contrary, both this world and the afterworld are complete worlds, not needing anything from outside." He provides arguments in *Asfār,* 9:202–5.

10. Ṣadrā denies substantial movement in more detail in *Sharḥ al-hidāya,* 99. He alludes to what he later comes to call "substantial movement" in 4.13, below, when he talks about the movement of existence from deficiency to perfection.

11. Note that "occurrence" translates *ḥudūth* and its derivatives. As noted, this important technical term is contrasted with *qidam,* "eternity." It refers to the fact that everything in the universe comes into existence within time.

12. Usually translated as "infinite regress," concatenation without end is considered an absurdity.

13. The saying is well known and is sometimes treated as a hadith; see Chittick, *Faith and Practice,* 83 and 218.

14. The "divine ones" *(ilāhiyyūn)* seem to be the same as the "deiform gnostics" *(al-ʿurafāʾ al-mutaʾallihūn)* mentioned earlier. Ṣadrā's use of the terms *ilāhī* and *mutaʾallih* in the *Asfār* suggests that he considers them synonyms. He refers only to three figures by name as "deiform"—Suhrawardī (six times), Ibn al-ʿArabī (once), and Porphyry (once). As for "divine," he uses it as an adjective for two sages—Suhrawardī (twelve times) and Plato (fifteen times).

15. In the *Asfār,* Ṣadrā provides some clarification as to what he means here by these definitions. He connects the discussion with the "fixed entities" *(aʿyān*

*thābita)* or "objects of [divine] knowledge" *(maᶜlūmāt)* discussed by Ibn al-ᶜArabī and his followers (which, as noted, are identical with the "quiddities" or "realities"). "In the speech of the masters of wisdom, the relation of the fixed to the fixed is 'sempiternity,' the relation of the fixed to the changing is 'aeon,' and the relation of the changing to the changing is 'time.' By the first they mean the relation of the Author to His names and knowledges; by the second the relation of His fixed knowledges to His ever-renewed *[mutajaddid]* objects of knowledge—which are the existents of the bodily cosmos in their entirety—through existential withness; and by the third the relation of some objects of His knowledge to others through temporal withness." *Asfār,* 3:147–48.

16. Literally "her." The Arabic pronouns here and in the following three paragraphs are actually feminine, because they refer back to the feminine word *nafs* (soul), not to the names of the archangels.

17. Apparently the manuscripts all have *yakūn* instead of *takūn,* but the subject is clearly *hiya.*

18. The use of the term *maqṣūd* here was made current by Ibn al-ᶜArabī, who calls man the "intended entity" *(al-ᶜayn al-maqṣūda)*—that is, the goal intended by God when he created the universe. Philosophers sometimes cite a maxim derived from Greek philosophy to make the same point: *Awwal al-fikr ākhir al-ᶜamal,* "The first in thought is the last in practice"—that is, the first thing to be thought about is the last to be actualized. God's "first thought" is man, made in his image and capable of knowing and loving him fully. Or it is the logos, the Muḥammadan Reality.

19. The "eightfold" journey is that of the seven planets and the fixed stars. By "seconds" Ṣadrā presumably means the sixty seconds of arc contained in a minute (the sixtieth part of a degree), which mark the gradual movement of the spheres in their journeys.

20. Ṣadrā provides a long philosophical exposition of human beings as the goal of creation and other beings as their leftover in *Al-Mabdaᵓ wa al-maᶜād,* 264–74.

21. I have been translating *naẓar* as "gaze" or "consideration," but here it clearly means something more. Ṣadrā has in mind an actualized vision of the truth, not human theories that may or may not be valid. *Naẓar* means literally to look and to gaze, and is used to refer to theological and philosophical theorizing in general, as in the phrase *ahl al-naẓar.* For Ṣadrā and others, the word can designate the fulness of vision that is achieved by the "theoretical intellect" when it reaches the stage of the Actual Intellect.

22. Ṣadrā seems to mean that "this period" is identical with the "six days" of creation that are mentioned several times in the Qurᵓān. In the Persian original of this passage, Bābā Afḍal explains the six days as follows: "In the same way, the Real wanted to show the human soul in bodily form with respect to the fact that it had a joining with the Real in its own shelter and was joined to those other souls. When it was about to appear in the bodily form, it fell into destruction, corruption, without-self-ness, and unconsciousness. In every level at which it arrived, many births appeared from it. In six days six things appeared. On the first day [there appeared] heaven and the stars—like the root, leaves, and seeds—in the respect that they have a joining with the Real; on the second day,

the pillar of fire with respect to its becoming mixed with the substance of the highest soul; on the third day the pillar of air; on the fourth day the pillar of earth; on the fifth day the pillar of water; and on the sixth day the generation of plants and animals." Chittick, *Heart of Islamic Philosophy,* 216–17.

23. Ṣadrā refers here to a hadith that he cited earlier (1.57).

24. *Three* here refers to Qurʾān 39:6: "He creates you in your mothers' bellies, creation after creation, in three darknesses."

25. Reading *lahu* for Yathribī's *lahum;* Ṣadrā has again modified the Qurʾānic verse to fit the grammar of his sentence, but Yathribī has corrected the text to follow the Qurʾān.

26. "Possibility" *(imkān)* is of course the opposite of "necessity" *(wujūb).* The latter belongs strictly to the Real *Wujūd,* which is existent through its own essence, whereas the former is the attribute of everything other than God. Inasmuch as a thing's existence does not belong to it, it is susceptible to evil, which is the lack of good—that is, the lack of *wujūd.*

27. The "smoke" is probably an allusion to Qurʾān 41:11: "Then He went directly to the heaven when it was smoke, and He said to it and to the earth, 'Come, willingly or unwillingly.'"

28. Aḥmad (2:176) and Tirmidhī (Īmān 18) have this hadith but with "cast" *(alqā)* instead of "sprinkled" *(rashsha).* Ibn al-ʿArabī commonly cites it, using "sprinkled."

29. *Ḥukm* here might be understood to mean God's "judgment" concerning the soul. However, that would be to put the burden on God rather than man. The point of the whole discussion is that the soul acquires properties *(aḥkām),* attributes *(ṣifāt),* and character traits *(akhlāq)* in this life and these then shape its destiny in the next life.

30. I read the verb as first form *(ṭahara),* despite the fact that "earth" (feminine) should have a feminine verb, because of the parallelism with the other two verbs and the tendency of many Persian authors to ignore the niceties of Arabic grammar. One could also read the verb as second form, *ṭahhara,* "he purified," and then "earth" would be the object rather than the subject.

31. The Kamada edition has *al-ghālibūn* in place of *al-mufliḥūn.* If this is correct, Ṣadrā conflated 5:56 with 58:22. The Yathribī edition makes no mention of this reading.

32. One might translate *al-shayṭān* here as "Satan," but this would give too much weight to the mythic background and ignore the parallelism with "angel." Ṣadrā's frequent use of the plural, *shayāṭīn,* as in the title of the previous chapter (and see also 1 n. 29), is further evidence that "satan" as opposed to "Satan" is sometimes the more appropriate translation. Later on in this chapter (para. 47) Ṣadrā even pluralizes Iblīs, which is almost always taken as a proper name. In *Al-Mabdaʾ wa al-maʿād,* 201–2, he explains the parallelism between angel and satan, inspiration and disquietening, and (God's) success-giving *(tawfīq)* and abandoning *(khidhlān),* and in the process cites the hadith, "There is not one of you that does not have a satan."

33. Like other philosophers and Sufis, Ṣadrā often criticizes following authority or imitation *(taqlīd)* in creedal matters *(ʿaqāʾid)* and encourages

instead its opposite, verification or realization *(taḥqīq),* which is to find the truth in oneself. He will have more to say about imitation in pt. four, chap. seven.

34. This hadith, not found in the usual Sunni sources or *Biḥār,* is probably taken from al-Ghazālī's *Iḥyāʾ*. If so, Ṣadrā has conflated two hadiths of similar purport. The first of these refers to the same Qurʾānic verse and reads, "Woe upon him who recites it and does not reflect *[tafakkur]* upon it" (4:617). The second gives the text that we have here, but in reference to Qurʾān 3:191, "those who reflect upon the creation of the heavens and the earth: 'Our Lord, Thou hast not created this in vain.'" In both places where al-Ghazālī cites this hadith, he explains the meaning of wiping the mustache with the verse. In one instance he says, "That is, he passes *[tajāwuz]* by it without reflection" (4:645). In the other he writes, "It means that he recites it but leaves aside thinking about it. He fails to understand the Sovereignty of the heavens, though he does recognize the color of the heaven and the brightness of the stars; but that is what the beasts also recognize. Thus, whoever is satisfied with this much knowledge is he who 'wipes his mustache with it'" (4:171).

35. Ṣadrā has in view here Qurʾān 3:7, which sets up a distinction between two types of verse. The first is *muḥkam,* which means firmly fixed, consolidated, and well made, and connotes being imbued with authority *(ḥukm)* and wisdom *(ḥikma).* The second is *mutashābih,* which means mutually similar, open to doubts, equivocal. In *The Qurʾān Interpreted* (London: Allen & Unwin, 1955), A. J. Arberry translates the two terms as "clear" and "ambiguous" and thereby suggests what has generally been understood from them. However, their exact meaning and the significance of the whole verse—which also mentions *taʾwīl* or "interpretation" in a rather ambiguous way—has been much discussed and debated, especially because the Qurʾān seems to be setting down here a basic principle for its own interpretation. Hence Ṣadrā is offering a plausible manner of distinguishing between the two types of verse in terms of two macrocosmic forces, angel and intellect, which correspond to the two microcosmic potencies that perceive universals. Intellect sees universals without intermediary and through identity with them, and sense-intuition sees them only within particulars and therefore in a distorted manner.

36. As already noted, to declare God ineffectual is to divest him of his attributes. Declaring him similar is to deny his transcendence and incomparability *(tanzīh).* Although Ṣadrā declares the illegitimacy of *tashbīh* here, he also recognizes in the *Asfār* that the correct understanding of *tawḥīd* depends upon the simultaneous assertion of both *tanzīh* and *tashbīh*—a position that Ibn al-ʿArabī takes as one of the cornerstones of his perspective.

37. That is, a knowledge received by way of suprarational intuition or divine inspiration, not ratiocination. "Unveiling" *(kashf)* is the generic term in Sufism for suprarational knowledge. "Influx" *(wārid)* means literally "arriver." Ibn al-ʿArabī tells us that the Sufis employ this word to designate "that which arrives in the heart from any divine name" (see his chapter on *wārid* in the *Futūḥāt,* translated in Chittick, *Self-Disclosure,* 148–50). Ṣadrā calls one of his treatises *Al-Wāridāt al-qalbiyya,* "Influxes in the heart." In explaining the book's name at the beginning, he writes, "I will explain to you some of the influxes

that have been cast to me in my inmost mind . . . [to which] I was called in my secret heart during my journey, and in which I imitate no one else."

38. There is a reference here to a hadith, a version of which is found in *Biḥār,* 60:243, that tells us that God planted the tree of Ṭūbā with his own hand.

39. *Maṣlaḥa* (advantage) is literally a place or an instance or a means of well-being and worthiness *(ṣalāḥ).* In other words, God does not create things to bring about corruption *(fasād).* If something seems to be evil, in fact there must be an underlying good that outweighs the evil, and this goes back to God's "wisdom," not to mention his mercy, which takes precedence over his wrath.

40. I have been translating *awliyā'*, with some hesitation, as "saints," but here the context forces me to go back to a more literal sense of the word. Thus "God's friends" in the next clause are God's "saints." The translation of *ṭāghūt* as "false god" is also problematic, and the eight Qur'ānic mentions of the term have given rise to a good deal of discussion among lexicographers and Qur'ān commentators.

41. Jalāl al-Dīn Rūmī, *The Mathnawī of Jalaluddin Rumi,* ed. Reynold A. Nicholson, 8 vols. (London: Luzac, 1925–40), bk. 5, vv. 1521–22.

42. The unusual expression "writing soul" is Bābā Afḍal's. In *Jāwidān-nāma,* he discusses it on two occasions prior to mentioning it in this passage, but Ṣadrā has not translated those sections, so its mention here seems odd.

43. The terms *al-ḥaḍra al-jamᶜiyya* (the Presence of Gatheredness) and *ᶜayn al-jamᶜ* (the Entity of Gathering) employed in this paragraph designate the first stage of the descent from God, which is identical with the final stage of the return to him. The expressions are derived from the writings of the school of Ibn al-ᶜArabī. Of course, the contrast between "gathering" and "dispersion" *(farq, tafriqa)* is much older in Sufi writings, but the earlier authors viewed these two from the perspective of the path to God; Ibn al-ᶜArabī and his followers also discuss them as ontological levels. From this standpoint, "gathering" refers to God or the Necessary Existence and "dispersion" to the world or the possible realm. More specifically, gathering pertains to the name *Allah,* which is called the "all-gathering name" *(al-ism al-jāmiᶜ),* because all the divine names and created realities come under its scope. In *Asfār* (2:331), Ṣadrā tells us that the Necessary Existence has no attributes and no descriptions and that *martabat al-jamᶜ* (the Level of Gathering) is the first level of existence that can be discerned as other than it. He tells us that this expression designates the same reality as several other terms derived from the writings of Ibn al-ᶜArabī's school—the Cloud *(ᶜamā')*, the Reality of Realities *(ḥaqīqat al-ḥaqā'iq),* the Presence of the Unity of Gathering *(ḥaḍrat aḥadiyyat al-jamᶜ),* and the Presence of One-and-Allness *(ḥaḍrat al-wāḥidiyya).*

44. This poem, frequently cited in Sufi works in similar contexts, is by the well-known scholar and vizier Ṣāḥib ibn ᶜAbbād (d. 385/995).

45. The Yathribī edition adds here the clause, "which is to say that they have reached dispersion," though it is not found in six of the manuscripts. It seems to be a copyist's interpolation for the sake of parallelism, and it contradicts the next sentence, which says that they "remain" in dispersion, which in fact is the state that they have in the world.

46. The saying is commonly attributed to Junayd.

47. This short section revises a passage from Ikhwān al-Ṣafā᾽, *Rasā᾽il,* 4 vols. (Beirut: Dār Ṣādir, 1957), 3:47–48. About half of the sentences are quoted word for word.

48. In its root meaning, *taqwā* combines the senses of fear and self-protection. In Qur᾽ānic terms, it is one of the highest human virtues. In rendering the superlative form of the adjective in the well-known verse, "Surely the noblest among you with God is the one 'with the most *taqwā*' " (49:13), Qur᾽ān translators have used expressions such as "most dutiful," "best in conduct," "most god-fearing," "most careful," "most righteous," "most deeply conscious," and "who best performs his duty." The central importance of the concept and the wide difference of opinion as to its exact meaning perhaps justify calling attention to it by employing a neologism that is evocative of the Qur᾽ānic meaning.

49. As noted earlier, for philosophers and Sufis, the issue in discussion of *ṣalāḥ* is not simply right activity and "righteousness," but rather transformation of the soul. The title of this work, *The Elixir of the Gnostics,* points to the alchemical transmutation that is the goal of the path.

50. Yathribī's edition chooses *ṣinf* rather than *ṣaff,* but I follow four of his other manuscripts because of the appropriateness of this Qur᾽ānic term in the context, rather than the rather philosophical *ṣinf.*

## Notes to Part Four

1. The term *limmī* (from *lima,* "why") is contrasted with *innī* (from *inna,* "surely"). The *limmī* or a priori demonstration begins with the cause and concludes with the existence of the effect. The *innī* or a posteriori demonstration begins with the effect and yields the cause. The former is considered superior, because it gives certain knowledge of its conclusion, whereas the latter can be mistaken, since there may be other causes that can explain the result just as well. In a similar passage in *Asfār,* 5:28, Ṣadrā uses the circularity of the spheres to show how one problem can be discussed in different respects by different sciences. The mathematical sciences prove through an *innī* demonstration, and the natural sciences by a *limmī* demonstration based on the "mutual similarity of the traces that occur to simple nature."

2. The discussion has to do with Aristotle's four causes—the material, formal, efficient, and final—the first two of which are "near," and the second two "far." In both cases that Ṣadrā is discussing, the investigator is seeking to prove that the spheres' movements, like the spheres themselves, do not undergo corruption.

3. I translate *fā᾿il* as "actor" rather than "efficient cause" to preserve the literal meaning of the Arabic expression and to avoid obscuring the connection with "act" and "actuality" *(fi᾿l),* "actual" *(bi'l-fi᾿l),* and "fully active" *(fa᾿᾿āl).*

4. On this expression, see the introduction, n. 32.

5. English usage suggests translating the word *ma᾿nā* here as "idea" or "concept." However, as noted earlier, *ma᾿nā* frequently designates a permanent

spiritual or intellective reality, as opposed to the unreal and passing "forms" *(ṣūra)* that appear as long as we continue to perceive things darkly through the veils of sense perception, imagination, and sense-intuition. Moreover, there is no reason to think that Ṣadrā is using the term "unveiling" in this paragraph in anything other than its technical sense—that is, direct vision of the spiritual realities. Ṣadrā is not suggesting that Porphyry thought up the idea of unification, but rather that he had experienced the reality of unification by actualizing his intellect and achieving conjunction with the Fully Active Intellect.

6. "Entified" existence is the sort of existence that things acquire when they become "existent entities" *(aʿyān mawjūda)* in the external realm. Here it is contrasted with imaginal existence, which is the existence of something as an image, or in imagination. More commonly it is contrasted with "cognitive" *(ʿilmī)* existence—that is, the existence of things as fixed entities *(aʿyān thābita)* in the divine knowledge or as forms in the intellect. The fixed entities are also known as the "nonexistent entities" *(aʿyān maʿdūma)* because they do not exist in the external realm.

7. *Ṭibāʿ* can be taken as a singular or as the plural of *ṭabʿ*. In general *ṭabīʿa* designates nature in a broad sense; *ṭabʿ*, nature as it pertains to individual instances; and *ṭibāʿ*, the combination of the natures that gives rise to a bodily constitution. Ṣadrā does not employ the term *ṭibāʿ* in the *Asfār.*

8. There is an allusion here to the doctrine of the "best of all possible worlds," debated at least since the time of al-Ghazālī.

9. "Essential" *(dhātī)* clearly means that which arises from the very essence and reality of a thing. The word is commonly contrasted with "accidental" *(ʿaraḍī),* which designates all the passing attributes that accrue to a thing. Since the text contrasts "essential" with "constrained," one might think that "essential" here means "autonomous," but that would be to ascribe too much self-control to things. The point is rather that God creates things by mercy and for mercy, and this bestows upon them a reality that can only draw them to mercy in the end. This is one of Ibn al-ʿArabī's common themes.

10. The Kamada and Yathribī editions have *hādhihi al-huwiyyāt bi'l-tawalludāt,* which is difficult to make sense of. Several of the manuscripts, including the Majlis autograph, correspond with my text, as does the same passage in Ṣadrā's commentary on *Yāsīn* (*Tafsīr* 5:171).

11. The pillars are the four elements, as becomes clear in the next paragraph, where water and fire are mentioned explicitly.

12. The mythic "salamander" dwells, of course, in fire.

13. This first sentence follows Bābā Afḍal's text, but the next five paragraphs digress from it. This is why Ṣadrā discusses the sheep as having all four legs bound and then having them released one by one. Only in "A Fine Point and an Allusion" does Ṣadrā return to explaining what is meant by the first sentence.

14. The reference is to the famous *ḥadīth qudsī,* found in *Biḥār,* Bukhārī, Muslim, and other standard sources, "I have prepared for My worthy servant what no eye has seen, what no ear has heard, and what has never passed into the heart of any mortal."

15. The hadith reads, "The folk of the Garden will enter the Garden hairless, beardless, [eyes] daubed with kohl, children of thirty or thirty-three years" (Tirmidhī, Janna 12; Aḥmad, 5:232, 240, 243). Ṣadrā comments on it in *Asfār,* 9:33.

16. Baba Afḍal's original does not connect the heavens and the four elements, and he gives a different version of the correspondence between the seasons and the elements, agreeing only on summer. In his view, autumn corresponds to air, spring to water, and winter to earth. Ṣadrā is tying the discussion into the well-known idea that the twelve constellations are divided into four groups of three each, according to the four elements.

17. From this sentence until "Another Fine Point," Ṣadrā is quoting and adapting a passage from Ibn al-ᶜArabī's *Al-Futūḥāt al-makkiyya,* 4 vols. (1911; reprint, Beirut: Dār Ṣādir, 1968), 1:294–96. The changes he makes usually simplify the text or eliminate digressions, and they have little effect on Ibn al-ᶜArabī's points. The few exceptions will be noted. At the very beginning, he drops the first clause, which situates the passage squarely in Ibn al-ᶜArabī's typical way of conceptualizing things—that is, in terms of the divine names. The original text reads, "Know that since God is named 'King' *[malik],* He ordered the cosmos as an 'empire' *[mamlaka]* is ordered."

18. On the basis of the analogy, one could translate *khawāṣṣ* or "elect" as "favorites" or "courtiers," but the expression is typically used in Sufism to distinguish Sufi adepts from the "common people" *(ᶜawāmm),* who may be the ordinary run of Sufis, or simply the non-Sufis, those who have not embarked on the path. The distinguishing characteristic of the elect is their constant remembrance of God, an angelic attribute. Instead of simply "angels," Ibn al-ᶜArabī's text has "the enraptured angels" (*al-malāᵓika al-muhayyama,* whom he will call later on in this passage "the enraptured spirits"). In many passages he identifies these with the "cherubim" *(karrūbiyyūn),* who will be mentioned shortly. Ṣadrā's version of the passage introduces the cherubim without explanation, and this causes a certain confusion, which will be explained in its place. Ibn al-ᶜArabī's regular readers would have caught the reference here to the "enraptured" angels and know that they are the same as the cherubim who come up later.

19. The Qurᵓānic inspiration for this discussion is 68:1: "*Nūn,* and by that which they are writing out." In this verse, *nūn* is written as a single letter *(n),* so it is taken as one of the mysterious detached letters that begin many Qurᵓānic chapters. However, some of the early commentators interpreted this as designating the word *nūn* itself, which can mean "fish" or "inkwell." See Murata, *Tao of Islam,* 153–54. In Ibn al-ᶜArabī's interpretation here, the name of the angel specifies its function as the inkwell containing the undifferentiated ink from which the Highest Pen is replenished.

20. Ṣadrā has abbreviated this passage, but he adds "world of His Decree" in order to bring in his own cosmological scheme. He has explained the Decree in 1.33ff. and mentioned its world in 2.45, 47.

21. In Ṣadrā's abbreviated text, the pronoun seems to refer to the Tablet, but there is no ambiguity in Ibn al-ᶜArabī's original.

22. Idiomatically, this last phrase would mean "silently or aloud." However, given Ibn al-ᶜArabī's attention to *ḥāl* as a technical term, we cannot assume that this is all that he has in mind. "State" denotes the ontological situation of a creature in relation to its Lord. Concerning the "tongue of the state," Ibn al-ᶜArabī writes in the *Futūḥāt,* 3.374.26, "When God turns toward the servant, He bestows upon him what he seeks from Him with the tongue of his state, which is the most eloquent tongue and the most direct expression." See his discussion of the three sorts of asking—by words, state, and preparedness—in *Fuṣūṣ al-ḥikam,* ed. Abū al-ᶜIla ᶜAfīfī (Beirut: Dār al-Kitāb al-ᶜArabī, 1946), 60.

23. In what follows, either the names or the functions of most of the mentioned angels are taken from Qurᵓānic verses.

24. The Inhabited House (mentioned in Qurᵓān 52:4) is said to be located in the seventh sphere directly above the Kaaba. Every day seventy thousand angels circumambulate it and pray in it, never to return. Sufi texts frequently identify it with the human heart, which is the focus of the angels' attention in the microcosm.

25. The words in brackets are from the *Futūḥāt,* and all the manuscripts indicate that they were dropped from Ṣadrā's text, possibly by oversight. If the text is left to read "those enraptured spirits," two problems arise. One is that the word *those* demands a reference, and there is no previous reference to the enraptured spirits. The second is that the text here identifies the enraptured spirits with the rulers, but their very name indicates—as Ṣadrā himself was well aware (cf. *Al-Mabdaᵓ wa al-maᶜād,* 267)—that they are so enraptured by the vision of God that they are not able to turn any attention toward creation. This is why, at the beginning of this passage, the text explained that God took one of the enraptured angels and separated it out from the rest. Only then did He give it knowledge of creation and call it Nūn.

26. Ibn al-ᶜArabī's list of human functionaries is a bit different, notably excluding the Imams. Ṣadrā, with a nicely Shiᶜite touch, cites this Qurᵓānic verse as a divine allusion *(ishāra)* to the connection between the Mother of the Book and the most excellent of the Imams. He employs the same verse in a similar way in a chapter of the *Asfār* called "Verifying the words of . . . ᶜAlī that have come to us, 'All the Qurᵓān is in the *bāᵓ* of *bismi'llāh,* and I am the dot under the *bāᵓ*.' " (7:32).

27. In Ibn al-ᶜArabī's vocabulary, the tenuities *(raqāᵓiq)* are subtle influences that tie the levels of existence together (see Chittick, *Sufi Path of Knowledge,* 406 n. 6). Ṣadrā explains that "realities" *(ḥaqāᵓiq)* dwell in universal, intellective existence with God, but they become manifest as "tenuities" in the lower levels of existence. So, "The tenuity is the reality with respect to conjunction." The realities stay with God, but the tenuities descend as imaginal apparitions and bodies. See *Asfār,* 8:126–27.

28. "Necessitates" may seem too strong, because it suggests that God is constrained to do something. However, Ṣadrā is not using the verb loosely. He has in view a well-known teaching that was first formulated clearly by Ibn al-ᶜArabī. No one can constrain God, of course, but God can constrain himself, which is precisely what he does in the mentioned verse, when he "writes" mercy for

specific creatures. Largely on the basis of this verse, Ibn al-ᶜArabī divides God's mercy into that of "favor" or "free gift" *(imtinān)* and that of "necessity" *(wujūb)*. The former is designated by the name *al-raḥmān,* which embraces all things, and the latter by *al-raḥīm,* which bestows its bounties on those who actualize the virtue of godwariness and do good works. See Chittick, *Sufi Path of Knowledge,* 130.

29. Sciences that are "noninstrumental" *(al-ghayr al-āliyya)* are known directly to the intellect without intermediary. The "instruments" or "tools" *(āla)* are the soul's faculties, the body's organs, and the various sciences that help the intellect come to actualize itself and know all things by knowing itself. Imagination and eyesight are tools of the soul, the eye is the tool of eyesight, and logic is the tool of wisdom. Ṣadrā writes in *Asfār,* 6:380, "The final goal of the science of logic is for it to be an instrument *[āla]* for the theoretical sciences, and these sciences, when taken in an unqualified sense, are noninstrumental, because their final goal is themselves. This is because they are the last, final goal of other, instrumental sciences."

30. By "traditions" *(āthār),* literally "traces," Ṣadrā clearly means sayings that have reached us, whoever may have uttered them. Bābā Afḍal's original is even vaguer in the ascription.

31. In Bābā Afḍal's original text, these words are simply his own explanation of the saying just quoted.

32. This is a hadith (Dārimī, Libās 4; Aḥmad, 2:50).

33. Compare *Asfār,* 7:9, where Ṣadrā also affirms that no one should imagine that the Prophet was imitating Gabriel in the way that a believer imitates the Prophet, because the Prophet had himself reached the truth.

34. The hadith is found in various versions in *Biḥār,* Bukhārī, and other standard sources. The fact that "John" slaughters death is not unrelated to the literal Arabic meaning of his name, "he lives."

35. Given the context, Ṣadrā employs the religious language. Elsewhere he makes it completely explicit that this "holy angel" is none other than the Fully Active Intellect. For example, in *Sharḥ al-hidāya,* 206, he writes that the acquired intellect *(al-ᶜaql al-mustafād)* is called by this name "because it is acquired from the Fully Active Intellect, which is called 'the spirit of holiness' *[rūḥ al-qudus]* in the language of the Shariᶜa. He is the teacher *intense in potencies* [53:5] and the one who confirms by casting revelation to the prophets. It is he who, when we conjoin with him, *confirms* us and *writes in* our *hearts faith* [58:22] and true sciences."

36. When the Prophet said this, he held up his hand with thumb and forefinger almost touching. The hadith is given in *Biḥār,* 2:263, 309; 16:256, as well as in Bukhārī, Muslim, and other standard sources.

37. Note the way that Ṣadrā supports his argument by employing the plurals of the words *jarīma* (offense) and *jirm* (body), both of which derive from the same root. This linguistic relationship can be understood to imply that having a body is itself an offense against the spirit, and the way to overcome this ontological sin is to adhere to the spirit and transmute the body into spirit.

38. The expression "fully active word" *(kalima faᶜᶜāla)* derives from the Arabic Plotinus (*Uthūlūjiyā,* Mīmir 8 and 10). Ṣadrā understands it to designate

the soulish and spiritual reality that gives rise to a bodily thing, or the form that in itself is disengaged but that appears to our senses and imagination as embodied in matter. He quotes two passages from *Uthūlūjiyā* on the fully active words and the manner in which they determine the elements, including earth, in *Asfār,* 9:268–69.

39. The hylic potency is also called "the hylic intellect," "the potential intellect" *(al-ᶜaql bi'l-quwwa),* and "the passive intellect" *(al-ᶜaql al-munfaᶜil).* It is the soul with respect to her innate disposition *(fiṭra),* which has the preparedness *(istiᶜdād)* to perceive every intelligible meaning. Ṣadrā explains that the name was given to the soul on the analogy of bodily matter, which is empty of all sensory forms but also receptive to them. Thus the soul's *hyle* or matter has no intelligible form whatsoever, yet it is receptive to every form. "If the potential intellect had a specific form, it would not have the worthiness to accept anything else, just like an inscribed tablet; rather, it is sheer preparedness." *Al-Mabdaᵓ wa al-maᶜād,* 262–63.

40. Ṣadrā seems to be alluding here to the several Qurᵓānic verses that speak of the folk of the Fire regretting the fact that they had not done good works in the world.

41. By this last sentence, Ṣadrā is suggesting that the paragraph is a direct quotation from "one of the commentators." However, it is probably a paraphrase of Fakhr al-Dīn Rāzī's words explaining Qurᵓān 6:61 in *Al-Tafsīr al-kabīr,* 8 vols. (Istanbul: Dār al-Ṭibāᶜat al-ᶜĀmira, 1307–8/1889–91).

42. A different version of this passage to the end of this chapter is found in Ṣadrā's commentary on *Sūrat al-sajda* in *Tafsīr al-Qurᵓān al-karīm,* 6:85–87.

43. The saying, "The *ṣalāt* is the *miᶜrāj* of the believer" is often treated as a hadith. Cf. *Biḥār,* 82:303, 84:255.

44. This short paragraph, not found in the original passage in *Tafsīr sūrat al-sajda,* alludes to one of the mainstays of Ṣadrā's teachings on *maᶜād.* Cf. *Shawāhid,* 289; *Asfār,* 7:93; 9:53, 258; *Al-Mabdaᵓ wa'l-maᶜād,* 454–58.

45. The clause in brackets, taken from the version of this passage in *Tafsīr sūrat al-sajda,* helps clarify what Ṣadrā is saying.

46. As noted earlier, the "actor" is the "efficient cause."

47. Ṣadrā often refers to the identity of knowledge and life, an identity which, he reminds us, is already explicit in certain Qurᵓānic verses (see, for example, *Asfār,* 9:176). In brief, as he puts it in *Al-Mabdaᵓ wa al-maᶜād,* 271, "Intellective perfection is the true felicity by which man actually comes alive without any need for matter to be intellectively established." He makes his basic point more bluntly in *Risāla sa aṣl,* ed. Seyyed Hossein Nasr (Tehran: Dānishgāh-i Tihrān, 1340/1961), 14, while commenting on the hadith, "He who knows his soul knows his Lord": "So, if someone does not have knowledge of the soul, his soul has no existence, because the existence of the soul is the same as light, presence, and awareness."

48. This discussion recalls Ṣadrā's famous axiom mentioned in the introduction, "The soul is bodily in occurrence, spiritual in subsistence" (cf. *Asfār,* 6:109; 8:345, 347, 393; 9:85; *Al-Shawāhid al-rubūbiyya,* 221). "Occurrence" *(ḥudūth),* the opposite of eternity *(qidam),* is "to come into being." Thus Ṣadrā

denies the "eternity" of the soul, but not its everlastingness. He uses the image of net and prey in a similar discussion in *Al-Mabdaʾ wa al-maʿād,* 315. He tells us that "they" have often used this image in explaining how the soul becomes connected to the body; he is probably alluding to Ibn Sīnā's *Risālat al-ṭayr* and the many subsequent versions of the same story. See Shokoufeh Taghi, *The Two Wings of Wisdom: Mysticism and Philosophy in the* Risālat uṭ-ṭair *of Ibn Sina* (Uppsala: Uppsala University Press, 2000). Ṣadrā states his own position clearly in *Asfār,* 8:393: "When the human soul climbs, is transformed, and is sent forth from the world of Creation to the world of Command, her existence becomes a separate, intellective existence that has no need for the body, its states, and its preparedness. The disappearance of the body's preparedness does not harm her in essence and subsistence, nor even in attachment *[taʿalluq]* and dominating power *[taṣarruf],* since her existence in the domain of occurrence is not her existence in the domain of subsistence. This is because the former is material, but the latter is separate from matter. Thus her state at her occurrence is not like her state at reaching perfection and coming home to the Active Origin. So, in reality, she is 'bodily in occurrence, spiritual in subsistence.' The likeness of this is the infant's need for the womb at first but its not needing it later, because existence has changed for it. It is also like the prey and the need for a net in hunting for it but the lack of need for it when the prey subsists with the hunter later. The corruption of the womb and the net does not contradict the subsistence of the infant and the prey, nor does it harm them."

49. In Ṣadrā's perspective, existence is of two basic sorts—interlinking *(rābiṭī)* and predicative *(maḥmūlī).* The second is the thing's own existence, whereas the first is an existence that is established for the thing, inasmuch as it is linked with something else. Examples of predicative existence would be the existence of the intellect and the soul, and examples of interlinking existence would include every accident that occurs for a substance (cf. *Asfār,* 1:78–82). He says what he is saying here in more straightforward language in *Al-Mabdaʾ wa al-maʿād,* 315, where he explains that the soul has two existences, one pertaining to the body and the other to her own essence.

50. Ṣadrā is alluding to the soul's existence in the afterworld once she has become a "separate" *(mufāriq)* substance. In this world, she is connected to the body through the body's "preparedness" (*istiʿdād),* which plays a major role in the manner in which the soul actualizes her potential, precisely because she is "bodily in occurrence." But once she comes to be "spiritual in subsistence," the body no longer plays a role in her unfolding. After the resurrection, she has an imaginal body, not a corporeal body, and this imaginal body has no effect upon her. Rather, it is the outward side or the image of her existence. Ṣadrā explains these points in many passages in various works, as for example in *Asfār,* 9:31: "The afterworldly bodies are the requisites of the souls, just as the shadow [is the requisite of] the possessor of the shadow. They are effused by the mere innovation of them by the First Real with respect to the active direction, without any sharing in this by the receptacles with respect to the direction of preparedness. Thus every soulish, separate substance requires an imaginal apparition that is configured from it with respect to its soulish habitudes,

character traits, and guises, without the intervention of the preparednesses and the gradual movements of the sorts of matter that are the case in the cosmos. The existence of the afterworldly body is not prior to the existence of the body's soul. Rather, the two are together in existence without the interference of either putting the other in place. This is like the togetherness of the requisite and what requires it, or the shadow and the object [that throws it]. Just as neither the object nor its shadow is prior to the other, so also neither obtains a preparedness for its existence from the other. Rather, this is by way of subordination and requisiteness. In such a way should be gauged the afterworldly bodies along with the souls conjoined with them."

51. "Lordship" here refers to philosophical theology.

# Bibliography


Arberry, Arthur John. *The Koran Interpreted.* London: Allen & Unwin, 1955.

Avicenna. *Al-Ishārāt wa'l-tanbīhāt.* Tehran: Maṭbaʿat al-Ḥaydarī, 1377–79/ 1957–60.

———. *Fī sirr al-qadar.* In *Majmūʿ rasāʾil al-shaykh al-raʾīs.* Hyderabad: Dāʾirat al-Maʿārif al-ʿUthmāniyya, 1953.

———. *Al-Taʿlīqāt.* Ed. ʿAbd al-Raḥmān Badawī. Cairo: al-Hayʾa al-Miṣriyya al-ʿĀmma li'l-Kitāb, 1973.

Bābā Afḍal. *Muṣannafāt.* Ed. Mujtabā Mīnuwī and Yaḥyā Mahdawī. Tehran: Dānishgāh-i Tihrān, 1331–37/1952–58.

Badawī, ʿAbd al-Raḥmān, ed. *Aflūṭīn ʿind al-ʿArab.* Cairo: Dār al-Nahḍa al-ʿArabiyya, 1966.

Bāqerī, Nāhīd. *Kitābshināsī-i jāmiʿ-i Mullā Ṣadrā.* Tehran: Bunyād-i Ḥikmat-i Islāmī-i Ṣadrā, 1378/1999.

Al-Bukhārī, Muḥammad ibn Ismāʿīl. *Al-Ṣaḥīḥ.* 9 vols. N.p.: Maṭābiʿ al-Shuʿab, 1378/1958–59.

Caspari, Carl Paul. *A Grammar of the Arabic Language.* Trans. W. Wright. London: Cambridge University Press, 1967.

Chittick, William C. *The Heart of Islamic Philosophy: The Quest for Self-Knowledge in the Teachings of Afḍal al-Dīn Kāshānī.* Oxford: Oxford University Press, 2001.

———. "On Sufi Psychology: A Debate between the Soul and the Spirit." In *Consciousness and Reality: Studies in Memory of Toshihiko Izutsu.* Ed. S. J. Ashtiyani et al., 341–66. Tokyo: Iwanami Shoten, 1998.

———. "On the Teleology of Perception." *Transcendent Philosophy* 1 (2000): 1–18.

———. *The Self-Disclosure of God: Principles of Ibn al-ʿArabī's Cosmology.* Albany: State University of New York Press, 1998.

———. *The Sufi Path of Knowledge: Ibn al-ʿArabī's Metaphysics of Imagination.* Albany: State University of New York Press, 1989.

Al-Dārimī, ʿAbd Allāh ibn ʿAbd al-Raḥman. *Al-Sunan.* 2 vols. Beirut: Dār Iḥyāʾ al-Sunna al-Nabawiyya, n.d.

Al-Ghazālī, Abū Ḥāmid Muḥammad. *Al-Arbaʿīn fī uṣūl al-dīn.* Ed. Muḥammad Muṣṭafā Abū al-ʿAlāʾ. Cairo: Maktabat al-Jundī, 1970.

———. *Iḥyāʾ ʿulūm al-dīn.* 5 vols. Beirut: Dār al-Hādī, 1992.

———. *The Remembrance of Death and the Afterlife: Book 40 of The Revival of the Religious Sciences.* Trans. T. J. Winter. Cambridge: Islamic Texts Society, 1989.

Gibb, Hamilton Alexander Rosskeen et al. *The Encyclopaedia of Islam.* Leiden: E. J. Brill, 1986–.

Ibn al-ʿArabī. *Al-Futūḥāt al-makkiyya.* 4 vols. 1911. Reprint, Beirut: Dār Ṣādir, 1968.

———. *Fuṣūṣ al-ḥikam.* Ed. Abū al-ʿĀlāʾ ʿAfīfī. Beirut: Dār al-Kitāb al-ʿArabī, 1946.

Ibn Ḥanbal, Aḥmad ibn Muḥammad. *Al-Musnad.* 6 vols. Beirut: Dār Ṣādir, n.d.

Ibn Māja, Muḥammad ibn Yazīd. *Al-Sunan.* 2 vols. Ed. M. F. ʿAbd al-Bāqī. Cairo: Dār Iḥyāʾ al-Kutub al-ʿArabiyya, 1952.

Ibn Sīnā. *See* Avicenna.

Ikhwān al-Ṣafāʾ. *Rasāʾil.* 4 vols. Beirut: Dār Ṣādir, 1957.

Jalāl al-Dīn Rūmī. *The Mathnawī of Jalaluddin Rumi.* Ed. Reynold Alleyne Nicholson. 8 vols. London: Luzac, 1925–40.

Kamada, Shigeru. *Morrā Sadorā no reikonron: Shinchi o motsu monotachi no reiyaku.* Tokyo: Isurāmu Shisō Kenkyukai, Faculty of Literature, Tokyo University, 1984.

Majlisī, Muḥammad Bāqir. *Biḥār al-anwār.* 110 vols. Reprint, Beirut: Muʾassasat al-Wafāʾ, 1983. Also on the CD-ROM *Nūr.* Qom: Computer Research Center of Islamic Sciences, 1999.

Morewedge, Parviz. *Essays in Islamic Philosophy, Theology, and Mysticism.* Oneonta, N.Y.: Global Publications, 1995.

Morris, James. *The Wisdom of the Throne: An Introduction to the Philosophy of Mullā Ṣadrā.* Princeton: Princeton University Press, 1981.

Mulla Ṣadrā. *See* Ṣadr al-Dīn Shīrāzī.

Murata, Sachiko. *Chinese Gleams of Sufi Light.* Albany: State University of New York Press, 2000.

———. *The Tao of Islam.* Albany: State University of New York Press, 1992.

Muslim ibn Ḥajjāj. *Al-Ṣaḥīḥ.* 8 vols. Cairo: Maṭbaʿa Muḥammad ʿAlī Ṣabīḥ, 1334/1915–16.

Nasr, Seyyed Hossein. *Ṣadr al-Dīn Shīrāzī and His Transcendent Theosophy: Background, Life and Works.* 2d ed. Tehran: Institute for Humanities and Cultural Studies, 1997.

Rahman, Fazlur. *The Philosophy of Mullā Ṣadrā.* Albany: State University of New York Press, 1975.

Rāzī, Fakhr al-Dīn. *Al-Tafsīr al-kabīr.* 8 vols. Istanbul: Dār al-Ṭibāʿa al-ʿĀmira, 1307–8/1889–91.

Rūmī. *See* Jalāl al-Dīn Rūmī.

Ṣadr al-Dīn Shīrāzī, Muḥammad ibn Ibrāhīm. *ʿArshiyya.* Ed. Ghulām Ḥusayn Āhanī. Isfahan: Kitābfurūshi-i Shahriyār, 1341/1962.

———. *Al-ḥikma al-mutaʿāliya fi al-asfār al-ʿaqliyya.* On *Nūr al-ḥikma 2* [CD-ROM]. Qom: Computer Research Center of Islamic Science, 1998.

———. *Al-Mabdaʾ wa al-maʿād.* Ed. Sayyid Jalāl al-Dīn Āshtiyānī. Tehran: Imperial Iranian Academy of Philosophy, 1976.

———. *Majmūʿa-i rasāʾil-i falsafī-i Ṣadr al-Mutaʾallihīn.* Ed. Ḥāmid Nājī Iṣfahānī. Tehran: Intishārāt-i Ḥikmat, 1378/1999.

———. *The Metaphysics of Mullā Ṣadrā.* Trans. Parviz Morewedge. New York: SSIPS, 1992.

———. *Risāla sa aṣl.* Ed. Seyyed Hossein Nasr. Tehran: Dānishgāh-i Tihrān, 1340/1961.

———. *Sharḥ al-hidāya.* Tehran: Lithograph edition, 1313/1895.

———. *Al-Shawāhid al-rubūbiyya fī al-manāhij al-sulūkiyya.* Ed. Sayyid Jalāl al-Dīn Āshtiyānī. Mashhad: Dānishgāh-i Mashhad, 1346/1967.

———. *Tafsīr al-Qur'ān al-karīm.* 7 vols. Qom: Intishārāt-i Bīdār, 1366–69/1987–90.

Suhrawardī, Shihāb al-Dīn Yaḥyā. *Kitāb al-muqāwamāt.* In *Majmūʿa fī al-ḥikma al-ilāhiyya.* Vol. 1. Ed. Henry Corbin. Istanbul: Maṭbaʿa al-Maʿārif, 1945.

Taghi, Shokoufeh. *The Two Wings of Wisdom: Mysticism and Philosophy in the* Risālat uṭ-ṭair *of Ibn Sina.* Uppsala: Uppsala University Press, 2000.

Al-Tirmidhī, Muḥammad ibn ʿĪsā. *Al-Jāmiʿ al-ṣaḥīḥ, wa huwa sunan al-Tirmidhī.* 5 vols. Ed. A. M. Shākir. Cairo: al-Maktaba al-Islāmiyya, 1938.

Wensinck, A. J. *Concordance et indices de la tradition musulmane.* 2d ed. 8 vols. Leiden: E. J. Brill, 1992.

# Index of Qur'ānic Verses

*For an explanation of the reference numbers following each phrase, see the note on internal references, p. xi.*

# Index of Hadiths and Sayings

# Index of Names and Terms

*About the Translator*

WILLIAM C. CHITTICK (Ph.D. University of Tehran, 1974) is a professor of comparative studies, State University of New York, Stony Brook. He specializes in Islamic intellectual history, especially the philosophical and mystical theology of the twelfth and thirteenth centuries as reflected in Arabic and Persian texts. He has also investigated the manner in which texts have been put into practice in the Sufi orders, which have dominated much of popular Islam down to the present.

Other publications by Professor Chittick include *The Sufi Path of Knowledge: Ibn al-ᶜArabi's Metaphysics of Imagination; Imaginal Worlds: Ibn al-ᶜArabi and the Problem of Religious Diversity; The Sufi Path of Love: The Spiritual Teachings of Rumi; Faith and Practice of Islam: Three Thirteenth Century Sufi Texts;* and *A Shiᶜite Anthology.*

*A Note on the Type*

The English text of this book was set in BASKERVILLE, a typeface originally designed by John Baskerville (1706–1775), a British stonecutter, letter designer, typefounder, and printer. The Baskerville type is considered to be one of the first "transitional" faces—a deliberate move away from the "old style" of the Continental humanist printer. Its rounded letterforms presented a greater differentiation of thick and thin strokes, the serifs on the lower-case letters were more nearly horizontal, and the stress was nearer the vertical—all of which would later influence the "modern" style undertaken by Bodoni and Didot in the 1790s. Because of its high readability, particularly in long texts, the type was subsequently copied by all major typefoundries. (The original punches and matrices still survive today at Cambridge University Press.) This adaptation of Baskerville, designed by the Compugraphic Corporation in the 1960s, is a notable departure from other versions in its overall typographic evenness and lightness in color. To enhance its range, supplemental diacritics and ligatures were created in 1997 for exclusive use in the Islamic Translation Series.

TYPOGRAPHY BY JONATHAN SALTZMAN

◆